Health, Technology and Society

A Sociological Critique

Andrew Webster

First pubished 2007 by
PALGRAVE MACMILLAN
Houndmills, Basingstoke, Hampshire RG21 6XS and
175 Fifth Avenue, New York, N.Y. 10010
Companies and representatives throughout the world.

PALGRAVE MACMILLAN is the global academic imprint of the Palgrave
Macmillan division of St. Martin's Press, LLC and of Palgrave Macmillan Ltd.
Macmillan® is a registered trademark in the United States, United Kingdom
and other countries. Palgrave is a registered trademark in the European
Union and other countries.

ISBN-13: 978–1–4039–9524–7   hardback
ISBN-10: 1–4039–9524–9   hardback
ISBN-13: 978–1–4039–9525–4   paperback
ISBN-10: 1–4039–9525–7   paperback

This book is printed on paper suitable for recycling and made from fully
managed and sustained forest sources. Logging, pulping and manufacturing
processes are expected to conform to the environmental regulations of
the country of origin.

A catalogue record for this book is available from the British Library.

A catalog record for this book is available from the Library of Congress.

10   9   8   7   6   5   4   3   2   1
16   15   14   13   12   11   10   09   08   07

Printed in China

Contents

List of Illustrations

Acknowledgements

I am very grateful to the range of colleagues who have provided me an opportunity to explore with them the ideas raised in this book. I want to express my gratitude especially to those at the National Europe Centre, Australian National University, Canberra, where I was based during the spring of 2006 as a Visiting Fellow, and where much of the core writing for the book was undertaken; thanks in particular to Simon Bronitt, Helen Fairbrother, Neil Hamilton, John Gage and Greg Tegart. I also want to thank colleagues in Sydney including Cathy Waldby, Ron Johnston, Kerry Carmody, and at Wollongong, Stuart Russell. In the United Kingdom, all those colleagues (too many to name) who were members of the Innovative Health Technologies Programme that I directed, have helped inform my thinking, as have my more immediate colleagues in SATSU at the University of York. Thanks too to Jill Lake and her team at Palgrave as well as those referees who read and commented on the original manuscript.

Finally, I want to thank my wife Helen and my two sons, Matt and Nick, for their support, company and forbearance while dad was yet again doing some writing.

University of York
January 2007

Understanding Innovative Health Technologies

Introduction

This is a book about one of the most significant social transformations of recent times. It is a book that explores fundamental changes in the way we understand and manage our health and our bodies, and how this understanding has been shaped by, and given expression through, developments in medical and related technologies. But it is also a book that is built on a strong sociological scepticism about how we should read these changes: we should not presume that they are necessarily progressive, nor always of value or utility. Nor should we expect that the technological promise of fields such as genetics and informatics will be made equally available to all, and when so, always happily embraced. Sociological scepticism also recognises that although many technological changes have global reach – at least in those modern societies that can afford them – they will be subject to vastly different local interpretations and uses.

A sociological perspective argues that these technologies and the techniques, models and assumptions on which they are based, are *given* meaning through the way they are tied into *other technologies and social practices*. This is true whether they appear in the most mundane (such as the stethoscope) or the most exotic (say the MRI scanner) of forms. The meaning of health technologies will also vary in different settings (from the clinic, to the home, to the Internet), and vary in the way they shape diverse notions of 'health' found within and between cultures. In this sense, technologies (not only of health but all fields) are best understood as an expression of, and thereby always expressed through, social relationships. It is for this reason that technologies have been described by Haraway (1997, p. 11) as forms of 'materialized figuration', inasmuch as they bring together (or configure) material, people and social meanings or as 'congealed social relations' (Grint and Woolgar, 1996). Technologies perform, or 'work' within the context of, as well as through, such relationships.

The book is also about how new technologies are engaged with at an everyday level where these relationships are played out, in, for example, the hospital setting, primary practice and the home. What do encounters with technology mean for the health practitioner and patient, and indeed for those who surround them, such as a patient's carers and wider kin? New techniques – such as a genetic test – may, for example, provide greater precision in regard to the diagnosis of disease susceptibility, but may have little to say about the likely experience of ill-health or actual degree of discomfort a person – or their family – might expect to have some time in the future. Will this reassure or create new anxieties for those involved? In this sense, medical technologies are two-sided: they provide new, more detailed, sources of information about our illnesses but at the same time new forms of uncertainty and risk. These relate not only simply to our understanding of the illness but also to the expectations that inform and guide the social relationships *through which* we define and manage it. If technologies are congealed social relationships, those that disrupt existing relationships can be especially problematic.

New health technologies not only disrupt relationships we have with other people, they can also redefine our relationship towards our own body and our sense of being well or ill, our sense of control over our body and its parts. As I have argued elsewhere (Webster, 2002, p. 446) these technologies can reinvent the boundaries of the body in space and time by reducing them to their basic biochemical or anatomical constituents and reconstructing then in novel ways. We shall see, for example, how this occurs in fields such as stem cells or digital telemedicine.

New fields of medicine might be expected to have this effect, but even when technologies are commonplace and everyday – such as the ubiquitous antenatal screening techniques used to test for fetal abnormality – this does not mean that their diagnostic or therapeutic value will remain stable: over time, the value of technologies changes, perhaps because of better ways of getting patient information, or delivering the treatment they provide, or through changing social expectations about treatment (particularly evident when patient advocacy groups seek access to experimental drugs). Moreover, the 'value' of medical techniques, devices or therapeutics (such as new drugs) is typically subjected to national (and international) evaluation, regulation and monitoring. These evaluations are anchored in wider social and political cultures, explaining the global diversity one sees in the regulation of fields such as stem cells research. This points more generally to ethical debate over new technologies and the very different perspectives that can be found between and within countries.

Apart from asking about the meaning, value, regulation and ethical implications of health technologies, a sociological perspective is also interested in the processes through which new health technologies are introduced in the first place, and what factors have shaped their introduction. Health and its definition depend not merely on a person's sense of well-being, but on powerful professional, commercial and institutional interests that capture health in order to define, control, exploit or deliver 'it'. Health technologies in this sense are developed as part of a much wider innovation system and indeed may well emerge from fields that have nothing directly to do with the conventional clinical management of health. This is the case, for example, in regard to the widespread introduction into health systems of information and communication technologies (ICTs) developed elsewhere and now deployed for information management purposes and treatment (as the growth of telehealthcare illustrates). In 2005, for example, the United Kingdom government established its national programme for information technology in the health services, 'Connecting for Health', that will link general practitioners, hospitals and pharmacists and allow the electronic transfer of patient records. In other words, technologies spill across fields and markets through the complex network of relations that mobilise them. This means that products on health share many features of products used elsewhere, while the convergence of high-tech engineering and information systems – such as the intersection between bioinformatics and nanotechnology – blurs the boundaries of what is to be regarded *exclusively* as a 'health' technology.

While these national (and indeed international) medical and commercial interests set the health agenda for many of us, it is also the case that as *consumers* of health, people capture health innovations for their own personal use, especially in fee-based health markets such as the United States, a model increasingly adopted across Europe and Pacific Rim countries. Online health advice and products (such as pharmaceutical drugs) as well as techniques (such as diagnostic tests), have helped to drive the expansion of consumer-led health. The Internet also allows people to subvert and circumvent national systems of regulation and differences in state provision for health. As we shall see later in the book, many people exploit this virtual world of health, whose territory extends way beyond that which is subject to the clinical gaze. And, of course, the body itself has become a site of consumption, especially through the huge market in body modification through 'cosmetic surgery' and what Conrad and Potter (2004) have usefully termed 'biomedical enhancement' that includes 'drugs, surgery and other medical interventions aimed at improving mind, body or performance' (p. 185). They also advise against our assuming that there is a clear divide between medical 'treatment' and these interventions, inasmuch as we might assume that the first relates to health need while the second to lifestyle choices. They point out that the boundaries between these two are 'movable . . . and highly contested' (p. 186).

While the Internet and consumer markets open up and increase the demand for more diverse health goods and services, it is nevertheless the case that there is a strong relationship between the profile of disease in modernity and the clinical technologies that are seen as most important and effective in managing disease. In this sense, the technologies mentioned above do not appear randomly: while it is certainly the case that some technologies appear in a rather ad hoc fashion, championed by individual clinicians, there is a clear structuring of health care, medical research and commercial investment around specific areas.

For example, US physicians recently identified the top five innovations according to their *relative* importance in the treatment of patients' disorders: these were MRI/CTC scanning, ACE inhibitors, Balloon angioplasty, the Statin drugs and Mammography (Fuchs and Sox, 2001). All five are related to the most common chronic and/or high mortality diseases of advanced consumer societies – cardiovascular disorders (angioplasty and statins), cancer (MRI, CTC and mammography), and hypertension (ACE inhibitors). In turn, in those countries where it is the state that acts as the main procurer and provider of care, there is a growing trend towards procurement according to certain standards (technical and clinical), targets and cost in these and other areas. This may constrain the adoption of medical innovation (as has been claimed, for example, in recent UK-based reports (e.g. Wanless, 2002). In market-based systems, such as the United States, new technologies have been much more quickly taken up in part because professional care is fee-based and specialist, and where patients are 'clients' with private health insurance, a physician competes with others in part through what state-of-the-art medicine they have on offer. Moreover, as insurance cover meets the cost of technical services (such as ultrasound scans during pregnancy) hospitals are more likely to encourage patients to have more scans, simply because they will provide a useful income stream for the hospital itself.

Whether we are speaking about socialised or privatised forms of care, similar patterns of illness and disease can be found in all affluent societies. The disease areas noted above are, of course, closely related to the ageing process and a general decline in bodily well-being, and universally mean that a large proportion of health resources are devoted to older members of the population. Health care demands are also high at the other end of the life course, where ante- and peri-natal care up to the first few months of a child's life account for a disproportionately large investment in health technologies through screening, diagnostics, testing, life support and so on. Increasingly, of course, illnesses of affluence and over-consumption – notably obesity – are growing at an alarming pace: in many countries almost 50 per cent of the population is classified as being overweight or obese (OECD, 2004). Whether it is at either end of the life-course or between, medical intervention to manage morbidity and/or to save life is always high-cost in terms of both the labour and technologies it demands (such as in intensive care units).

This raises the question of resourcing for health interventions and who pays for it: the consumer or the state. In most socialised health care systems, such as the United Kingdom and Australia or mixed systems such as Sweden or the Netherlands, the state often sets a cut-off point or threshold beyond which the burden of ill-health or disease should be met by the private individual rather than through state provision through national taxation. In addition, most advanced states encourage their citizens to buy into private health insurance: for example, although Australia provides universal access to health care regardless of their ability to pay, almost 45 per cent of its population also have private health insurance (Hilless and Healy, 2001). The demographic shift towards a greater number of older people in the population as a whole will increase this trend towards private insurance. Increasingly, governments are encouraging patients, and their carers, to become more responsible for their own health, aided by devices that can be used by patients themselves in their own homes. This is especially true for the management of chronic illness, a potentially huge drain on the state. Self-care is, of course, likely to be politically framed in terms of a discourse of patient 'empowerment' rather than one of saving money. These trends towards self-administered medicine have implications for the traditional relationship between doctor and patient, as we shall see later in the book when we examine what I call 'the new sick role'.

This brief introduction has sketched out some of the main areas of interest that are to be explored later on and that indicate the complexity that is health technology today. But how far, we can ask, is this complexity significantly different from medical technologies of the past? That is, are we seeing today some sort of qualitative shift in their character and use, the way we make sense of them, or is there much that they have in common with the past? It is to this question that we can now turn.

New technologies, new health?

It is useful, first, to say something about what many regard as innovative health technologies. This cannot be presented as a straightforward list, for this would be to presume in advance some *intrinsic* quality of novelty that can be identified in some, but not other technologies. Instead, we need to understand what it is that people perceive as new about these developments and why.

One way of identifying what might be regarded as good candidates for innovative technology is to look at those areas receiving disproportionately large levels of public and private funding upstream, in the research labs of corporations and universities, or those appearing in documents of a health policy world that spends all its time scanning the 'horizon' for 'disruptive' technologies. We are also likely to find these same technologies populating the pages of science journals, the press, TV and the Web. Here we can find a range of developments that appear time and again; the more common of these are:

- Genetics-related developments (especially the advent of new technologies for genetic diagnosis, testing and screening; gene therapy; pharmacogenetics and pharmacogenomics; and neutrigenomics);
- informatics-based systems used for monitoring the individual – such as biosensors or telecare; telemedicine deployed for diagnostic (through imaging/ultrasound) and therapeutic purposes; and information systems used to manage clinical data about patients;
- tissue-related, such as tissue engineering and (adult or embryonic) stem cells research and therapy;
- Let us look at each of these in turn, focussing in particular on why each of them is regarded as transformative, at least according to those that develop them and bring them into the health care system.

Genetics-related developments

Traditionally, medical genetics has been mainly focused on the inheritability of single gene disorders related to a mutation in a person's DNA that is passed from one generation to the next. There are different degrees of risk of inheriting such disorders according to whether the genetic mutation is 'dominant' (such as in Huntingdon's disease where if you inherit the genetic disorder the disease will appear) or 'recessive' (as in cystic fibrosis or sickle cell anaemia) where you may simply be a 'carrier' of the mutation without it being 'expressed' as – an ultimately fatal – illness; here you need the defective gene from both your parents to succumb to the disease. A third form of genetically inherited disorder is known as X-linked and refers to single gene mutations (related to muscular dystrophy, for example) found only in the sons of women who carry the mutation.

The determination of these types of disorder is based as much on taking a thorough family history as it is on genetic testing, and the latter has been used for many decades in medicine. These tests are used to determine the likelihood of a disease and its relative severity (in part derived from the so-called 'penetrance' of the genetic mutation). In the particular area of reproductive genetics, techniques used include using microscopy simply to see whether there are additional chromosomes (as in Down's syndrome), testing a mother's blood chemistry for an over-expression of enzymes produced by the mutation, or removing by amniocentesis some of the amniotic fluid carrying foetal cells and testing them in the lab for markers linked to mutations. Information on family history is especially important in later onset diseases such as breast cancer.

How, then, might developments in 'the new genetics' differ from these conventional genetic techniques? The areas noted above – new diagnostics/testing/screening, gene therapy, pharmacogenetics/genomics and neutrigenomics – all depend for their novelty and applicability on the results of the Human Genome Project, the sequencing of the long chains of deoxyribonucleic acid (DNA) that make up the human genome. This mapping 'project' was begun in 1990 and was completed in draft form in July 2000, and a more developed version again in 2004. The more recent map is, perhaps ironically, presented less as a blueprint of the genome from which it would be possible to read off genetic mutation and its effect on the body, and more as a useful reference point through which gene hunting is made possible. Even so, it was this map, more than anything else, that has inspired claims that new genetic information would transform medicine.

Genetics would no longer be primarily reserved to working on diagnosing single gene (or monogenetic) disorders: instead *multifactorial* disease would become the new target, whereby illnesses and diseases caused by gene–gene or gene–environment interaction would now be understood, a move away from a focus on managing disease to preventing it arising in the first place. Where the disease already existed, this could be treated through gene therapy, modifying a person's DNA such that they would no longer produce the mutations that made them chronically or fatally ill.

The sub-field of pharmacogenetics, which goes back many years, has now been transformed by the HGP, primarily because it has become possible to identify those genotypes that are more, or less, responsive to drugs. In theory, it heralds the era of so-called personalised medicine.

More recently, food and genetics have been directly linked in the field of neutrigenomics, that applies genomics to diet: primarily it seeks to understand the relationship between a person's genome and how a specific diet might help mitigate or pre-empt the onset of genetic disease (Kaput and Rodriguez, 2004). It also examines the genetic basis of food organisms themselves in order to produce 'functional' food products that have a beneficial effect on health. This is attracting major investment in the commercial sector and the emergence of hybrid food/drug companies keen to cash in on high value-added (i.e. profitable) goods in a health-conscious consumer market.

These developments associated with contemporary genetics have been said to mark a sea-change or 'revolution' (European Parliament, 2001) in medicine. There are three changes which receive most attention:

1. *The diagnosis and treatment of both single and multifactorial disease.* Single gene disorders, such as Huntingdons, have been impossible to treat other than in a palliative sense: the onset of the disease is inevitable, such that, as McEwan (2005) so elegantly and terrifyingly notes, 'the brilliant machinery of being is undone by the tiniest of faulty cogs, the insidious whisper of ruin, a single bad idea lodged in every cell' (p. 94).

Gene therapy could, drawing on genomic information, develop techniques that would make good these single gene disorders. At the same time, it is suggested that medicine will be increasingly centred around tests for late-onset multifactorial diseases, those diseases individuals might get in the future. The medical practice this *predictive* testing generates, therefore, will not so much focus on concrete complaints and pains, but *risk-assessments* of diseases to which individuals (including the pre-born) are susceptible and which they might only obtain later on in life. Genetics research is now being related to a wide range of pathologies including cancer, diabetes, coronary heart disease and mental illness. Sociologically, however, this move towards risk assessment rather than the management of actual symptoms can generate new forms of uncertainty for both the 'patient-to-be' as well as clinicians (Bharadwaj et al., 2006). It could also be hugely expensive for socialised health care systems, such as that found in the United Kingdom, if risk assessment were to be based on the DNA profiling of all 600,000 babies born each year, in order to be used later in life to confirm a patient's genetic risk diagnosis (HGC, 2005).

2. *The development of target disorders.* Key to this is a move in medicine away from looking at clinical manifestations (the phenotype) of illness and disease to the underlying genetic causes of diseases. Many diseases share some molecular features at the genetic level. As a result, this might lead to the redefining of disease categories once perceived as similar or quite distinct on the basis of clinical symptoms. From a sociological perspective, this re-classification of disease could have major implications for existing professional boundaries and clinical practice, while creating ever-greater pressure towards a reductive geneticisation of illness and indeed of social problems more generally (Lippman, 1991; Hedgecoe, 2004). How far this type of tidy reductionism is sustainable is open to question, however, not least because within bioscience itself there is an increased recognition of the instability and complexity of genetic information.

3. *The targeting of drug-based treatments.* The possibility of targeted drug treatments is related to two areas of pharmaceutical research, namely, pharmacogenomics, how knowledge of the genetic composition of diseases themselves, such as cancer, can enable the development of a particular drug to target the mutating gene; and pharmacogenetics, a more precise understanding of how a person's particular genetic make-up (or 'genotype') affects the response they make to a specific drug (Webster et al., 2006). Some common drugs, such as warfarin, have a very narrow 'therapeutic index', which means that the most beneficial and non-toxic effects of the drug are limited to those patients with a particular genotype. So pharmacogenetics could, if fully realised, not only reduce unwanted side effects for patients but also lead to the more effective (therapeutic) use of drugs. Drugs are of course commercial products subject to international regulation: so we need to ask how might the advent of pharmacogenetics change the way in which corporations develop new drugs and regulators oversee the safety and efficacy of drugs?

Informatics-based system and e-health

Information systems are a key part of all social systems and are central to the reproduction of social order, forms of control and the exercise of power. This is true in health as it is in politics, education, the media and so on. The role of information in health and medicine today has to be seen in the changing context within which the information system more broadly has changed, especially over the past 30 years or so. Just as the HGP has been seen to transform genetics, so the 'information revolution' of the 1970s and beyond has been said to radically alter the meaning, scope and purposes of data, its flow, management and complexity (see e.g. Forester, 1984; Rozsak, 1986; Webster, 1995). This in turn has had a major effect on the ways in which health information is classified, sought, and deployed within and outside the clinical setting.

Late-modern societies are characterised by impersonal interaction, individualisation (Beck, 1992) and the disembedding of social relations (Giddens, 1990; Lash and Featherstone, 2002), across spatially extensive boundaries and networks (Castells, 1996) through a global communications media, driven by the World Wide Web. These changes have depended on key shifts in the ways in which information technologies (IT) are configured and the capacity that they have to manage information itself. Miles (2002) has argued that in the 1970s IT facilities were few, large (mainframes), and detached from one another. Subsequently, the 1980s saw the growth of IT devices (PCs), of many (and much smaller) sizes, with limited (two-way) communication between them being the norm, while the market was opened up through the deregulation of telecommunications and the arrival of satellite television. The 1990s saw the rapid growth of the Internet and Web as 'information superhighways', with technical links between the Web, email and G3 mobile phone systems. In the twenty-first century IT is now regarded as being embedded within the physical and virtual environment: wherever we turn we find IT systems at work, often invisibly so. This is what is meant by 'ubiquitous computing' deploying 'ambient intelligence' (Ducatel, 2000). Information of all kinds is handled as digital data: this makes it easier to transport information from one device to another – a move from centralised information processing to mobile and interoperable processing systems.

These developments have been particularly evident and exploited in some core social institutions within the 'virtual' or 'e-society' (Woolgar, 2002) and expressed in e-government, e-learning, e-commerce, and, of relevance here, *e-health*. E-health refers to a mix of digital technologies whose function is to diagnose, monitor, store and relay information about health, the patient, and the huge volume of management data-flows that characterise national health systems today. They reflect a time of audit, standardisation, technocracy and ambitions towards more effi-cient systems for managing health resources. As I have argued elsewhere (Webster, 2002, p. 450), the contemporary medical world is becoming increasingly 'informaticised'.

These digital technologies are networked, mobile and extensive. We can see a rapid expansion of embedded systems incorporated into bodies themselves as with biosensors, devices that convert a biological response into a digital electrical signal which can then be tracked remotely and logged by a central server monitoring a person's condition – such as their blood pressure. As Virilio (1998) remarks, we 'have to cope with technology inhabiting us. "Smart pills" are developed which are able to transmit information on nerve functions or blood flows to distant monitoring facilities' (p. 53). Ultimately, so extensive will our technological embodiment be that Virilio believes we will become 'citizen-terminals' where we are 'decked out to the eyeballs with interactive prostheses' (p. 20).

At the same time, the training of new medics need no longer solely rely on physical bodies – dead or alive. The physical link between the person, body and health is challenged by the arrival of cybernetic medicine where supercomputers are deployed to produce models of '*in silico*' organs, organ systems and eventually the 'Virtual Human'. Medics today are being trained online and in the computer suite through software programmes that generate virtual bodies rather than being required to learn their craft using cadavers or volunteers.

E-health is also found within buildings, such as 'smart homes' for the elderly or the chronically ill, including the monitoring and remote imaging systems used in telecare and telemedicine. Clinical data (inscribed within an Electronic Patient Record) is itself being incor-porated into massive information handling systems such as the United Kingdom's 'Connecting for Health' programme, or the Australian 'Health-Connect' initiative (both rolled out in 2005). The United Kingdom programme is the most ambitious system being introduced worldwide and is designed to give 30,000 British doctors access to patient records, that will (it is hoped) by 2008, support five billion transactions a year, including online decision-support.

Beyond the formal health system, more and more people, through increased domestic access to the Internet are using the Web as a source of health care information. As Fox et al. (2002, p. 4) note, more peo-ple go on line in the United States to secure health information than do visit their physician. Nettleton (2004) describes the emergence of 'e-scaped medicine', suggesting the formation of a new health information landscape occupied by virtual 'wellness managers', 'expert patients' surfing the net, health seekers in chat rooms and so on, signalling at the same time a move away from, an escape from the domain of orthodox medicine itself. As she says:

> Medical knowledge is therefore no longer exclusive to the medical academy and the formal medical text. It has 'escaped' into the networks of contemporary info-scapes where it can be accessed, assessed and re-appropriated. Rather than being concealed within the institutional domains of medicine, knowledges of the biophysical body (hitherto medicine's most sacred object) seep out into cyberspace. (p. 674)

These developments, as with any disruptive technology, generate not only new types of social relationships – to our bodies, to and between medics, to the state – but also new risks and threats. For example, telehealthcare can be said to have contradictory effects: on the one hand it is deployed in order to enhance patients' autonomy (e.g. by allowing them to remain at home); on the other hand for it to work patients must be compliant to be remotely 'activated' through a distributed information system infrastructure (Mort et al., 2003). Patient carers are caught up in this process at the same time and required to carry an ever-increasing burden of responsibility for health. Or again, the volume and flow of information creates new risks with regard to an individual's rights to privacy and concerns over who has authorised access to patient information. This is especially so in the United States, where privacy laws are less strict than they are in the European Union.

Whatever the risks and opportunities afforded by informatics, its transformative potential seems clear, and indeed it gains greater momentum through its tie-in with those developments in genetics noted above. In fact, the relationship between the genetic code of DNA and the digital code of software is critical to the future of bio-medical science. As Hine (1998) has observed: 'without [informatics] all the accumulated knowledge [related to genomic research] would be a disorganised heap as unreadable as the genome itself' (p. 42).

The third, and final, area we can consider that is seen to herald a major shift in the configuring of health and medicine concerns the field of tissue engineering and stem cells research. Hine's reference to a 'disorganised heap' might well describe the problems faced by biomedical scientists trying to understand, stabilise and use 'wet biology': tissues collapse, cells do things differently than expected, and the media used to grow them may well contaminate them or produce false readings. So there is considerable effort spent in trying to sort out, classify, standardise and organise this biological micro-world, whose main features are sketched out below.

Tissue-related biomedicine

Most bioscientists working in the tissue engineering field use the term 'regenerative medicine' to capture its hopes and aspirations: that is, they hope to engineer the properties of tissue and cells so that they might be introduced into a patient in order to regenerate damaged or non-functional tissue – such as bone, cartilage, blood cells and so on. In many areas, this research combines biological tissue with synthetic materials. This has been used, for example, to create new tissue used for the treatment of ulceration and skin lesions often associated with diabetes, or for the treatment of serious burns, or the repair of bone fractures (Faulkner et al., 2003).

Stem cell research has two main wings to it: work on adult stem cells which stretches back more than 40 years, and the much more recent (and socially contentious) embryonic stem cell research. The potential advantages of stem cell technologies include the potential to cure currently incurable conditions, such as Parkinson's disease (carrying McEwan's 'insidious whisper'), to mend damaged organs such as the heart and spine, and to provide an important new advance in drug toxicity testing, based on human models rather than animal models that have in the past proved unreliable.

Adult stem cells (alternatively known as 'somatic stem cells') serve to reproduce through maintenance and repair the specific tissue/organ within which they are found. If these cells can be isolated and extracted from oneself (autologous) or other people (allogenic) they can be used therapeutically to treat disease. For example, research in bioscience labs is being undertaken to identify those cells that function as heart muscle that could then be introduced into a patient suffering from chronic heart disease to repair damaged tissue. Such cells, it might be suggested, offer the heady promise of replacing self with self.

An adult stem cell's functionality is primarily determined and limited to that part of the biological system within which it is located, though recent research suggests that these cells might be coaxed into differentiating to form other cells. It is this capacity – this potential – that is the defining characteristic of embryonic stem cells. Unlike somatic cells these are special kinds of cells that have the unique capacity to renew themselves indefinitely and to give rise to specialised cell types. While adult cells perform a specific function, an embryonic stem cell remains uncommitted until it receives a signal to develop into a specialised cell. These stem cells vary in their properties. At the earliest stages of development of a foetus, up to about eight cells, all the cells are 'totipotent' (meaning they can develop into every type of cell needed for human development, including extra-embryonic tissues [that is the placenta and umbilical cord]). Once the blastocyst stage is reached (50–100 cells) embryonic stem cells (ES cells) can be derived which are said to be 'pluripotent'.

This class of stem cell, which is not only found in embryos at the early stage of development, but also in some foetal tissue, has the potential to develop into almost any of the 200 or so known cell types, although not into extra-embryonic tissues. Embryonic stem cells come from donated 'spare' embryos created as a result of *in vitro* fertilisation (IVF) programmes. Clinics offer IVF services to couples who have been unable to conceive, the clinical technique depending on the production of 'supernumerary' or surplus eggs, some of which can be taken for experimental purposes. Another type of stem cell, human embryonic germ cells, are derived from medically terminated pregnancies; these stem cells which come from the foetus in a later stage of its early development are not known to be pluripotent.

The first reported isolation and growth of pluripotent stem cells from early human embryos was made in 1998. Since then, the field has grown rapidly, though it has yet to deliver clinically therapeutic results. While adult stem cells are derived from mature tissue, here biomedical science might be said to be sourcing tissues from 'the very margins of (pre-) human life' (Waldby, 2002, p. 313). It is the clinical possibilities associated with ES cells that can be seen to constitute a radical break with existing biomedical science. The cloning of these cells and their cell lines in contemporary research breaks the direct physical relationship between bodies, tissue and its subsequent use: this contrasts with conventional transplantation for, in that case, organs donated from one person are used by one other person to sustain their life (as in heart, lung or kidney transplants). In contrast, stem cell donation derived from IVF treatment has no single recipient. Cell lines can be cloned indefinitely and be encouraged to differentiate into one form of tissue rather than another, and introduced in many different patients. The nearest medicine gets to this at present is in blood donation, where those of a particular blood group will be able to use blood of the same group from someone they have never met. But this is only ever blood: stem cell differentiation allows for the very possibility of creating such blood – or in theory any other 'tissue' – in the petri dish.

If this is to be achieved, however, the cells need to be stored and maintained, their quality ensured, and the biological and clinical standards that they must meet set down very precisely. This is the job of the new institutions known as tissue or stem cell banks found across the world today, that act as repositories for the new ES cell lines developed in bioscience labs in Australia, India, the United Kingdom, United States and so on. The procurement and banking of human tissues has become a major logistical task, surrounded by extensive regulatory and ethical provisions and codes. These new institutional structures are themselves indicative of the novelty of ES research.

We have seen, then, how the new genetics, informatics and tissue engineering/ES research disrupt existing and open new clinical possibilities while at the same time creating new socio-technical relationships. As such they are important candidates for sociological scrutiny. In each case, however, we have noted that they do not drop from some bioscience lab in the sky but are based on earlier scientific and technical developments already found 'on the ground'. So our questions as sociologists are less about the precise technical shifts they mark, important though these are, but more about the sense in which they are part of, and enabling conditions for, a transformation in the wider relationships between health, technology and society. What sort of questions might lie at the heart of such a sociological analysis?

Developing the sociological critique

There is a rich sociological literature exploring health, illness and, more recently, health technologies (ESRC, 2005) and their role in shaping the relationship between health practitioners and patients (e.g. Hanlon et al., 2004), the embodied sense of illness and disease (e.g. Flowers, 2001), the meaning and classification of disease itself (Kerr, 2005), and the wider professional and regulatory changes that characterise modern health care systems (e.g. May et al., 2004; Salter et al., 2004).

Prior to this more recent work on health technologies, there had been a much longer tradition in social theory that located health squarely within the wider structural and cultural dynamics of society.

Foucault (1975), for example, was interested in the ways in which knowledge, power and social control was produced and reproduced through the clinic: the clinical 'gaze' determines the basis on which identities are defined and classified, so sorting the mad from the sane, and the medium through which people become an object for scientific 'subjectification'. Without such discourses, these classifications and the divisions between normality and abnormality they create would not have existed: madness is a discursive product. More recent work exemplifies the play of classification processes: for example, Prior et al. (2002) show how those presenting with breast cancer fall on one, or another side of the threshold for treatment and clinical monitoring. Such classification reflects not only the conventions of scientific expertise but also the 'political calculus' that determines the rationing of health resources in the field of oncology. Similarly, Lippman (1992) has explored the way in which illness has become re-classified in terms of contemporary genetics discourse. Some can ask then whether the new technologies produce different types or forms of 'political calculus', as the relation between classification, disease risk and its management change the structuring of health care delivery?

Sociologists have also been interested in the ways in which patterns of social inequality are reflected in patterns of disease and the availability of health care. Bury (1997), Bartley (2003) and Stacey (1988) for example have examined the distribution of morbidity and mortality against social class, gender and the allocation of health resources. How, we might ask are these structural patterns of health mediated by the new technologies sketched out above: will, for example, the introduction of e-health exacerbate or ameliorate access to health care and advice?

In parallel, and perhaps not surprisingly, work in the field of the sociology of science and especially science and technology studies (STS) has become increasingly interested in examining the role of technologies in (re-)defining the meaning of health, disease and the role of the clinic (as in Casper and Berg, 1995; Berg and Mol, 1998; May and Ellis, 2001; Brown and Webster, 2004). More historical studies in this tradition remark too on the move away from an interest in the patient *per se* to disease and the technologies that can control it, or, in Pickstone's (2000) words from 'biographical' to 'techno-medicine'. Others observe how this shift has been driven by private corporations keen to exploit innovative technologies in the biomedical market, especially in the United States. This defines the move away from a public health framework for medical provision, to one which has become increasingly obsessed with 'miracle technology' – the creeping fetishisation of technology, hardware and gadgetry (Blume, 1997). Pharmaceutical and wider health care industries whose products populate the high street, the clinic and the home, operate in global and local markets, and engage with government and regulatory actors in such a way as to ensure their goods and devices are usually well-received (Abraham and Lawton Smith, 2002).

One important feature of 'technomedicine' is its capacity to keep people alive when they might otherwise have died, most obviously illustrated in the life-sustaining power of the intensive care unit (Lock, 2002). Less dramatically, technomedicine also ensures that there are more chronically sick than ever before, as drugs and devices keep the body going. Bury (2000) has noted how the demographic shift towards a greater number of older people in the population simply magnifies this 'problem', such that the focus of many in medicine has shifted from 'treatment and cure' to 'management and care' (p. 267). Technology ejects people from acute and fatal disorders into long-lived chronic illness.

In such circumstances, the meaning of someone's illness and its place in defining their personal identity becomes key: chronic illness is likely to form a key component of a personal biography or life story. Indeed, the focus on personal illness 'narratives' has been a key feature of much medical sociology. In the past – and still today – narratives have been anchored in the expectations associated with the sick role and the way medicine, having identified the causes of ones problem, provides a cure or treatment for it. Today this curative model is accompanied by a growing medical discourse and patient narrative centred on risk: instead of identifying symptoms and their treatment, doctors are increasingly identifying possible risks and creating a large number of the so-called worried well, those with no symptoms but who may succumb to illness in the future (Bharadwaj et al., 2006). How do these developments create new senses of illness and the body at the level of personal experience?

In light of the above, what then can we say provides the core issues that would inform a sociological critique of the relations between health, technology and society? Such a critique, I suggest, would explore and challenge the implications of medical technoscience with respect to:

- the socio-economic factors shaping innovation and how these affect the structuring of health care delivery;
- the patterns of inequality in morbidity and mortality;

- the public and private institutions that are investing huge amounts of political and economic capital in existing and novel areas such as genetics, informatics and tissue engineering fields;
- the regulation and control of new medical technologies;
- embodied knowledge about and experience of health and disease.

These are the main issues that underpin the rest of this book. Though they are directly and explicitly tied to debates surrounding technologies per se, they need to be understood as part of a wider range of structural and institutional changes characterising contemporary societies that are not restricted to the field of medicine and health. These include the growing individualisation of our lives, the changing relationship between lay and expert knowledge, the increasingly globalised contest over (health) rights and resources, and tensions between the political regulation and economic promotion of innovation by the state. Where possible, I will broaden the focus to include reference to these wider themes throughout the book.

Returning more specifically to medical innovation, I have argued elsewhere that we can see developments in technoscience in terms of three broad but related changes that have opened up clinical medicine to new influences and actors. These I have called the *socialisation of medical innovation*, the *socialisation of clinical diagnosis* and the *socialisation of clinical implementation* (Webster, 2002). The first refers to the ways in which lay people are enrolled as *active participants* in the development of new technologies from their very earliest stages of development. This is not simply as volunteers for clinical trials, but as users encountering health services and goods beyond the clinic. Health innovation is dependent on socially and spatially distributed and mobile systems that are less and less contained within the walls of a clinic. The 'where' of medical innovation becomes as important as the 'what' to which it refers precisely because the very rationale of the innovation is that it is – as Giddens (1991) might say – time-space distanciated. And this distanciation is given increasing impetus through the role of the state as procurer of medical innovation: it will seek to secure those new technologies and interventions that relocate care and its delivery to non-clinical settings.

The second change refers to the fracturing of the medical monopoly over the meaning of health and disease, especially through the arrival of what has been called a 'new medical pluralism' (Cant and Sharma, 1995) and what Giddens (1991) has called the 'reskilling' of lay people in their engagement with, definition and management of health and illness (Hardey, 1999). The third change refers to the ways in which lay people are required, but also perhaps actively embrace a turn towards taking greater responsibility for making new health technologies 'work': IVF is a case in point. As Roberts and Franklin (2004) show in their study of IVF clinics and the use of pre-implantation genetic diagnosis (PGD) to select embryos that are not carrying genetic mutations, PGD only 'works' where the prospective parents are active participants in managing and accepting the chronic uncertainties that still prevail with this treatment.

These three processes have then redefined the spatial, experiential and epistemic boundaries of conventional medicine and the clinic. I will be returning to each of these later in the book as we explore the implications of 'technomedicine', framed by the broader sociological issues noted above. The critique must be the attentive context of use of technologies to reflect any notion of technological determinism across different contexts (be these clinics or countries). It must explore the ways in which users (patients, carers, clinicians etc.) make sense of technologies and how re-order the meaning of health. It must examine the expectations and hopes that surround them, and the subtle and not so subtle forms of inequity and insecurity they create.

There is one area that will figure in only a minor way in this book and this relates to the ethical aspects of the new technologies. This is clearly a crucial issue and one that has led to a massive growth in literature that asks what are the effects of these systems on the rights of the individual and on the obligations of the state. Much of this growth has been in the field of bioethics particularly the so-called ELSA (ethical, legal and social aspects) of contemporary genetics. This text is a sociological and not ethical critique: where I do discuss ethics it will be to note the ways in which ethical and scientific discourses *co-evolve* as quandaries are resolved, boundaries redrawn, regulatory goalposts moved. Regulatory agencies change as they redefine what is possible and permissible, what is proscribed and what off-limits.

Structure of the book

The book is made up of seven chapters. The material for these chapters is informed by UK research that I was privileged to help steer as Director of the Innovative Health Technologies Programme supported by the ESRC, but also by a much wider body of literature. After this introductory chapter, the next two (linked) chapters explore some of the main institutional and organisational drivers that lie behind the emergence of new health technologies. Chapter 2 examines the role played by two actors – the clinical professions and the state – that have historically been and are today central to the process through which new health technologies are crafted, developed, deployed and evaluated. The state/profession relationship was tied to a range of factors associated with the regulation of medicine, the emergence of the welfare state, the standardisation and delivery of care at primary (general practitioner) and secondary (hospital) levels, and broader public health programmes that were tied to preventative medicine (such as vaccination). Both national and international government agencies (e.g. the World Health Organisation, the European Union) seek today to invest in technologies in such a way as to provide more effective as well as more efficient systems of health care. The mantra of the day is 'evidence-based medicine', that is health care that can be shown to be based on robust and reliable information and research. This is then supposed to guide clinical practice on the ground. For their part, clinicians either individually through their own research or collectively through their professional bodies, develop and oversee the use of novel techniques in the clinic.

Paralleling state and professional groups in the production of new health technologies is the wider corporate innovation system that plays a key role in producing them, the private sector of pharmaceutical and ICT firms and those operating in the made up especially of medical devices markets. Chapter 3 summarises the main changes in the role of corporate innovation in shaping the meaning of disease and health disorders and their treatment. The largest firms are of course global actors and will try to ensure that their products sell equally well wherever possible. At the same time, these firms are well aware that their markets can vary considerably. This may result from different procurement regimes (from fee-based, market systems through to fully socialised (national) health systems), different ethical regimes and differential abilities to pay (for drugs etc.). The globalisation of health technologies does not, therefore, necessarily mean among less prosperous countries the globalisation of a standard price that health procurers or individuals must pay for a specific product or technique. This is especially true in the area of pharmaceutical drugs where government health authorities in a number of high-income countries determine a reimbursement level which drugs suppliers complain is much too low. This complaint has often been made, for example, by US drugs companies against a number of richer European states. The chapter will explore the role of private sector innovation in the key areas sketched out earlier: genetics, informatics and tissue engineering. In turn it asks about the role of the state and regulatory regimes (national and global) that are charged with the task of managing risk and fostering innovation.

Chapter 4 discusses current social science literature on the body and our engagement with and management of illness, disease and treatment in light of the changes described in the preceding chapters. Most importantly, this leads to a revisiting of the long-established literature on 'the sick role' and 'illness behaviour'. This work has been central to much of medical sociology but has tended to neglect the role of technologies (other than in the specific field of reproductive medicine) and has, understandably, been confined to conventional doctor–patient relations and narratives found therein. New technologies reshape the relations/ their narratives and thereby render new possibilities regarding the sick role itself.

This leads us, in Chapter 5, to consider what might new technologies mean for the delivery and management of health care? The Chapter is especially interested in issues surrounding primary and secondary care, and is so on a comparative (international) basis. Computer aided support systems (increasingly commonplace in health delivery – such as the United Kingdom's NHSDirect, or the internationally common CASS tools used in patient care planning and so on) disturb boundaries between professional and patient, redefine the professionals expertise, and create both tensions between as well as empower those involved. In technology-rich environments such as these, nurses' interaction with decision support leads to some unanticipated outcomes. I go on to ask what sort of discourses of governance have been created to oversee and regulate a more heterogeneous and risk-laden health care system.

The penultimate chapter will explore what I call the 'new sick role', wherein patient and activist groups mobilise this role in different ways to both secure or repel medicalisation. I also examine what happens when the role is denied to those who seek it and how new technologies can create competing definitions of what a condition might mean for different patients.

The final chapter will summarise the broad themes of the book and return to wider debates within social science theory about the 'technologisation' of health culture and the loss of traditional trust within expertise. It argues that innovations today have disturbed the body, medicine, health/illness experience relationships and suggests that health, like many other arenas of social life, is as Bauman has argued, increasingly and chronically disembedded from conventional community, professional and institutional relationships. Despite such shifts, I return to the question of 'novelty' and show in the chapter how we need to assess both the discontinuities and continuities in health technologies and their deployment, and that both aspects characterise the ways in which patients and practitioners experience innovative health technologies.

The Dynamics of Biomedical Innovation

Introduction

One of the areas of contemporary biomedical science that is attracting huge clinical, commercial and government interest is tissue engineering and stem cell research. In many ways the scientific tasks that have to be addressed in this field act as a useful analogy for the social and economic tasks that must be undertaken in *any* area of innovation if the promise of research is to be translated into health care delivery. To see why this analogy is useful we need to sketch out the field itself.

Tissue engineering has a number of different research targets (typically differentiated by areas of interest such as bone, cartilage, skin, neurones and so on, all of which are subsumed within the general heading of 'tissue'). Research has two complementary objectives, either the repair or the regeneration of damaged tissue within a patient (*in vivo*). Much of the current work depends on using animals to model, test and validate techniques that can then be used in humans, indeed there are already tissue engineered (TE) products available that have been approved by regulatory agencies: in the United States, for example, the federal Food and Drug Administration (FDA) has approved skin and musculoskeletal devices for use in clinical trials.

A crucial step in the TE process is the construction of a synthetic 'scaffold' or matrix that will act as the framework through which new tissue will grow and be incorporated within the body. There are a whole range of problems that need to be resolved relating to tissue rejection, integration of the scaffold, the functionality of the repair once integrated and so on. If in addition the scaffold is to be 'seeded' with stem cells to facilitate regeneration then additional problems arise; will the cells do what they are supposed to do and not have toxic or carcinogenic effects in the body? So engineering the scaffold or 'matrix' is difficult, to say the least.

But, apart from meeting these technical problems, the success of the field will be as equally dependent on the construction of what we can think of, by way of analogy, as a *social* scaffold that will act as the vehicle through which regenerative medicine becomes more widely established. This metaphorical 'social matrix' is made up of diverse agents – patients, clinicians, regulators, politicians, voters, lawyers, the media and other actors – who will determine whether or not TE is integrated in the wider *social* body of clinical practice and care. Just as the biological matrix needs to mobilise biochemical and genetic agents to function, so the social matrix has to be built in such a way that the 'growth factors' for the field *as a whole* can be effectively mobilised.

This requires social (and not simply tissue) 'engineering', illus-trated, for example, by a law introduced in California in 2004, known as 'Proposition 71'. The success of this piece of legislation depended on the mobilisation of California's tax-paying voters, and a public rela-tions campaign that relied heavily on the support of Christopher Reeve, the former Hollywood *Superman*, who saw in embryonic stem cell research a cure for his own paralysis caused by a horse riding acci-dent. The new legislation was in response to the US Federal position President Bush's administration had adopted some years earlier that, driven by the 'neo-conservative' lobby, had placed major restrictions on the field because of claims made about the moral status of the embryo from which such cells would be derived. The new law required an amendment to California's state constitution and a raft of enabling legislation. The legislation supported the establishing of a new institute for regenerative medicine, and authorised the raising of a special bond paid by Californians to the tune of $300 million per year for ten years. Unusually, the funds are overseen by a citizens' financial group, working in tandem with the state auditor.

Proposition 71 (now law entitled the 'California Stem Cell Research and Cures Act') illustrates in a rather dramatic way how a 'social scaffold' can be built to bring life to a field, here 'vascularised' by the flow of political and economic resources.

The California case is not unique: similar stories could be told about the more, or less, successful attempts to build new 'social matrices' through which new fields grow. The debates within the European Parliament over the ethical boundaries of TE, the deliberations within the World Health Organisation (WHO) about the global standards that should shape the field – all point towards the way in which what might be regarded as external to the field of science are in fact being deeply implicated or inscribed (Akrich, 1992) in the very fibres of the scaffold about to be implanted in the body. This bio-social 'scaffold' is no longer simply a useful metaphor but a description of a process that is true of all areas of health innovation and was there all along, and needs to be seen as the *mutual construction*, or what the sociology of science would call, 'co-construction' of the material and the social.

As such, whether in the United States, Europe or elsewhere, things can go wrong; the biosocial scaffold can fail. Simply because resources are mobilised on behalf of new technologies does not guarantee that they will 'work'. The introduction of new information systems in the British health service have been beset with ongoing problems that are both social and technical in nature. One reason for this is that such systems need to be standardised around an agreed technological platform and yet allow for existing systems to be interoperable. Moreover, British health care is highly devolved through its Local Trust system (with over 700 such bodies in primary, secondary and ambulatory care) whose priorities can differ. Although it may be a nationalised (free at the point of care) system it is far from a nationally integrated system.

Even if new health technologies are seen to work, they are likely to generate new questions that the clinical professions and the state must answer: long-term uncertainties will remain about TE products relying on embryonic stem cells, since they may well generate pathological side effects (such as cancer) that will be difficult to detect and difficult to isolate from other (say environmental or dietary) carcinogenic effects. And even when more modest and controllable technologies are introduced – such as the 'statins' for managing cholesterol levels as a cardiovascular therapy – these will ensure more people will make more long-term demands on the health system simply as they get older.

In light of the discussion above, this chapter focuses on two, inter-dependent, social actors who have played a key role over the past hundred and more years in developing and managing new health technologies. These are the clinical professions and the state. They both figured strongly in the TE story from California as they have done elsewhere. Private corporations (both large, such as the pharmaceutical industry, and smaller firms developing new devices and techniques) are a third social actor shaping innovation, and related to this is the growth of the consumer market for health. I will discuss these commercial aspects separately in Chapter 3.

The clinical professions are a source of much health innovation precisely because of the role the clinic itself has played since the beginnings of medicine as a site for experimentation and trial of new therapies or 'interventions'. Physicians have long enjoyed considerable professional discretion to develop or deploy new devices, treatments or diagnostic techniques. The clinic is not only a site for testing new ideas but also the place where expertise can be most effectively displayed, not least through the use of a range of clinical instruments and procedures to determine a patient's condition (once his or her medical history has been taken). Indeed, in fee-based systems where patients are effectively 'clients', clinicians mark out their specialist expertise through the use of state-of-the-art techniques: this has been most marked in the United States where competition between physicians has fostered over the last century a rapid growth in biomedical technologies.

This process has a powerful feedback effect, given greater momentum through the development of formal training and skills requirements to practice as a medic. Today medical schools around the world demand that their students are exposed to a wide range of biomedical systems in their clinical training. Moreover, the conventional university/clinical school link provides a bridge between emergent innovation in the lab and clinical practice, even if only in the form (at least till additional funds are available) for small-scale pilot studies or trials.

The state, our second social actor shaping medical innovation, has played a crucial role in funding and co-ordinating the provision of health resources in different countries. Health policy is shaped by government and delivered through public sector health agencies operating at international (such as the WHO), national, regional and local levels. It would be wrong to presume that policy made centrally cascades down through different levels in some sort of coherent, rational way. Rather, health policy can be fractured and fragmented and there may well be tension between local and state priorities, especially true, for example in federal political systems such as those of the United States and Australia. Many countries' health programmes are also a mix of public welfare and private or quasi-market health insurance systems, as health is both a political priority and a profitable commodity, the proportion of national expenditure on health continues to grow in real terms year on year. Much of this is to do with the increasing costs of chronic illness and (the associated) ageing population, as well as health as a 'lifestyle choice' outside of the orbit of the clinic itself.

Innovation in health is seen by the state as a way, in principle, of checking this inexorable rise in costs through, for example, novel techniques that can diagnose illness earlier and so act to pre-empt or prevent the onset of disease, or health information management systems that can act to remotely monitor patients outside of clinical settings.

Given this, the state defines the boundaries of what it is prepared to support or what are defined as health 'needs' that it must meet, what is to be passed to private insurance, what can be presumed to be the provenance of individual self-care and what can be placed onto the shoulders of 'informal carers' who look after relatives with poor (typically chronic) ill-health. Much of the latter is highly gendered work that women are expected to take up looking after partners or elderly relatives.

State support for innovation tends to be driven by these allocative, resource-related criteria and is regulated through a whole panoply of policy discourses and devices. One such is the subscription to support innovation that is demonstrably 'evidence-based', to which we shall return later, another is to seek to manage and regularise innovation through establishing national standards that set the terms on which it is to be introduced. This attempt to control innovation can be seen as part of the wider social disciplining of health, medicine and indeed 'life itself' through forms of 'surveillance' (Armstrong, 1995) and 'governance' (Rose, 2001, 2004) that order and regulate 'biopolitics' (Foucault, 1988). I shall explore these issues later.

In what follows, I outline some of the main features that characterise the role that, first, the medical profession and second, the state, have played in fostering health innovation, restricting my discussion to advanced industrial society. I then show, especially with respect to the role of the state and its political culture, how a similar innovation may meet very different responses, such that health technologies are shaped and mobilised in quite distinct ways according to diverse socio-cultural contexts. I conclude by asking whether the role of the state and professional medicine as a source of innovation is in principle limited compared with the private health industry, the focus of Chapter 3. First, though, we need to challenge the view that many might hold, namely, that medical innovation follows some linear and always progressively better 'path'.

Medical innovation: take-up and efficacy

There has been a long-standing debate over the contribution that has been made by medical innovation to health improvement. Reference is often made, for example, to McKeown's (1976) classical (and highly controversial) analysis of the limited contribution that medicine has made to population health in general. Using historical data on the decline of mortality rates reflecting a decline in the virulence of infectious diseases, McKeown argued that much progress has been made over the past century through general improvements in public health but especially in nutrition and diet across the population as a whole, than through the changes wrought by increasingly sophisticated health technologies (see Harris, 2004). Such improvements are directly linked to reductions in overall levels of poverty than, he argued, to specific medical/health interventions. Medical sociologists (e.g. Bury, 1997; Graham, 2000, 2005) and social epidemiologists (e.g. Wilkinson, 2005) have argued in a complementary way that health improvements are also about broader changes in social structure and a more equitable distribution of income and wealth.

McKeown's work was subject to strong critique from medical historians and public health analysts who stressed the importance of key interventions to reduce disease, such as anti-tuberculosis programmes in the United Kingdom and the United States (see e.g. Fairchild and Oppenheimer, 1998). Moreover, it is clear that technical development in medicine has occurred that now enables clinicians to undertake quite routinely what have been in the past highly dangerous procedures. Heart transplants or brain surgery are cases in point. Moreover, McKeown's analysis related to an historical context that no longer obtains with respect to the control and management of diseases of the twenty-first century. For example, a recent Australian government report (Australian Productivity Commission, 2005) points to the beneficial impact of health technologies in regard to disorders such as cancer, heart disease and asthma (noting, for example that 'medications for asthma have resulted in a 28 per cent decline in mortality from the condition in Australia over the 1990s' [p. xlii]).

Such innovations rely on ever greater technical sophistication and clinical skill, an extensive range of support sciences (such as immunology or pathology), a supportive regulatory environment, perhaps most important of all, willing patients who in the early stages of a technology act as 'moral pioneers' (Rapp, 1999) negotiating the choices, risks and hazards of these new techniques on behalf of others.

On the other hand, the increasing sophistication of health technology to probe, rechart and redefine pathology may serve to *generate* new forms of disease, as Foucault (1988) has argued in regard to the role of screening in health care: this can simply produce the asymptomatically ill, as in screens for hypertension in assessing blood pressure levels. Innovative technologies here create and define diseased bodies and do so for people who have no sense, no lived experience of being 'ill'. To this extent, health innovation is generative of new uncertainties that cannot, as risks, be easily calculated. Moreover, in this sense, as Beck (1992) or Giddens (1990) would argue innovations simply create new problems precisely as they seek to resolve existing ones. Much of the success of biomedicine has been in coping with acute medical problems but in doing so has often (clearly not always) relocated patients from a dangerously acute to a chronically sick condition.

Innovation is not therefore straightforwardly progressive or effective in what it produces. In fact we need to explore, as suggested earlier by the analogy of the 'social matrix', the ways in which its efficacy and effectiveness are socially constructed, thereby why some medical technologies succeed and some fail or indeed why some – such as drugs – do both. Innovation does not speak for itself. It is not quickly or easily adopted simply because those who design and develop it believe it to be the solution to a (perceived) problem. We need then to ask what processes influence the take-up of new technologies, and later, in a return to McKeown's question, explore debates over the relative effectiveness of new techniques.

Take-up

Early contributions towards an understanding of the spread of new medical technologies have focused on different factors. Coleman et al., (1966) argued that innovation depended on new technologies being supported by elite members of the medical profession who act as 'opinion leaders' and enrol other doctors into new techniques. This analysis (of the take up of the then new drug tetracycline) stressed the role of social networks and the communication therein and presented innovation as a form of social contagion across the medical community. Those with good ties to the innovation network were more likely to adopt the new drug than those isolated from it. Rogers (1995) 'diffusion theory' focuses attention on five factors shaping the perceived merits and so likely adoption of new clinical technologies, namely, their 'relative advantage', 'compatibility' (with existing technology), degree of 'complexity', 'trialability' and 'observability'. Echoing the Coleman study, more recent work has stressed the ways in which the adoption of innovation reflects a social learning process by those following in the footsteps of first adopters (e.g. Burke et al., 2005).

While opinion leaders are clearly, by definition, important social actors who might encourage favourable views about medical innovations, there are various weaknesses in this approach. One is its presumption that innovation is necessarily progressive and that poor adopters are in some sense conservative or entrenched in outmoded technologies. This clearly begs questions as to the net value of new systems and to why resistance might well, in some circumstances, be a perfectly rational response. Another limitation of the approach is that the unit of analysis is the individual or groups of individuals in clinical networks. Little or no attention is given to the role of more structural dynamics at work, such as professional pressures to conform to practice elsewhere, or to the process through which organisations take up new technologies as a result of economic, regulatory or even legal reasons. Innovative drugs, such as the statins, have been shown to have become widely taken up precisely for such reasons (Will, 2005).

Over time, as new innovation becomes normalised, take-up and use has been shown to display an 'S-shaped' curve, where slow, limited early adoption, leads to a second stage of more rapid widespread take-up, followed by a gradual tailing-off in new usage. At the same time, the utility of some technologies depends on their being taken up by many people quite rapidly, such that a point of critical mass is secured. This is especially true of information and communication or media technologies used in medicine that require many users if they are to be efficient.

Partly as a result of this, it is frequently the case that some technologies – such as those we find in global communications systems or in national health information systems – exhibit a strong directionality or 'path dependency' as alternative options get closed off by designers, manufacturers and users, creating a feedback process that embeds a particular technology in a wider social system. As Williams and Edge (1996) comment, 'earlier technological choices pattern subsequent development' (p. 867; see also Rip, 1995, p. 419). Mina et al. (2004) have shown how innovation paths reflect innovating networks made up of clinicians, engineersand patients who identify innovation problems along the way – a series of 'problem sequences' – that define the problem and its solution. Overtime these solutions tend to converge towards a dominant one around which a process of social closure is seen (Bijker, Hughes and Pinch, 1987). This closure around a relatively stable set of devices and practices does not happen 'automatically' but as a result of negotiation and sometimes conflict over competing corporate, regulatory and public interests (see Webster, 2004a). The process through which innovation is taken up has, of course, been compared to the process of biological evolution (see e.g. Ziman, ed. 2000) though there are questions to be raised here about the ways in which innovation is, 'selected', what shapes its 'diversity' and the level and form of what I would suggest can be called the *innovation granularity* that we attend to as a marker of real change and novelty (see also Pavitt, 2003). That is, sociologically we have to see innovation and technical change as happening across different networks and at multiple levels, some low-level and relatively modest in technical shift but which together may produce a higher order innovative change that can have quite transformative effects. This can often happen when new functionality is introduced into everyday existing systems – such as photographic devices into mobile phones.

At the same time, there are also always likely to be *localised* versions of technologies that may differ from that promoted as 'the global standard': these may prevail in a niche market for some time, or founder, not because they are necessarily technically less efficient or effective, but because they may relate to *existing* technologies and social practices less well. Moreover, we need to understand how technological trajectories and path dependencies often depend on the 'co-construction' or co-evolution of new social institutions within wider innovation systems (Edquist, 1997). We can see this today in the emergence of new types of regulatory institutions that have had to combine previously separate regulatory functions in order to manage the risks associated with new hybrid biosciences (as is true of tissue engineering, discussed in Chapter 1, that combines mechanical with wet biology engineering; see Faulkner et al., 2003). How new technologies are regulated also expresses local regulatory regimes and will vary across different national political systems; Salter (2006) has shown how this is the case for the regulation of new technological developments associated with research in the field of embryonic stem cell science. I return to this question of regulation in Chapter 3.

Efficacy

One might presume that the widespread adoption of a health technology is a reasonably good indication that it must 'work', is effective (in terms of relative cost/benefit analysis) and efficacious in terms of actually performing a specific function well. But what counts as failure or success of a clinical intervention can often be difficult to define, especially in managing chronic disorders such as cancer: does the chemotherapy work, and what sort of criteria should be used to determine this? Sometimes drugs that have the desired biochemical effect on the body can produce side effects that can be experienced as a worsening of the disease itself. This has been observed, for example, with respect to the effect of drugs – a cocktail known as HAART (Highly Active Anti-Retroviral Treatment) – used to manage AIDS. Disease, illness and their management or cure are shaped by the contingencies of the body as a living organism, experienced and understood in terms of feelings, emotion and beliefs that construct 'narratives' of illness and its symptoms and what it means to 'get better'.

That medicine works on living systems also means that success in coping with pathology in a part of the body can be accompanied by sudden failure elsewhere, which may be terminal; hence the surgeon's cliché that 'the operation was a great success but unfortunately the patient died'. This may be caused by infection, by the effect of anaesthesia on the patient, by 'complications' such as shock and so on.

But such vagaries have been with medicine since its beginnings. Indeed, seeking medical treatment in the sixteenth century from say the 'barber-surgeon' was a highly dangerous step to take if one were suffering badly, though in some settings, such as the battlefield, such practitioners provided one's only hope for survival. Today, the professionalisation of medicine across diverse fields each with a range of techniques of growing sophistication and precision, such as key-hole surgery, means that medical intervention is safer, extensive in scale and number, deployed according to clinically tested procedures.

The growth of medical technologies and their spread, as well as the higher expectations that patients and primary care practitioners have of them – that they are safe and work – has not meant that they have gone unregulated. On the contrary, precisely because medical technologies have had the capacity to develop rapidly and expensively, the state has sought to rein them in. One way this has been attempted, but with only limited success, has been through the employment of health economists asked to undertake 'health technology assessment' (HTA) of existing or proposed health innovations. The state's desire to manage the potential economic and legal risks associated with innovation has seen priority being given to 'early warning' about the likely impact of a new development. Such ambivalence reflects a common preoccupation with scrutiny, audit and surveillance that prevails in modernity (Bauman, 2000) and a decline in the technocratic confidence that marked medicine and indeed most fields of science between the 1950s and 1970s.

Critique of HTA from within medical sociology has been limited (see Faulkner, 1999). But some of the questions that have been raised about HTA (see Lehoux and Blume, 2000; Webster, 2004) relate to its tendency to review technologies as discrete innovations rather than, as is often the case, part of wider integrated systems; its presumption that it can deploy a similar methodology in measuring 'success' across diverse medical fields; its failure to engage with more qualitative measures of evaluation, and more generally, its failure to recognise that evaluation is a contested terrain involving different sorts of evidence related to different sorts of context (such as the experimental derived from clinical trials, evidential, derived from existing clinical practice, and experiential, based on patients' experience of an intervention). There has been some attempt within the HTA discipline to respond to these criticisms (Giacomini, 2005) and develop more sophisticated methodologies that provide for more complex evaluation attentive to context (Briggs et al., 2006; Gabbay and Walley, 2006). But as Blume (2005) has argued, the HTA field developed within a specific political context (that promoting evidence-based medicine and the claim to be able to generalise results from one study) and this has limited what it can do. In many ways, the sort of data deemed key to the HTA world reflects the interests of more powerful actors within government and health delivery: certain 'variables' used for assessment are deemed relevant others not so, much of the latter relates to context of use and how, ultimately, the patient benefits. Blume has argued strongly that HTA neglects the political, social and ethical dimensions of new technologies, and has argued for a more socially and politically informed process of assessment.

Prior to the arrival of HTA analysis of new technologies, patient experience was a matter that had been taken up by clinicians, who recognised that though the biomedical outcome had been achieved (say a lowering of blood pressure), the sense of wellness for the patient had not changed. This led in the 1970s to the development of 'Quality of life' (QoL) measures, which as Armstrong (2006) has argued, recognised the need for more sensitive therapeutic markers of the patients well-being than simply those of lives saved or lives extended. That is, they were designed to try to capture the patient's subjective experience of health and the value of health interventions, with respect, for example, to their being able to live as 'normal' a life as possible. However, as Armstrong also shows, QoL measures (of which there are now over 800) are a contested area, since they act as 'social evaluations of the "good life" and these will both change over time and are likely to differ for different people and groups in the population' (2006, p. 238). Again, the social construction of what 'works' or has beneficial effect is evident, and thereby points to an important role that sociology could and should play in this area.

Complementing the HTA and QoL approaches to evaluating the merits of a new health technology has been the use of randomised clinical trials (RCTs) that test a specific intervention – say a new drug, device or diagnostic test – across a target patient group. RCTs are designed to identify the safety and efficacy of interventions and are organised as a sequence of 'phases' from pre-clinical tests, through to a full trial on the target patient group. The objective of such trials is not only to test a new (or indeed existing) intervention but thereby to provide a more rigorous basis on which clinicians can be advised what to use, when and with what groups of patients. The assumption is, as with QoL measures, that these results can be generalised across equivalent populations beyond the trial group. Clearly, the warrant for this depends on the ways in which the initial sample was derived, and how representative this is of those for whom the intervention is ultimately aimed at.

Criticisms made from within social science of RCTs have focused on this question of representativeness, noting that drugs trials often begin with healthy, young, typically male volunteers in determining the toxicity of new compounds. Even then, such volunteers can experience severe side-effects and, not surprisingly, down the line, following approval such drugs can have major adverse effects on those prescribed who do not conform to the norm built into the sample population. Adverse drug reactions – the side effects of taking drugs that have been approved by regulatory agencies – are a major source of morbidity and mortality; in the United States in 2004 they accounted for 104,000 deaths (Webster et al., 2005). This in part is a result of the combined effects of drugs – the problem of 'polypharmacy' especially significant among older patients being treated for multiple, and not one, condition. Moreover, RCTs assume stable pathologies or diseases that can be addressed by standardised treatments, inappropriate therefore for metal health or more behaviourally based interventions (Slade, 2001).

Despite the various criticisms that have been made of these three forms of evaluation – HTA, QoL, and RCT, the holy trinity of evidence-based medicine – they are used more and more heavily by health agencies in affluent states to assess the merits of health innovation. These three different forms of evaluation act not only to evaluate existing health technologies, but also shape how new technologies are being developed. Health innovators are aware that these evaluations will be used to determine the relative merits of their product or procedure, and endeavour to design them in such a way as to anticipate and meet the criteria against which they will be judged. In other words, such criteria are, as the sociologist of science Akrich (1992) would argue, 'inscribed' within the very innovation itself. As she argues,

Designers thus define actors with specific tastes, competences, motives, aspirations, political prejudices, and the rest, and they assume that morality, technology, science, and economy will evolve in particular ways. A large part of the work of innovators is that of 'inscribing' this vision of (or prediction about) the world in the technical content of the new object . . . an attempt to predetermine the settings that users are asked to imagine. (1992, p. 208)

However, we should not thereby assume that this attempt is always successful or indeed based on a proper understanding of the target patient group. In fact, as Blume (1997) has shown with respect to his study of the cochlear implant used to treat deafness in children, the deaf community were highly critical of the implant technology not only because of its costs and side effects, but also because designers presumed no value should be accorded to the use of sign language and the distinctive deaf culture that the community holds in high regard.

Furthermore, where the design of a technology inscribes (i.e. presumes) specific contexts of use, but that technology is deployed in a different setting, we can expect that users will struggle to give value to it in the way envisaged by the innovator. A good illustration of this is the study by Heaton et al., (2005) of the use of life-sustaining technologies for seriously and chronically sick children, devices originally developed for use in a hospital setting. The meaning, combination, use, effectiveness and efficacy of the devices and systems (such as assisted ventilation and intravenous feeding) are quite different when these devices are deployed in the home, where complex care regimens have to be managed by the children's families (including siblings) in conjunction with statutory and voluntary services. Many such technologies work only through constant monitoring and intervention which in the 24/7 nursing shifts of a hospital is more easily achieved. Parents were also responsible for preparing the equipment and providing supplies: the responsibilities and demands on parental time were extensive. As Heaton (in Seymour 2006) observes, 'While families were, to varying degrees, able to incorporate aspects of the care regimes into their everyday routines, at the same time, they experienced a range of difficulties as a result of the time demands of the care regimes being incompatible with other domestic, institutional and social schedules' (p. 138).

While the sociological importance of context of use is therefore key to understanding how technologies are experienced and seen to 'work', it is also necessary to broaden our focus and ask wider questions about the priorities served by medical innovation systems more generally. Here we need to attend to the *structuring* of health care delivery rather than simply to specific issues about context per se. That is we can ask what broader social utility is produced by a biomedical model of health innovation that, as Bury (1998) notes produces a system devoted on the one hand to high-tech biomedical care and on the other management of chronic disease – from a regime of 'treatment and cure' to 'management and care' (p. 267). There have been a number of radical critiques of contemporary biomedicine, such as that of Zola (1997) and also Illich (1975) who in his book *Medical Nemesis* observed that 'The medical establishment has become a major threat to health' (p. 11). The principal target of Illich's attack was medical expertise which through professional monopoly and credentialism controls the meaning of health and knowledge about it, denying alternative sources of understanding or treatment. Moreover, Illich believed the biomedical model and its expert-base obscures the structural reasons that lie behind ill-health, more to do with the unequal distribution of social and economic resources, including health itself rather than a random distribution of pathology: in the United States, for example, 45 million residents are excluded from health care insurance and provision (CCU, 2002).

Such criticisms are not the sole preserve of radical social scientists such as Illich. Recent commentary from within medicine itself raises similarly strong doubts about the social utility – or what has been called 'the fidelity of health care' – of contemporary medicine. Woolf and Johnson (2005), practitioners in US family medicine, argue that few innovations make the 'break-even point' at which they provide a real gain to health care. They note that 'industry's technological advancement finds support with the American public, which marvels over scientific discovery and technological breakthroughs. Robotic devices and genome mapping are more thrilling than bland quality improvement efforts, such as reminder systems and organizational redesign, irrespective of whether the latter saves more lives' (p. 550).

And indeed, policy-makers themselves, acknowledge the limits of medical innovation and its ultimate social utility: as the Australian Productivity Commission noted, it is virtually impossible to conclude that a particular technology will *always* be cost effective or, for that matter, not cost effective – this will depend on who is receiving it and the cost effectiveness of available alternative treatments' (2005, p. xlv).

This exploration of the take-up and efficacy of health innovation has, I hope, shown how both are socially shaped and contested as process and measure. The notion that the sort of medical innovation that characterises biomedical science is unequivocally beneficial or meets social needs cannot be sustained without major qualification. Here the legacy of McKeown's work discussed above remains, for it is clear that when considering the relationship between medical innovation and health it is important to consider at the same time much wider questions about the distribution of socio-economic resources across social class groups. As Colgrove (2002) has argued, McKeown's work 'challenges public health professionals . . . to find ways to integrate technical preventive and curative measures with more broad-based efforts to improve all of the conditions in which people live' (p. 727). This has important implications for health policy and especially the measures and evidence used to demonstrate real health improvements. As Graham (2005) has argued, it is vital to distinguish between evidence relating to general improvements in health (such as related to decline in smoking overall) and evidence relating to persistent health inequalities across the social classes.

Drawing on some classic and more recent analyses, I have also argued that innovation needs to be mobilised across complex networks, that in doing so, its success and efficacy is defined according to criteria that, unhelpfully, fail to address social context properly, and that the resource deployed on biomedicine is structured in such a way that some health needs remain unmet. It is now time to explore health technology in more detail and ask what role is performed by the two main drivers of innovation being considered in this chapter, the clinicians and the state.

The clinical professions, the state and innovation

In understanding the role played by the medical profession in fostering innovation, it is important to consider two inter-related dynamics at work: those relating to forms of knowing that clinicians have deployed and those relating to professional control and expertise within and between clinical disciplines. The second will occupy most of the discussion below, so let me sketch out briefly some key debates about medical knowledge and the forms it might take.

Pickstone (1992, 2000) has provided an historical classification of the forms or 'ways' of knowing that have shaped medicine's engagement with the body and its pathologies. He suggests that there are five ways of knowing – hermeneutics, natural history, analysis, experimentalism and technoscience – that shape medical practice and which though prevalent at particular times in history, from the seventeenth century to the present day, can in certain circumstances coexist in the clinic. Hermeneutics refers to the early text-based rhetoric of medicine that was limited in the extent to which it actually physically intervened in the body; natural history to a way of knowing that links the body to wider cultural beliefs or paradigms of nature and the world; analysis to the increasing rationalisation of medicine as it sought especially to understand the properties and effects of its procedures, such as the basis of chemical compounds used to treat ailments; experimentalism to that form of knowledge based on trial and error, on the use of inventive devices and new measurements that could form the basis of diagnoses; and finally, 'technoscience' which refers principally to current laboratory and industrially based medicine that draws on a very wide range of technologies – such as genetics and informatics – to quarry pathology and the very structures of the body itself.

Pickstone's key point is that there is an affinity between different ways of knowing in medicine, the sorts of technologies that are used, and the sense in which medicine is positioned as a 'science' (Pickstone, 2005). These ways of knowing foster the development of new techniques and procedures within the clinic and create the basis for experimental, diagnostic and applied medical techniques of growing sophistication.

As such techniques developed so too have the specialisms within medicine, forming an occupational division of labour. As Atkinson (1995) has noted, responsibility for patient management gradually extended beyond the single physician to various medics in specialties and sub-specialisms managing the patient through a complex and technical division of labour and 'medical talk'.

Foucault's analysis of the 'clinical gaze' provides a useful link between the epistemic work of writers such as Pickstone and those within medical sociology who have been concerned to understand the professionalising occupational strategies that have been key to the power of orthodox medicine. In his book *The Birth of the Clinic* Foucault (1975) argues that a powerful myth or cultural discourse grew in the Enlightenment period (he speaks primarily of France in his examples) around the power of the clinician's diagnostic, observational 'gaze', a way of seeing that could penetrate the body's (pathological) secrets and problems. This way of seeing is less to do with Pickstone's epistemic categories of knowledge and more about powerful cultural repertoires of expertise that early medicine laid claim to. Observation was, subsequently, codified through learning and teaching in early medical schools, and this produced the observation-learning model that prevails in medical training today. The language of medicine – and especially the notion of divining the patient's 'medical history' – was crucial to the transformation of the clinical gaze from the immediacy of the clinical encounter to a science that was context-free. As Foucault puts it: codifying the patient's problem via a case history 'authorizes the transformation of symptom into sign and the passage from patient to disease and from the individual to the conceptual' (p. 114).

The problem with the Foucauldian perspective on the clinical gaze is that, though critical of the discursive power this holds, he offers no alternative to this, for to do so would be to contravene one of his over-arching philosophical principles, that there is no foundation for critique that is not itself simply another form of discourse. It is this that has attracted considerable criticism from feminist scholars (see e.g. Bordo, 1993, 1993a) who seek to identify the malestream, highly gendered nature of orthodox medicine, and thereby to offer in place a new way of seeing that is neither sexist nor impositional. Feminist analysis has been especially concerned to critique medical innovation within the reproductive domain, seeking to demonstrate that it is here in particular that women find the most patriarchal forms of medical knowledge and practice (Stanworth, 1987; McNeil et al., 1990; Wajcman, 1991). More recent work has focused attention on how the 'medicalisation of childbirth' has been shaped by the expansion of new prenatal genetic screening and tests (Ettore, 2002). There has been considerable debate in this literature about the sense in which reproductive technologies increase or constrain women's control over reproductive choices (whether for example to continue with a pregnancy, to seek IVF treatment, and so on). New technologies open up possibilities and have been said to be empowering (Davis-Floyd, 1994) yet pose new dilemmas for women and their partners, and even pose new risks for women's health (Lippman, 1999). A recent analysis of women's experience of being counselled about the possibility of their carrying a child with Down's Syndrome emphasises how new clinical tests (using ultrasound scanning) and the risk prognoses they create produce uncertainties for women, and indeed, genetic counsellors themselves (Lewando Hundt et al., 2006). At the same time the more tests become routinised in the clinic and results more quickly available the more pressure there is on women to make ('responsible') decisions according to a more restrictive clinical model, despite prognostic uncertainties.

This field of reproductive technology provides a good example of how the three ways of seeing that have been sketched out above come together in clinical practice. Pickstone's discussion focuses on the *epistemic* character of medical knowledge (what counts as knowledge), Foucault's on the *discursive*, cultural power that medical knowledge (and the 'gaze') enjoys in society, while the feminist analysis identifies how that knowledge is *gendered*. Epistemic, discursive and gendered ways of knowing inform the everyday practice of the clinic but also have helped to configure the sorts of innovation choices and uses that to mark the history of medicine. They have fostered technologies that are extremely powerful in their ability to reduce, penetrate, open up and engineer the body.

But these ways of knowing have also been developed in quite systematic ways, coordinated through ways of organising knowledge and its technologies and techniques. This is where we turn to the role of professionalisation as an important factor shaping the pattern of medical innovation.

Mention was made above of the growing division of labour in medicine. A hospital today is likely to house over a hundred different clinical professions focused on discrete pathologies, deploying diverse techniques and acting in more or less 'specialist' ways. The historical origins of this division of labour and the place of technological innovation within it vary considerably from one country to another. In the United States medicine was (and indeed still is) a fee-based system and practitioners secured patient clients through a competitive medical market. Competition led to growing areas of specialisation and the promise of providing clients with the 'latest' technologies and knowledge – both, as Abbott (1988) has observed, 'the currency of competition' (p. 102). In the United Kingdom, in contrast, the doctor either occupied a primary care role as general practitioner or enjoyed a more powerful position through membership of the various 'royal societies' that licensed medics. In this latter context, technology did not serve as a defining and competitive feature of one doctor against another, and indeed, new technologies or discoveries were sometimes actively resisted by establishment medicine, or accepted only on terms that served professional interests. This was especially so if the source of the innovation was outside professional medicine, as for example, was the physicist Roentgen who discovered X-rays in 1895 (Caufield, 1989), or if, as in fields such as epidemiology, new science and innovation could serve interests other than those of medicine, such as government bureaucracy or other non-clinical professionals. And one should not assume that certain innovations are natural candidates for quick adoption: early anaesthesia was objected to by some physicians because they claimed that pain, especially in labour, had diagnostic value.

Most writing in the sociology of the medical profession has focused on the question of power and the role of medical science in reproducing such power over time (e.g. Carr Saunders and Wilson, 1933;

Friedson, 1970a, b). Starr (1982) provided one of the more detailed socio-historical analyses of the rise to power of the American medical profession stressing the role that medical science played in securing public and government support for the clinician. This had been especially the case in the United States and across Europe at the beginning of the twentieth century through the advent of bacteriology, and anaesthesia and antisepsis for surgery.

This close links between medical science and professional practice was fostered not least by the combination of teaching and research that characterised medical training in the United States and, later Western Europe. Such training sought not only to ensure new recruits were conversant with current technical knowledge, but also could demonstrate an ability to handle and manipulate, as experts, indeterminate understanding, where judgement and experience came to the fore. Foucault's 'clinical gaze' resonates here, as does Turner's (1995) observation that expertise pretends 'a distinct mystique which suggests that there is a certain professional attitude and competence that cannot be reduced merely to systematic and routinized knowledge' (p. 133). The ability to play off yet balance these technical (or codified) and indeterminate forms of knowledge characterised the profession for much of the twentieth century (Jamous and Pelloille, 1970).

> However, as Wailoo (2004) has shown, developments in health-related areas of science, notably virology and epidemiology, moved the focus of innovation from clinically-inspired and controlled development to wider public health agencies: as he says, they . . . exemplify the vital relationship not of doctors and patients, but of science, public policy, and the health of populations. These new sciences became integral to a wide range of health crises and discussions – the polio trials, the relationship between smoking and cancer, and so on – health discussions in which the medical profession was active, but not necessarily central. (p. 646)

Health was being drawn on a much larger canvas than that provided by medicine itself, and the developments in the latter part of the century in bioengineering, the physical and molecular sciences occurred as much outside of as within medicine. Indeed, as noted in Chapter 1, the recent review of US physicians' most indispensable innovations – those that deal with their most common problems – indicates the importance of the basic sciences outside of medicine and the role especially of the bioengineering and pharmaceutical industries. To recall: the most important on the list were magnetic resonance imaging (MRI) and CT scanners, ACE (Angiotensin-converting Enzyme) inhibitors, balloon angioplasty and statins. These relate to neurological, carcinogenic and cardiovascular problems, the most prevalent disorders in affluent states. The first of these, the MRI scanner was developed for medical use by a chemist (Lauterbur) and a physicist (Mansfield). Clearly, as we saw earlier in the work of Metcalfe and Romlogan, medical scientists and clinicians were involved in fostering and mobilising these innovations but they did not drive them. Now such technologies are routinely deployed, though the more expensive (notably the MRI scanners) typically available only on a regional basis.

That the source of much innovation from the 1960s onwards has derived from sources outside of the clinic has also meant that the profession has had, especially in this past decade, to accommodate external measures of effectiveness and efficacy – as we saw above – sometimes referred to as 'scientific-bureaucratic' medicine (Kuhlmann, 2004). In part this is driven by the state's concerns over both the costs of such innovation and the associated pressure towards greater standardisation of clinical procedures and interventions. Standardising practice and use of innovation has become increasingly important and in principle, poses a threat to the non-codified, indeterminate expertise of the medic to deploy therapies and devices as he or she sees fit. However, recent studies of the medical profession (Kuhlmann, 2004; Salter, 2004) provide good evidence for the resilience of medicine to accommodate and negotiate, at least among the more senior professions (rather than, say, among nursing or paramedical groups) what such standards mean in practice.

Even so, the growing costs of what we should call biomedical innovation and the importance of public health has brought the state into centre stage in both driving and managing innovation. Table 2.1 below indicates the growth in real terms of national expenditure on health for selected OECD countries, while Table 2.2 summarises the proportion of expenditure on medical technologies, excluding pharmaceutical drugs.

The table not only shows the doubling or even, as in the United States and France tripling of national expenditure on health, but the significance of the proportion of this accounted for by the pharmaceutical industry. The public purse accounts for roughly three quarters of expenditure except for the United States where the drop is accounted for in terms of private health/fee-based payments made directly by consumers. The overall US total is, however, much higher

Table 2.1 National Expenditure on Health as percentage of GDP (gross domestic product)

Country	1960	1980	2003	Of which public expenditure in 2003 comprises (%)	Of which pharmaceutical expenditure in 2003 comprises (%)
Australia	4.1	7	9.3	67.5	14
Canada	5.4	7.1	9.9	69.6	16.9
France	3.8	7.1	10.1	76.3	20.9
Spain	1.5	5.4	7.7	71.2	21.8
United Kingdom	3.9	5.6	7.7	83.4	16
United States	5	8.7	15	44.4	12.9

Source: based on *OECD Health Data* 2005

than any other OECD country. In 2005/2006 the total expenditure on the UK NHS was just over £82 billion, and by 2007/2008, the budget will be £92.6 billion.

Table 2.2 below captures that proportion of national expenditure on health care devoted exclusively to investment in and procurement of medical devices, instruments and technologies (such as telemedical systems). Compared to the drugs bill, this is relatively modest, not least reflecting the smaller firms and markets involved.

Much of state expenditure on health relates to meeting the salary costs of medical and ancillary staff and capital and equipment needs. The growing links between the state and the biotechnology, pharmaceutical and medical devices industries, and more recently corporations working in the information and communication technologies (ICT) sector have produced a much more complex innovation environment, indeed not simply what (with particular reference to the United States) was originally called a 'medical–industrial complex' (Ehrenreich and Ehrenreich, 1970; Relman, 1980) but a medical–industrial–state complex. We shall be exploring this more fully in the next chapter. Here we can focus on the more general ways in which the state has intervened to shape the sorts of medical innovation typical of affluent states.

First, health has become a major component of the economy with respect to employment, production and emergent innovation. Technologies originating outside of the formal clinical setting now cut across and are embedded in health care systems, such as the ICT systems

Table 2.2 Percentage of health care spent on medical technologies

Country	Percentage
Germany	8.6
France	6.5
Spain	6.1
United States	5.1
United Kingdom	4.5

Source: UK House of Commons Health Select Committee (2005)

being introduced to monitor and manage health care. The industrialisation of health in terms of capital investment from both public and private sectors for goods and services has made health a source of both public good and private gain. In the United Kingdom the Department of Health is introducing a national 'information spine' that will integrate electronic patient records and provide for fast access to medical details for health practitioners. It has contracted the major ICT corporation, BT, to provide the infrastructure for the programme (known as 'Connecting for Health'). Innovation in e-health is one of the major priorities of the state, promising faster, remote and in theory more cost-effective care. I return to the introduction of e-health later in the book.

Second, the state has a legal duty to ensure that health innovation is safe and efficacious, in part because of the amount of public expenditure devoted to it and thereby demands from public audit offices that this is well spent. Government also has to meet a growing compensation bill from patients whose treatment as been found to be negligent: innovation here – such as the growth of computer aided support systems to assist clinical practice – is seen as one way of ensuring procedures meet certain standards, precisely by constraining clinical autonomy: too much 'mystique' can be a bad thing. Relatedly, in the very recent past, the state has had to introduce tighter controls on the research conducted by clinicians after a number of scandals over use of human tissue without permission, falsification of data and inadequate regulation of drugs trials. These cases will be explored more fully in Chapter 5, though here we can note that they can have extensive ripple-effects and create broad public mistrust in science and health innovation.

Third, the state seeks to foster innovation that can reduce its overall costs: one area that is notable here is current interest in pharmacogenetics. Pharmacogenetics involves various (genetic and other) tests to determine whether a person is a good or poor metaboliser of a drug, and if so, it should be possible to adjust the dose given to the patient to maximise best use and benefit of the drug, or, in some cases, determine that a patient with a particular genetic profile (their 'genotype') should not be given the drug at all as to do so could produce major, if not fatal, side effects (Webster et al., 2005; Pirmohamed and Lewis, 2004). If this technique were to be fully developed it could reduce the state's drugs bill. In the United Kingdom this amounts to around £7 billion per year, of which about 80 per cent is spent on branded drugs from the major corporations such as GSK, Merck, Roche and so on. The Department of Health is keen to identify savings, but at present can only target off-patent generic drugs. Even so, these still cost around £1.5 billion per annum.Innovation in the pharmacogenetics area could reduce this considerably, and the Department has funded clinical research in the field.

Pharmacogenetics is in fact part of a wider state investment in genetics research and innovation, notably in areas such as genetics testing, diagnostics and gene therapy. Again, this has seen a major investment in the United Kingdom following the publication in 2003 of the Department of Health's White Paper on genetics in the NHS; the state seeks to co-ordinate and promote such technologies across the research and practice-based clinical system, though, as I discuss in Chapter 5, translating research from the clinic to the 'bed-side' can be highly problematic, as suggested earlier in my discussion of the innovation process more generally.

The more the state fosters innovative techniques the more it has to determine precisely where its responsibility lies in terms of development, delivery and payment for them. Health resourcing by the state has always a political calculus, as noted in Chapter 1. Managing innovation is never simply organisational but always political: innovation is, as Barry (2001) has argued, part of a 'political machine' and, while reflecting the technical competences of the nation-state, creates new challenges for the legitimacy of the state and its technical priorities and ambitions.

Finally, as noted above, the state plays a public health role and here the social and political dimensions of innovation are particularly evident. Public health requires governance and regulation of populations in order to manage disease (such as HIV or SARS) and now must do so in global terms given population mobility. Again, we will return to this in Chapter 5.

Contrasting innovation environments

So far the chapter has described the social process of innovation – the social matrix of actors, networks and institutional structures (here professions and the state) – through which new technologies are developed. In this section, I show how variation in this social matrix inevitably produces different innovation outcomes with respect to the ways in which new technologies are taken up. To limit the debate, I focus on the role of political and especially regulatory environments that have responded to the 'promise' and hype of stem cells research, and as a result have been more or less enabling of innovation in this field.

In Europe there are considerable differences in the response to stem cells science. Some countries, such as Austria, Italy and Germany have been reluctant, indeed resistant, to its full embrace, while others, in part through articulating very comprehensive regulatory oversight, have been very accommodating to stem cells research, most notably the United Kingdom. What explains these differences? There are powerful religio-ethical factors that play a part in creating the broadly hostile reception therapeutic cloning has received from catholic/southern European countries. And these may be deepened by the recent inauguration of the very conservative Pope Benedict. However, the pattern of response cannot be explained solely in these terms, since Spain, for example, does permit derivation of stem cells from embryos, and indeed within Spain (Andalusia) regional plans are under way to establish a stem cell bank and allow therapeutic cloning. Ireland and France, strong Catholic countries, are also promoting research in the area.

In order to explain these diverse responses, as Jasanoff (2005) argues, we need to attend to the ways in which existing normative discourses about science are embedded in wider political cultures and practices, and how, thereby, science and politics are engaged in ongoing exchange and mutual stabilisation. This echoes an argument I made over a decade ago (Webster, 1991) when I suggested that we can understand how policy-making responds to new technologies and their perceived costs and benefits, risks and uncertainties, if we locate science policy within the wider political arena. Then I drew a distinction between the structures and processes of decision-making, contrasting structures that are rights-driven, pluralistic/devolved and non-hierarchical with those that tend to be more bureaucratic and top-down, and decision-making processes that are more or less open and contested, more or less expert-led. Together this produces the model as shown in Table 2.3, populated with illustrative countries.

Table 2.3 Political cultures and S and T policy-making

	Pluralistic/devolved	**State-led**
Open and contested	USA/Spain/Sweden	Netherlands Germany Austria
Closed with low public scrutiny	UK/Belgium	EU accession states/France/ Japan

As suggested above, some countries may have a loose, pluralistic structure through which the planning process for science is developed.
Others may adopt a much more centralised, directive style, the corpo-
ratist approach found in Germany. Or again, the adversarial science
politics of the United States contrast with the expert-led committee
system in place in the United Kingdom (see also Salter, 2006).
Overtime, there may be movement across the matrix, as political cultures respond to new challenges and demands made of them. This can
lead to social experimentation in policy-making, as was seen in the UK
government's 'GM Nation' exercise between 2002 and 2004, which
in practice opened up the policy debate on agricultural biotechnology
to wide lay participation. Such experiments are always dependent on
how far government sees them as constrained by and accountable to
within existing institutional structures or providing the basis for the
development of genuinely new ones. The British government adopted
the former line from the start, such that the outcomes of the debate
and the sense of public impact on it were always likely to be limited, as
has been seen (Pidgeon and Poortinga, 2006).

Applying this model to stem cell research we can see that it is similarly shaped by the different structures and processes within European
policy-making. The UK culture allows for incremental and expert-led
policy-making that has provided a context supportive of embryonic
stem cells research while the Spanish regional government structures
and devolved power allows for alternative positions to be adopted
locally, which then feedback on the state at a national level. More open
yet centralised cultures that combine strong bureaucratic regimes tend
toward conservatism in policy-making, as is illustrated by German and
Austrian reluctance to support embryonic stem cell programmes.

The model is offered simply as a heuristic device inasmuch as there
are likely to be occasions when countries do not neatly fall within one
category. But it does suggest how different political cultures may be

more or less likely to adopt more or less ambitious policies about the boundaries of stem cells research. The iterative, expert-led policy in the United Kingdom has been built on the political consensus surrounding the earlier Warnock Inquiry (Warnock, 1984), and has produced an extensive body of regulatory and advisory codes of practice that far from constraining science give it the room to develop in a gradualist way. Elsewhere, boundaries are defined through more formalised, public debate that lead to explicit national policy decisions that must appeal to a wider constituency of interests, as in the Netherlands or Sweden. However, where devolved decision-making is possible – as in the United States and Spain – legitimacy can be more locally crafted and framed, as in California's Proposition 71 (with which we opened this chapter) and more recently in Massachusetts and Andalusia.

The implications of the argument are that innovation, though driven by similar actors, is always so within specific contexts, here important political and regulatory ones. Health research, such as stem cells science, is, like any other field, configured by these socio-political processes and the priorities and interests they serve. This leads to a broader question relating to the way innovation serves public and/or private good interests? I return to this in the concluding chapter of the book, but with regard to the broad question of the chapter – what drives biomedical innovation? – we might ask whether the 'quality' of such innovation differs when it originates from the private rather than the public sector?

What might quality imply here? Quality is best seen in terms of sustainable health innovation that can be seen to be demonstrably a (therapeutic, curative, preventative) public good. Herein, lies the possibility of a critical but constructive intervention by social scientists in the health policy arena. Claims made on behalf of novel innovation, by both public and private actors can be assessed against such criteria. But some health economists argue that the primary driver for much of the health innovations seen over the past 50 years has been the private sector, for while the public sector may be good at initiating inventive ideas or prototypes, it is poor in taking these through to full development. However, there is evidence of the public sector leading innovation in public good areas that has been successful, even if commercial interests have moved in to commodify such fields: this is true of vaccines (Blume, 2006), prosthetics (especially, for example through their tie-in with minimally invasive surgery; Anderson et al. (2007) and wheelchair design (Woods and Watson, 2005). It is an important task for sociology and related social sciences to explore what characterised these fields and their innovation networks, if we are to see an expansion in the innovation potential of public health systems.

Conclusion

This chapter has explored what I have called the 'social matrix' of medical innovation. In doing so, a number of key arguments have been advanced. First, that innovation is co-constructed across diverse actors and networks; that its diffusion and take up depends on its being successfully mobilised across such networks; that even then, what counts as its efficacy is in turn a matter of negotiation and contestation, subject to increasing attempts to discipline the form and use of new technologies and procedures through the trio of HTA, EBM and QoL metrics. Second, I discussed the role of clinicians in shaping developments in medical technology, relating this to both 'ways of knowing' and 'ways of organising', through professional strategies, the science and practice of medicine. I argued that the clinicians' role as drivers of new technology has been overtaken by the state and the private sector in the past 50 years, yet, even so, that medics are still able to gate-keep and manage the way in which new systems are incorporated into health care. I outlined the economic, regulatory and enabling role of the state and the problems it must confront. Third, I described, through reference to stem cells, how diverse political cultures configure and open up or close down innovation paths through the regulatory positions they adopt, indicating how science is always highly politicised within the political machine. I described a model of policy-making that I suggested can be used to understand this diversity and would suggest could be used to help explain nation-states' response to all forms of technoscience innovation, not just that found within health.

I concluded by arguing that more work in the sociology of innovation needs to be undertaken to explore the capacity of the public sector to produce innovation that meets public good needs. This echoes the criticisms noted earlier in the chapter with respect to the net gains (or lack thereof) relating to much that passes for medical innovation today.

In conclusion, it should be clear that the relationship between health, technology and society is neither uniform across different societies, nor stable within any one society. The scale and significance of the relationship has meant that it has become a major site for economic investment, political surveillance, and in contrast growing demand from lay and patient groups for more accountable, accessible and affordable therapies. This last point – where health becomes an item of consumption in a wider market-place, takes us to the theme of our next chapter, where we look at the role of the corporation, the market, and the consumer of medicine and how national and international agencies have sought to regulate these.

Corporate Health, Markets and Regulation

Introduction

Take a walk down any high street in a relatively prosperous city and note the variety of shops that are in some ways connected with health. Apart from the pharmacists selling (among other items) over-the-counter medicines and licensed drugs, there are alternative health stores, organic food stores, sports and keep-fit outlets, clinics for that healthy tan (and in Australia clinics to advise on skin cancer caused by such tans), leisure companies selling 'active holidays' and so on. Add to this high street parade of stores the virtual health sites on the Internet superhighway, and it is clear that health has become as significant a site for social and material consumption as the car, clothing, food, education or housing. And, of course, the 'consumption' of health is often precisely in response to other, regarded as harmful forms of consumption, such as overeating, poor nutrition, or alcohol and tobacco abuse.

Sociologists working in the field of consumption studies emphasise the ways in which consumerism and the consumer society have become central to lifestyle, social identity and social status (Miller, 2001; Fine, 2002). However, while we might seek fulfilment through consumption it is typically a highly alienating experience (and often environmentally damaging). Rather than providing a source of stability, consumption creates unstable, postmodern identities and, indeed, compulsive buying has, as you might expect, now been medicalised as an illness (Lee and Mysyk, 2004). At a wider level consumerism is said to generate an individualistic and fragmented social structure that dilutes the pre-existing social class hierarchies characteristic of industrial society. The objects of consumption are themselves highly plastic in their meaning, effect and utility – jeans can mean many things (Fiske, 1989) – and are promoted by manufacturers and advertising agencies with specific markets in mind, both local and global, as Ritzer's famous text on the 'McDonaldisation' of the world suggested (Ritzer, 1998).

Work on the sociology of the body provides an important link between consumption and health, since it shows how the body itself has become a 'project', a site where considerable personal investment in time, effort, grooming and body disciplining is required. As Shilling (2002) notes,

> people are now no longer able to take their bodies for granted when they are healthy, but are faced with multiple models of body maintenance from which to choose . . . . In this context, the need to develop a healthy, adaptable and instrumentally efficient body has become an important variable in social success. (p. 627)

This too feeds higher levels of consumption of products that are designed to enhance the body and thereby become a target for the manufacture of goods (such as vitamin pills) and services (such as sports and fitness centres). Given this volume of consumption activity, it is not surprising that major companies are involved in the health sector today, not only those in the pharmaceutical sector, but in a much more widely defined health and leisure industry. These companies play an important role in shaping the demand for health and in creating new illnesses, failings or deficiencies that the consumer, and the patient-as-consumer are encouraged to buy into. This chapter discusses the main features of this world of corporate health, and examines in particular, the emergence and role of the medical–industrial complex (MIC) and within that the role of the global pharmaceutical sector, and the ways in which the state both fosters yet regulates private corporate interests in health. On the basis of material presented in this chapter, I argue that though there are tensions emerging between health corporations and an increasingly critical public, the fragmentation and delegation of state policy to local, global and personal responsibilities and the state's support for 'bio- (and indeed "info-" capitalism' make it highly unlikely that calls for greater controls over what I call here 'corporate health' will succeed.

Corporations and health markets

In exploring the role of the private sector, it is important to differentiate between a number of areas within which investment is made.

There are three which define much if not all of the activity: first, there are firms involved in developing novel products, such as therapeutic drugs, or new technologies (such as medical devices or robotics); second, there are corporations providing health care services (which may be contracted by government agencies), and various forms of actuarial advice, notably in the health insurance market; and finally, firms providing infrastructural support for other organisations that provide the actual health service itself. Examples of this last group are those global firms supplying the platform technologies for telehealthcare in a number of different countries, such as IBM Health, BT and Telstra. Another important feature of these areas of investment is that corporations have sought to vertically and horizontally integrate their goods and services across different markets, and in doing so repositioning themselves as general health and lifestyle companies, rather than ones simply providing a specific product to a discrete sector of the market. This has led to a growing number of mergers across the sector as a whole.

Many corporations also operate at a global level not least as a result of the growing geographical integration of markets and increasing across convergence national state regulation of these markets (as in the EU, for example). This is especially true for product-based firms (such as drugs companies) rather than those providing services, precisely because the market for services is much more context and culturally specific. It also reflects the fact that services have been typically the preserve of the state. Within national boundaries, this goods and services distinction is much less apparent. The growth of public–private partnerships has opened new opportunities for private investors, in terms of both capital build programmes (for new hospitals or other facilities) and service provision. In poorer countries of the world, the imposition of 'liberalised' markets and health care by international funding agencies has created new, profitable but highly uneven and unequal health markets for firms, while weakening local public provision for health. In a recent study of the role of the World Bank in promoting the interests of US corporate health in Latin America, Iriart et al. (2001) show how the introduction of 'managed care' programmes in Mexico and neighbouring states has enabled US firms to occupy a key intermediary position in the administrative and insurance-related aspects of health delivery. The Bank's loans to Latin American governments come with strings attached, namely 'structural adjustment' that typically involves a cut back in public services: as the authors note, 'The purpose of these policies was to reduce state participation in the financing, administration, and delivery of services, and to enhance the role of the private sector' (p. 1247). This privatisation of health care in developing countries has occurred elsewhere, such that, even though the absolute amount may be comparatively small in global terms, as a proportion of expenditure on health, poorer countries spend a *higher* percentage of their (low) income on *private* health care than richer countries (see Mackintosh and Koivusalo, 2005).

Corporations seeking to expand their markets look for those areas that are, as Chakraborty and Harding (2003) put it, more or less 'buyable', that is more likely to allow easy access, a speedy exit if things go wrong, and where possible goods or services that are relatively stable with respect to demand. Those most buyable include drugs, diagnostics, hospitable support services and ambulatory clinical care. As they enter these markets firms develop new products and services that can meet both existing and new demands, while at the same time, seeking to encourage ever greater use of the well-established products. This in part explains the extensive evidence of 'over-use' of health technologies in some settings – such as ultrasound scans during antenatal care – which can lead to greater chance of harm than good to the patient. The market for health as lifestyle product is as large as that for more conventional medical goods, and firms now provide drugs such as Viagra to improve sexual performance, manage diet, check obesity and cope with a range of allergies. Of course, how such drugs 'perform' is not simply the result of the biomedical compound on which they are based, but will depend on the ways these drugs are *given* potency – the social scripts of what Viagra does are key to any success it might have (see e.g. Mamo and Fishman, 2001).

In Chapter 1 it was argued that there were three fields in which we can find forms of health innovation that both continue to build on yet offer radical breaks from the past. These are *genetics, informatics* and *tissue engineering*. Inasmuch as they offer both continuity and change, they are potentially profitable though risk-laden arenas into which firms are moving. Much of the novelty will depend on research and development undertaken in corporations in tandem with researchers in medical schools and bioscience departments and centres in academia.

In the *genetics* field there are three areas which are of central strategic importance for firms keen to secure their medium and long-term position in the health market: these are pharmacogenetics, genetic diagnostics/tests and the bio banking of genetic information. These represent the basis of future genetic medicine inasmuch as the first should provide the basis for a drugs industry that targets the genetic origin of disease rather than managing the symptoms of it as now; the second, spinning out from this and from the research conducted on the human genome identifying genetic 'markers' (now about 1500) for different disorders, should provide a crucial intermediary technology that translates corporate science from the lab to the clinic; the third, biobanking, should, in theory, bring even greater value-added to the industry by long- term analysis of genotypic and phenotypic information that ties genes to lifestyle, illness patterns and a whole range of demographic information of immense use to companies, with respect to their clinical trials, targeting drugs for specific population groups and fine-tuning regulatory submissions made to drug approval agencies.

Not surprisingly, therefore, it is these three areas within genomic medicine that have attracted a high proportion of investment by biotechnology, gene-based and pharmaceutical companies, and in turn seen major activity with respect to the patenting of genes and genetic technologies. Gene patenting (a right granted in the United States since 1980) has been highly controversial with respect to companies' claims to 'own' what are regarded by critics as part of the 'genetic commons' (see World Social Forum, 2005), as well as disputed by bioethicists and lawyers in terms of the infringement of individual human rights (Laurie, 2002; Nuffield, 2002). Patenting has also been seen to delay or constrain the introduction of new research into clinical settings (Quigley, 2002) and has been criticised by scientists who to their surprise find that the results of their work are claimed to be covered by patents already held by companies (Waldholz, 2000). This criticism has not, however, stopped such patents being granted, and currently, there are over 4 million patents held or filed by biotechnology and pharmaceutical firms worldwide. Many of these were filed in a patent rush during the 1990s by new firms keen to secure intellectual property in genetics and so to attract venture capital investment: the actual function and utility of the patented gene was often unknown. Today the principal patent offices, such as WIPO, and the regional equivalents in the United States and Europe require some evidence of utility, that is, that patent claims must include how the inventive step might be of use. However, as Calvert (2004) has shown it is exceedingly difficult to identify precisely what functionality gene sequences may have, especially in biological terms, that is, in the very materiality of the gene itself. In response, many biotech firms file patent claims based on the *information* they claim the gene provides: however, this attempt to patent information has met with strong resistance from scientists working in the public sector, who argue that information be regarded as a public good.

Patents provide formal legal rights through which knowledge claims (inventions and discovery) can render private economic returns to an individual (or organisation). As such, they work against wider collective notions of social rights or justice that critics of gene patenting advocate. They play an important role in the new biocapitalism (Lock, 2001) and are, thereby, part of what May (2000) has called the 'new enclosures', echoing the first enclosures of the early agricultural revolution that removed collective access to farmland.

Clearly, there is substantial investment by biotech firms in genetics research because of the potential for profit such innovation is expected to bring. There have been some significant therapeutic developments made since 1980, but these are much fewer than the hype would suggest. Evidence by Nightingale and Martin (2004) summarised in Table 3.1 shows that only 12 drugs based on recombinant proteins have significant global markets and many of these markets have taken 10 to 20 years to build. This, they argue, speaks to a much more gradual and limited impact of genetic innovation on biomedicine, despite the extensive patenting noted above. Biocapitalism is, then, thriving but unevenly so, and its clinical value much less apparent than the

Table 3. 1   Therapeutic proteins with sales >$500 in 2002–2003

Product	First launched by	Annual sales 2002/2003 ($ million)	Launch date
Recombinant therapeutic proteins			
Recombinant human insulin	Lilly	5340	1982 (US)
Recombinant human growth hormone	Genentech	1760	1985 (US)
Interferon alpha	Roche & Schering-Plough	2700	1986 (US)
Erythropoeitin	Amgen/Johnson & Johnson	8880	1989 (US)
Granulocyte colony stimulating factor	Amgen	2520	1991 (US & EU)
Blood Factor VIII	Bayer	670	1992 (US)
Interferon beta	Berelex (Schering AG)	2200	1993 (US)
Glucocerebrosidase	Genzyme	740	1994 (US)
Follicle Stimulating Hormone	Serono & Organon	1000	1995 (EU)
Blood Factor VII a	Novo Nordisk	630	1996 (EU)
TNF receptor binding protein	Amgen	800	1998 (US)
Lutenising hormone	Serono	590	2000 (EU)

promotional hype found on the Web and in the biotech trade journals would suggest.

Let us now turn our attention to the three areas in genetics noted above which are attracting new levels of interest and investment from corporate health. Pharmacogenetics, as mentioned in Chapter 1, involves the search for genetic information related to what are known as single-nucleotide polymorphisms (SNPs, pronounced 'snips'). These affect the function of enzymes in the liver, playing a crucial role in the way drugs are metabolised in the body: having a particular SNP profile will mean that a patient is a good, bad or poor metaboliser of a drug. In theory, therefore, dosage levels for a drug could be modified and made much more accurate for different patients with particular profiles, so enabling the arrival of 'personalised medicine'. As a recent study (Webster et al., 2005) shows, there are about 60 firms investing in the area, split fairly evenly between the large pharmaceuticals, such as Roche, and smaller biotech firms. There are various ways in which the technique has been deployed, primarily to help filter drugs for safety and efficacy during clinical trials, and to a lesser extent developing pharmacogenetic tests for existing drugs prior to their being prescribed. There is very limited commercial interest in the latter, since this may well erode a company's drug market. Moreover, this field of biocapitalism has to contend with reluctance among clinicians to adopt pharmacogenetics because of its cost, time to test, the relative value of information provided and the fact that there are already existing techniques (such as blood tests) for determining likely response to drugs. This links back to a point made in Chapter 2 that take-up of new technologies depends on whether they are seen as a marked improvement on those already available. In short, the role of pharmacogenetics in shaping drug delivery systems is still uncertain, carrying both clinical and corporate risk.

The second area, diagnostic tests and screening, has become of growing importance to corporate health. In many countries including the United States and United Kingdom, tests can be advertised and sold direct to the public, without any formal quality check. Global pharmaceutical companies, such as Roche, Beckton Dickenson and GSK, manufacture these tests as well as smaller biotech firms such as Sciona and Gene Link. Most recent evaluation of the tests indicates they have very limited clinical value and may generate unnecessary anxieties about possible but unlikely prospective diseases. One area that has attracted strong corporate interest is DNA paternity testing. These tests are being used by private individuals in increasing numbers to establish family blood ties to resolve disputes over who carries the legal and economic responsibilities for children. Here the technology offers a forensic certification of familial relations.

In the United Kingdom the Human Genetics Commission (2003) advised the government to restrict the sale of genetic tests direct to the public because of fears it had about their safety and value, but more significantly concern over the fact that there was no formal regulation of firms, reflecting anxiety over the governance of corporate health. Private diagnostic companies saw the HGC's advice as a threat to their market and offered self-regulation instead, though the UK government is still to make its formal response to the report. The UK corporate activity in this area is in fact quite limited, compared with the United States and Germany both of which have large commercial sectors. This situation may well change, however: as part of its drive to promote greater over-the-counter (OTC) access for patients to medicines previously only available through general practitioners, the UK government published The Medicines (Advertising) Amendment Regulations in 2004. The new regulations allowed advertising of OTC test kits for genetic disorders.

At the same time however, there appears to be a strong political investment among UK genetic advisory agencies, regulatory bodies such as NICE, the NHS and the Department of Health itself, that predictive tests should, as the 2003 report argued, be regarded as the preserve of the clinician not the private marketplace. These boundaries between the public and private are drawn as a result of the play of political, economic and professional networks that vary between countries. In the United Kingdom they reflect the concerns as well as dominance of a nationalised health service. Hopkins (2003) has also argued with regard to the development of cytogenetic tests that these have been heavily dependent on the craft skills of NHS clinicians developing techniques that work. He argues that it would be highly unlikely that firms could capture and standardise such skills, not least because 'these skills will continue to be too complex to fully automate and that clinical scientists will maintain their control of the technology, leaving firms at the periphery' (p. 26).

The final area considered of key importance to the long-term utility of health genetics relates to the curation and analysis of biological samples and digitised genetic data in large-scale bio banks. Such banks are being established as public, private and hybrid organisations across the world (see Lewis, 2004). There are a variety of banks serving different purposes, some focusing on banking tissue from specific population groups carrying certain disease profiles in order thereby to determine what gene/disease areas to target. Others are more encompassing and seek to capture what we might call representative DNA, that is genetic material from across the population, along with their past, present and future medical histories and lifestyles. The United Kingdom and the United States have recently established banks of this second type. Other banks can be found in Canada, Estonia, Finland, Iceland, Norway, Sweden and Singapore.

The UK Bio bank intends to recruit 500,000 volunteers aged between 45 and 69 from GP and hospital patients to donate blood samples and information about their health, medication and lifestyle. This 'phenotypic' information can then be linked to their DNA genotypes and in theory provide links between genes, disease and lifestyle. Initiated in 2002, the bank only announced the first collection of samples in January 2006, reflecting the social, political and organisational difficulties it has had, and no doubt will continue to face, not least in securing sufficient and reliable phenotypic information.

One of the central areas of contention has been a question over the status and ownership of the data a bank holds and the information it renders. This is a common concern in the establishing of databases but it was one that was highly politicised in the United Kingdom through the public scandal over the removal, retention and use of deceased children's organs and tissues by clinicians at the Alder Hey Hospital in Liverpool (House of Commons, 2001). The Department of Health, Medical Research Council and Wellcome Trust, the principal funders of the bank, were anxious that such controversy would be visited on the new bank simply by association. A prolonged consultation and period of review of ethical and governance concerns served to garner broad support in principle for the bank, though securing enough GPs to recruit patients proved problematic. Unlike the US bank which will, if asked, give information to donor participants about possible future disease they may contract, such as cancer, the UK bank will not provide any feedback.

More contentious have been those banks (unlike the UK Biobank) that have given exclusive access to private companies of the genetic and related information they house (indeed had such an arrangement been made in the United Kingdom the bank would have been much less likely to gain support). These include most notably the Icelandic Health Sector Database and the US-based company deCODE Genetics. The company was interested in securing access to a population group whose genetic make-up and genealogy was relatively well-documented: the information that could be developed from this could then be sold on to third party drugs companies. DeCODE approached the Icelandic government in 1997 and recommended the establishing of a national database. Subsequently, in 2000 deCODE was given, through Act of Parliament, full access to the emerging database which, uniquely, intends to carry the health records entire Icelandic population (c. 280,000). This (anonymised) data is then to be linked to genetic information provided by volunteers. The company also sold to Roche exclusive access to this genetic information through which they could develop new drugs. The Icelandic government met with considerable hostility from clinicians and patient groups, criticisms ranging from lack of patient consent (which had simply been 'presumed'), the exclusive rights to market the data that were given to deCODE and Roche and concerns over third party access to the data, especially by insurance companies. Commenting on the debate, Sigurdsson (2001) notes,

> This was a volatile mixture of messy ethical questions, lofty medical and economical promises, and politics, in a society which possessed neither a vocabulary nor tradition to discuss biotechnology, bioinformatics or the regulation of biomedical research, and certainly had no international models with which to discuss novel genomic database issues. (p. 105)

Even so, many Icelandic citizens and patients sought to opt-out of the 'presumed consent' enshrined in the Act, and by 2004 between over 20,000 had done so. The more opting-out occurs, the more this compromises deCODE's commercial stake, and indeed, there is more recent evidence to indicate that the firm has repositioned its interest away from the collection and analysis of the full population dataset, towards searching for specific gene/disease relation in which Roche would be more interested and through which a faster return on their investment might be made. So while in practice it may not be the case that Iceland is, as Lewontin (1999) argued, making 'its entire population into a captive biomedical commodity', it is clearly evident that the deCODE bio bank case:the potential tension between private and public good bioscience (see Chadwick, 1999). At the same time, the Icelandic case, and indeed all other bio banks, illustrate what Gottweis (2003) has called the emergence of a new 'biopolitics'. In the past, states secured information on whole populations as part of an agenda that sought to manage health as a collective endeavour through, for example, national policies on reproduction, public health and hygiene. Bio banks are, in contrast, tied into the growing individualisation and geneticisation of health as risk susceptibility to disease. They also give more momentum to the decorporalisation of the body (Brown and Webster, 2004) where patient samples are transformed into serum, blood samples, DNA and digital versions thereof to be accessed and used by multiple actors including drugs firms, clinical scientists, insurance companies, universities and so on.

In regard to *informatics*, our second main field, the structure of corporate investment is more diverse, and reflects a technology that is markedly different from bioscience and genetics. Rather than being long-term and so depending on more radical shifts in innovation, informatics is much more continuous, incremental developmental, that is, quick to market, typically with a two-year product life cycle. While much is made of the development of e-commerce in the form of business-to-consumer markets, the e-based activity between businesses is much higher, perhaps by a factor of ten (Miles, 2002).

In broad terms, one of the most significant developments influencing how society accesses and uses ICT systems is the arrival of broadband of ever-greater bandwidth capacity across fixed and mobile networks. This has had major implications for the scale, scope, speed, storage and accessibility of remote and proximate information; in the area of e-health these characteristics have been seen to be of central importance in what, as noted in Chapter 1, I have called the 'informaticisation' of health (Webster, 2002).

Corporate e-health has to be seen as part of the wider pattern of investment in the cyber economy. Over the past decade the expansion of ICT-based systems has been rapid and extensive leading to a deepening of capital investment in informatics throughout the economy of affluent states. As prices have fallen in real terms and quality and capacity increased the dependency of economic systems on informatics has grown, and while enabling growth, this has also created new risks and crises when systems fail or products cannot cope with the complexity they themselves create. Some have argued that these developments herald the arrival of an 'information society' or, as Castells (1996) prefers 'informational' society, emphasising the centrality of information in radically transforming life in regard to sources of productivity, power and property. Such arguments should not, however, lead to the conclusion that information is thereby a new force for equality, for not only are ICT systems unevenly available on a global scale, but can also serve to reproduce or create new inequalities and disadvantages (Stanworth, 1998; Golding, 2000).

Health is itself a highly complex socio-technical system and informatics has been introduced to both manage and improve it and to

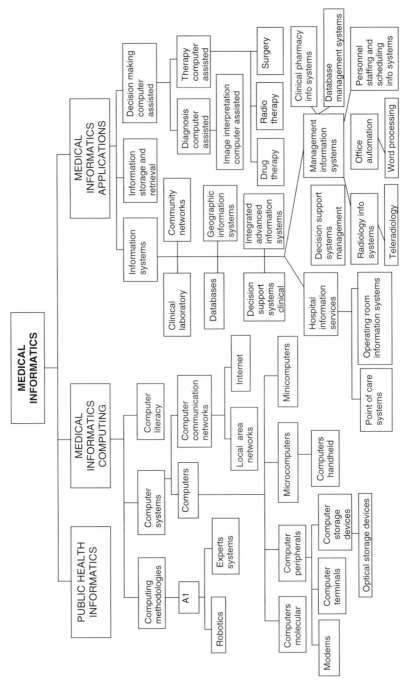

Figure 3.1 Medical informatics systems

Source: Pagliaria et al., 2005

reduce its costs. Some sense of this complexity is conveyed by the map of the medical informatics world found within the United Kingdom's NHS system (see Figure 3.1).

Private corporations providing ICT goods and services have moved into the medical informatics field with the support of government agencies or through selling directly to healthcare providers. The main areas of corporate investment can, as Ballon et al., (2003) have suggested, be differentiated into four main areas. These are summarised in Table 3.2.

The principal corporations investing in these areas are global organisations such as Microsoft, BT, Nokia and Intel. These combine hardware, software and communications systems and so can access these four different market niches with a range of generic and customised technologies. Corporations seek to lock customers into their products to secure stable long-term markets, and do so through designs that constrain how they are used, what Bijker and Law (1992) have called the 'obduracy' of existing socio-technical systems. This lock-in, or path dependency, makes it difficult for competitors or smaller firms to enter the market with genuine alternatives, and they too become part of a supply chain to the larger corporations.

Is there, then, something that we might call 'info-capitalism', paralleling that of 'biocapitalism' discussed above? Clearly there, at a general level, major global corporations that make profit through the sale of products and services to both public and private consumers, such as the banking and financial sector. The impact of ICT systems in industrial and service sectors as a whole has been shown to reduce costs (especially of labour) through greater flexibilisation of work, part-time and contract work, and loss of long-term stability. There are too

Table 3.2 Corporate investment in e-health

Health domain	Corporate health focus
Prevention	Lifestyle applications (e.g. weight management)
Cure	Diagnostic, monitoring systems (ambient intelligence)
Care	Smart homes/ hospital monitoring systems
Health information management	Platform technologies for whole health care systems

patents and other intellectual property rights associated with both hard- and software, and licensing arrangements constrain who can and who may not use systems. In addition, we can see various forms of technically derived but financially driven lock-in: Miles (2002) observes, for example, that 'many of the newer users of the Internet are effectively "locked in" to particular portals by the financial and learning costs associated with changing service provider' (p. 21). This is part of what he calls 'the fencing of the electronic frontier', reminiscent of May's notion of the 'new enclosures' noted above.

Indeed, info-capitalism has been argued by Castells (1996) in his notion of 'informational capitalism', is also suggested by Schiller's (1999) work on 'digital capitalism' (primarily a critique of the capitalisation of the Internet) and by BurtonJones (2001) notion of 'knowledge capitalism' (exploring the centrality of knowledge and 'knowledge management' in the contemporary economy) and none of these texts examine the role of info-capitalism in the context of health. The degree to which information has transformed capitalism per se has been challenged (see Webster, F., 2000, 2002). Even so, many of these arguments could usefully be applied here. Most importantly, as elsewhere, information systems and their capacity for fast, massive and time-flexible information storage, access and relay have become defining features of information management, and in health have been central to the development of the electronic patient record, and are becoming more important in clinical delivery, such as picture archive and communication and clinical decision support systems. State agencies procure these systems from corporations according to specifications that are supposed to meet user needs. Typically these require ongoing modification to ensure compliant and integrated networks, difficult to achieve across nationwide or even regional contexts of application.

There are a range of questions that have been raised about corporate health as provider and potential user of health information, similar to those linked to biocapitalism. These relate to control over information held in systems, data protection and privacy, whether system providers can access information even if anonymised for third party users (such as market research agencies or insurance companies), and the way these issues reflect the commodification of health information and knowledge, deepening and extending the means through which private capital can generate new forms of value (Gane, 2003).

At the same time, it is important to note countervailing processes at work restricting and constraining the capacity of private capital to exploit health information. State regulation and legislation are key barriers to this, as are clinician and patient group challenges to third party access. Moreover, e-health, especially through the Internet, has been shown to be enabling or empowering of patient and health consumers more generally to check and seek alternative sources of information, product or service (Hardey, 2001; Nettleton et al., 2005). Indeed, patients can learn through the Internet about services or therapeutics available in other countries but not available locally (either because of high costs or regulatory restrictions) and buy them over the Web, or can challenge health agencies to provide them locally (Fox et al., 2005). The possibility of patients opting out of state provision through Web-based private means compromises regulatory control and the public health intelligence required for effective epidemiology.

Informatics, in sum, is a key site for corporate health and one that has growing profitability attached to it, principally with respect to the provision of large-scale information platforms on which smaller, more localised technologies can build, and through which smaller firms can find a slot on the supply chain. State agencies around the world are buying into these systems to improve health care and its management though the extent to which this will actually reduce costs on health budgets is questionable. Monitoring systems can be extremely costly, and patient anxieties and sense of insecurity about their health could well generate high levels of demand when the objective is to moderate them. Moreover, ICT systems can lead to the distribution of health delivery across various health practitioners in time and space and thereby open up questions about the meaning of 'treatment' and who is to be held accountable for it. There is also the possibility of clinical errors being 'digitally embedded' and so, as a result, amplified in a health management system – just as credit card errors can become entrenched and difficult to resolve in banking systems. The informaticisation of medicine both through state and private sector activity may also raise questions in the future about the status and value of non-digital sources of information.

The final field to be discussed relates to *tissue culture* within which can be included bioengineering and stem cells technologies: how does corporate health engage with these related areas of biomedical and clinical practice? At present this is a much more precarious and uncertain investment target for corporations compared with both genetics and informatics. Some indication of the reason for this was given in the opening pages of Chapter 2 where I discussed in brief California's Proposition 71 and the social and technical labour that has had to be expended to build a sufficiently robust 'social matrix' through which stem cells research – and so long-term commercial investment – might be stabilised. In more sociological terms, we can reframe this as a problem of 'purification' for both industry and regulators (see Brown et al., 2006; Faulkner et al., 2006): what precisely is to be defined as a human tissue engineered product that can then be the basis for a sale and a regulatory statute? As Faulkner et al., argue, uncertainty over this has created a regulatory vacuum across the European Union (EU), and thereby problems for secure capital investment.

Much of the difficulty in commodifying this area relates directly to the biological, experimental, and clinical understanding and management of this much messier world of wet biology, which cannot be as easily captured and redefined as bio-information as have the fields of genetics and informatics. Even so, the clinical and commercial potential associated with these developments have been strong enough to generate large-scale investment in the field, from both state and private sources. The United States has seen higher levels of corporate investment in tissue engineering than elsewhere over the past 15 years or so (Lysaght and Reyes, 2001) with investment levels currently around the $1 billion per annum, despite the fact that relatively few profitable products are on the market.

One of the principal drivers for this level of interest is the pressure, as Waldby (2002) puts it, on existing 'tissue economies', the supply and demand for organ transplant and other more conventional forms of tissue replacement (such as blood donation). Tissue engineering promises to provide unlimited supplies of lab cloned rather than patient–donor derived tissue. In theory this could then be used therapeutically to treat pathologies of the brain (such as Alzheimers), heart, lung or any other of the organs of the body. Embryos are often the source of such tissue, and the cell lines they produce distributed across a range of research and clinical settings for experimental or therapeutic use. Waldby and Mitchell (2006) observe that the relationship between donor and eventual use is much more complex than found in more conventional forms of donation (driven by classical conceptions of civic responsibility), such as giving blood. As they say, 'a single donated embryo may form the starting point for several immortalised cell lines that can be copied, divided, sent to laboratories and clinics around the world, and eventually used to treat an open-ended number of patients, Tissue donation is thus transformed from an act of direct civic responsibility between fellow citizens into a complex network of donor-recipient relations' (p. 22). And to ensure tissue is repositioned such that its status as 'human' can be set aside, Waldby and Mitchell point to the ways in which tissue is reconfigured as 'waste' to both distance it from donors and release it into global circulation.

At the same time, however, extracting and using tissue is technically an extremely difficult and risk-laden enterprise and many clinicians have expressed serious reservations over the hype and promise of human tissue-cell engineering. State investment continues to grow and focuses increasingly on so-called translational research, research that will translate basic science into clinical practice. In the United Kingdom, for example, government has funded a 'stem cell initiative' supporting five 'centres of excellence' and a national 'stem cell production unit' that will undertake the translational work on a pilot basis. As with many such initiatives, this is Treasury supported because of a perceived development gap, but involves the private sector as partner, notably the Stem Cell Foundation supported by venture capital and the pharmaceutical industry. The Department of Health, leading on this initiative, is well aware of the exaggerated promise often associated with the field, and commenting on this says, 'although it is reasonable to anticipate that some new stem cell therapies will be developed within the next decade, we must also accept that it is probable that this area will take several decades of small incremental advances in science and medicine to come to fruition' (see DoH, 2005).

This completes my discussion of the three fields that mark out the key market areas for corporate health today. All three show similar processes at work, relating to:

- the commodification of personal and population-based genetic information;
- the drive to capture and distil such information through definable property rights held as patents;
- and through such a process purify, reduce, make mobile and so exploit such information across different markets, nationally and globally;
- common to all too is the role of the state as enabler of private investment and regulator of its products.

Moreover, there are strong networks between public, private and professional organisations through which basic science is co-constructed and fashioned for more applied, clinical settings. These ties, especially between corporations and physicians have been seen as being central to what has been called the medical-industrial complex, and it is to this that I now turn as a specific aspect of corporate health.

The MIC complex

The notion of the MIC was first introduced by Ehrenreich and Ehrenreich (1971). It is perhaps not surprising that the term was first coined in the US context where ties between health corporations and physicians, insurance firms, health equipment suppliers, finance houses and construction companies have been extremely strong, and form a 'complex' of relations that serve corporate health interests. Subsequently, various writers have developed the original MIC thesis, notably Navarro (1976), Relman (1980), Krimsky (2003) and Kassirer (2005). Navarro argued that the health care system in capitalist states serves the interests of private capital. In managing disease, in fostering medical education and research, and the development of drugs and medical devices, private capital's interests are served both through the maintenance of a healthy workforce and a market for health and health-related goods and services such as private insurance or the outsourcing of hospital catering and cleaning. More generally, the state has, he claimed, represented health and illness as a matter of individual or personal choice and lifestyle rather than a direct result of structures of inequality, thereby hiding the social determinants of poor health.

The more recent work exemplified by Krimsky and Kassirer focuses attention on the strength of academic-industry ties between researchers and companies and the conflict of interest this can generate, as well as the direct influence firms have over doctors through gifts, corruption and various indirect forms of pressure and persuasion. While these writers provide powerful evidence of ties between industry and academia, these are not restricted to the field of health, nor should we see them as solely initiated by a predatory industrial sector. On the contrary, throughout the world, public sector institutions, notably research-intensive universities, have been actively encouraged to commercialise their own research results, through which they can secure additional income and thereby be less of a burden on the state.

While consultancy has been the predominant form of academic commercialisation, today various forms of commercialisation are encouraged through industrial liaison offices co-ordinating entrepreneurial and marketing activities. Much of this was prompted by legislative changes during the early 1980s in the United States and then Europe, that allowed public sector establishments to retain income from state-funded research. This led to new forms of collaboration between industry and academia, such as the establishment of strategic research alliances in the United Kingdom of a more long-term nature between academics and drugs companies (Webster and Constable, 1990; Webster, 1994). Research groups and universities increasingly manage and organise their research as if it were a business that operates to generate revenues, though managing science as academic research on the one hand and patentable intellectual property on the other has been shown to be highly problematic (Packer and Webster, 1996).

Corporations find strategic advantage in collaborating with institutions in the public sector. It provides firms with links to expertise and skills, acts as a source of help and advice, and allows firms to keep abreast of emerging knowledge fields without carrying out in-house research. Although industry funding of public sector institutions still makes up a minority percentage of their overall funding, the penetration of commercial market values has been seen to extend well beyond specific instances of industry-academic collaboration. As Hill and Turpin (1994) argued over a decade ago, '[T]he commercial marketplace is [now] sitting inside the processes that forge the global constitution of society's knowledge rather than standing alongside and drawing from society's knowledge capital' (pp. 335–336). Not surprisingly, scientists and others (such as Krimksy) who believe that this happening has challenged such commercialisation activities on the basis that they ultimately undermine the benefits of public good research by focusing on short-term (market) goals. The public sector 'reservoir of knowledge' becomes contaminated by private interests.

In regard to health, the influence of the industry on medical practitioners and scientists has been growing, especially in regard to the biotechnology and pharmaceutical sectors. This can be demonstrated through analysis of joint patenting and publication (Anderson, 1996) or other collaborative links: Martin et al. (2000) showed that 60 per cent of leading European gene therapy researchers had commercial ties in 1999. In regard to the United States, the pattern of linkage between biotechnology firms and health science researchers has been extensively documented by Blumenthal and his colleagues. In a series of papers over the past decade (see e.g. Blumenthal et al., 1996, 1997; Louis et al., 2001; Campbell et al., 2004) they have explored a range of links including: consulting relationships (such as joining corporate health boards), equity (shareholding) links with joint academic-corporate spin off firms, industrial support for training of academics, and 'gift' relationships such as 'discretionary funding, equipment, food, trips to meetings, biomaterials etc.' (Campbell et al., 2001, p. 6). Their surveys report that almost half of US health science research in the top 50 research-intensive universities received gifts from industry.

Blumenthal argues that such linkages are important to the science base and bring a range of benefits to all concerned, but stresses the need to consider where and when they generate conflicts of interest for publicly funded scientists. These include the risks of biased results when supported by industry. For example, one study reports that there is 'a statistically significant relationship between industry sponsorship and pro-industry conclusions' (Bekelman 2003, p. 456; see also Webster, 1994).

Clearly this is an important issue that raises analytical questions for sociologists exploring the commodification of science as well as policy questions for science agencies themselves. In regard to the latter, for example, one can point to the controversy in the United States over the public sector Scripps Institute that had arranged collaboration with sign-off rights to the drugs firm Sandoz. This provoked the National Institutes of Health to demand a revision to the original contract to ensure that the intellectual property that Sandoz could extract from Scripps would be limited (see Science, 1993). This ruling has now become the NIH benchmark for all current linkages. More recently, the NIH has also produced guidelines for academics regarding what particular types of contracts should be struck with those in industry so as not to stifle the dissemination of research. However, the NIH *itself* was subject to Congressional inquiry in 2004 after news reports that some of its senior scientists were receiving significant gifts and related benefits from drugs companies. The inquiry revealed, for example, that one researcher was paid $517,000 in various benefits from Pfizer over a five-year period without reporting that income to NIH. As a result of the inquiry, the NIH placed a moratorium of one year on any new links between its staff and the biotech/pharmaceutical industry, and demanded a discontinuation of existing ones. The ruling generated considerable hostility from senior NIH scientists.

These cases of conflict of interest raise wider issues about trust and the accountability of publicly funded science, and where political and ethical thresholds need to be drawn beyond which conflicts will arise. There is evidently a notion at work here of a pool of knowledge into which one can 'commercially' dip (within limits) and this is indeed one of the most common views held of how academia can be (legitimately) exploited. Much depends on where boundaries are drawn and indeed how they are seen as being more or less permeable to cross-cutting influences. There has been some attempt in science policy studies to develop a new theoretical model of how academic/industrial/government ties are best understood. This is seen to comprise a 'triple helix' of relationships (Etzkowitz and Leydesdorff, 2001), though the helix concept seems to be much less critical of these ties than the earlier MIC model has been.

Apart from evidence relating to links between academia, industry and the state, other research (building on original work by Starr, 1982) points to the way in which public health organisations have themselves become increasingly subject to the process of 'corporatisation'. This refers to ways in which these organisations, such as hospitals, or clinical centres offering specialist services, become 'profit centres', providing contracted services to local and regional purchasers. In the United Kingdom, the state has introduced a range of reforms to NHS that involve the 'marketisation' of services, and a move towards independent and semi-independent 'foundation trusts' and the anticipation that users will be charged for services (Donaldson and Ruta, 2005). In the United States, 'managed care companies', such as Health Management Organisations (HMOs) and Preferred Provider Plans, contract the services of almost 90 per cent of physicians to deliver services and establish the terms of which services care to be made available and from whom they may be sought. In addition, health insurance companies have increasing control over what services can be delivered to patients through their intervening horizontally between hospital, patient and physician. These developments can be seen throughout Europe and elsewhere, and reflect two processes at work: the desire by the state to manage and constrain health care budgets (and professions), and the related move towards privatising health care costs where possible. I shall return to this issue of marketisation and indeed what has been regarded as privatisation in Chapter 5.

Much of the commentary above refers to the role of pharmaceutical companies within the MIC. It is important to recognise the contribution they have made in developing new compounds and improving health: antibiotics, vaccines, pain-killers, anti-hypertensives and so on, have played a major role in therapeutic health care. At the same time, their influence on medicine and medical priorities has been subject to extensive critique, not least as a result of their close ties to the state's principal health agencies. The following comment makes the point very strongly:

> The Department of Health has not only to promote the interests of the pharmaceutical industry but also the health of the public and the effectiveness of the NHS. There is a dilemma here which cannot be readily glossed over. The Secretary of State for Health cannot serve two masters. The Department seems unable to prioritise the interests of patients and public health over the interests of the pharmaceutical industry.

While one might expect the source of this to be a radical critic of the industry, in fact it comes from the UK House of Commons Health Committee in its inquiry into the influence of the industry on the health service (HoC, 2005, p. 6). In response, the government dismissed the criticism saying that the interests of the public and of the industry were not mutually exclusive (see Abraham, 2005). Critics of the MIC would declare that such a response was inevitable given the close relationship between state and industry. While the evidence points to this, it is also true that the state must act and be seen to act to regulate industry both to bolster public trust and meet international regulatory requirements. At times it does so quite contrary to corporate health's collective or individual interests. For example, government health authorities in a number of high-income countries determine a reimbursement level that they will pay the industry for the drugs they supply. Many drugs companies protest this is set too low, a complaint often made by US drugs companies against European regulators. A related but distinctive approach adopted by Germany and some Canadian provinces has been 'therapeutic reference pricing' where a branded drug is compared with its generic (off-patent) equivalent and a 'reference price' set based on comparison of the most and least expensive. Since its introduction in Germany in 1989, the price index for health service drugs has fallen by 30 per cent (Kanavos and Reinhardt, 2003). In the United Kingdom the Department of Health controls the price of drugs the NHS pays to firms through an agreement known as the Pharmaceutical Price Regulatory Scheme. The most recent version of the agreement (in 2005) required firms selling more than £1 million of drugs to the NHS to reduce their bill by 7 per cent.

The largest firms are of course global actors and will try to ensure that their products sell equally well wherever possible. At the same time, these firms are well aware that their markets can vary considerably. This may result from different procurement regimes (from fee-based, market systems through to fully socialised (national) health systems), different ethical regimes or differential abilities to pay (for drugs etc.). The globalisation of health technologies such as drugs does not, therefore, necessarily mean the globalisation of a standard price that health procurers or individuals must pay for a specific product or technique. Globalisation also means that in terms of meeting the costs of research and development of new drugs (claimed to be a disputed $800 million per compound), companies are increasingly looking to cheaper locations in which to run clinical trials for their drugs, such as Eastern Europe. Of course, the regulatory context of such regions simply adds weight to the questions critics raise about trials elsewhere, namely, how much information do trial participants receive, what risks are there from taking the drug and with what are the new compounds being compared?

The globalisation of the pharmaceutical sector means that they have sought new markets in emerging states that have relatively affluent, though, as a proportion of total population, small, health consumer markets and public health programmes which they can buy into and manage. This strategy is evident in the more prosperous Latin American countries such as Brazil and Mexico (Jasso-Aguilar et al., 2004). It is also a strategy that has been made more possible as a result of international trade agreements introduced by the World Trade Organization's General Agreement on Trade in Services (GATS) and the regional Free Trade Area of the Americas (FTAA) that have favoured the 'liberalisation' of health markets and created difficulties for public health care organisations to control the basis on which local health care services are provided.

This leads us to the more general question of the capacity and interests of state agencies, within national and international arenas, to regulate corporate health and the MIC.

Regulating corporate health

The role of regulatory agencies with respect to the state's management of corporate health is complex and extensive both within countries and at an international, indeed global, level. In this concluding section to the chapter I can only sketch out some of the main features of this role, and where appropriate illustrate this complexity at work.

At a general level, the sociology of regulation has been concerned with the way political and legal institutions discipline and control populations, organisations and individuals with respect to a number of concerns central to the state. These relate to matters of *right* and the regulation of *risk*. In regard to the former, states regulate property and ownership rights, trading rights, civil and moral rights, and thereby legislative, statutory and more informal controls – processes more to do with 'governance' than government – that protect them. In terms of risk, states have to manage these as part of what Beck (2000) calls the 'logic of control which dominates modernity' (p. 215). Regulating corporate health swings around debates over the balance of these rights and the management of perceived risks associated with new drugs, therapies, devices etc. This involves negotiation between firms, regulators, citizen groups, professional bodies, patients and state policy-makers about the appropriate forms of regulation to be deployed in a health care system. Such forms of regulation are more than ever shaped by international agencies.

At the same time, as the closing section of Chapter 2 argued, we need to attend to the diversity of political cultures that shape regulatory decision-making and through which rights and risks are defined: the rights and risks of stem cell research, as I suggested, are quite different from one country to the next. Moreover, within any one country, we should not expect that regulatory policy is marked by coherence and integration. Regulatory systems develop incrementally and unevenly, and often find the political question of defining the boundaries of public and private rights and risks hugely problematic. They do not, therefore, deploy the 'logic of control' in some systematic and rational way, though the more bureaucratic political cultures of countries such as Germany like to think they do so. And finally, we should not expect that because policy is designed to tackle a particular scientific and technical issue, there will inevitably be some convergence across countries because 'the science' demands this. On the contrary, while there are important examples of international harmonisation of policy, sociologists of science point to significant differences in the way 'the same' scientific problem is handled from country A to country B. I will illustrate this shortly with respect to work on the licensing of drugs in the United States and Europe.

Corporate health is, of course, dominated by the pharmaceutical industry in terms of scale, capital value, research spend, the political resource and leverage it commands and its impact on national health budgets and economies. But corporate health is not only a manufacturer of drugs and devices but also of risks. Medicines have long been a site for state regulation, though during the nineteenth and first half of the twentieth century most regulation was not state-based but profession-based through clinicians and medical researchers through a self-regulatory process, while the industry itself was subject to little or nor formal regulation per se It was the impact of a major crisis in trust in medicines brought about by the thalidomide catastrophe in the early 1960s that prompted a much more interventionist state regulation of medicines, part, indeed, of what has been seen to be the emergence of 'the regulatory state' (Majone, 1994).

The regulatory state has had quite distinct careers either side of the Atlantic. During the late 1960s through the 1980s, regulation became a key feature of US political culture generated by a series of controversies surrounding science and a loss of public trust in federal and state agencies. During the same period European regulation was much more modest in scale and scope, but from the 1990s onwards, the political culture of Europe shifted significantly. This was, according to Vogel (2004) a result of three factors: much greater public support for health and environmental matters, growing competence in the regulatory agencies themselves and paradoxically, a series of regulatory failures that had damaged public trust in the political machine.

International regulation of corporate health has grown apace during this past decade. Again, the primary focus has been on medicines because of concerns over the safety and efficacy of drugs. One of the most significant developments globally has been the 'International Conference on Harmonisation' (ICH), initiated by a conference in 1990, now an international network of regulatory agencies and major pharmaceutical companies from the United States, European Union and Japan determining standards with respect to the scrutiny and approval of drugs. The ICH provisions have been adopted more recently in Canada and Australia and by the WHO.

The ICH's very composition reflects the close ties between industry and regulator, a good illustration of the MIC at work (Abraham and Reed, 2002). This encourages moves towards faster and more effective regulation but at the cost of proper scrutiny. Abraham (1995) has provided a detailed history of pharmaceutical regulation in the United Kingdom and the United States and systematically explored the licensing regimes regulating drugs approval on either side of the Atlantic and the health risks generated by uneven and often poor scrutiny of data on the adverse effects of new compounds. More recent work (Abraham and Davis, 2005) points to the inconsistency of decision between the two with respect to licensing of new drugs, with the US Food and Drug Administration being slower to approve new drugs compared with the United Kingdom, which meant that many unsafe drugs entered the US market than did that of the UK (Martin et al., 2006). One of the key points common to Abraham's long-standing analysis of drugs pharmaceutical regulation is the ways in which regulatory agencies and the political institutions of state more generally, favour a 'politics of technology as progress versus hazard' (Abraham, 2002, p. 229). Much of this derives from the close relations between industry and medical authorities and the wider profession. In some contexts this has, paradoxically, meant that data held by firms is less likely to be accessed or indeed accessible, taken more on trust. For example, the House of Commons 2005 Inquiry drew attention to the fact that the ICH standards which are binding on the United Kingdom's regulatory body, the Medicines and Healthcare products Regulatory Agency (MHRA), prevent the agency obtaining access to audit reports on clinical trials data unless they suspect 'serious non-compliance' with local UK standards associated with patient care. As the Select Committee remarked, 'This amounts to a Catch 22 position: the primary evidence of serious non-compliance would be in the audit report, but regulators may ask to see that report only if they suspect serious non-compliance. Surprisingly, the MHRA expressed no concerns about the issue' (HoC, 2005, p. 78).

While international standards such as the ICH act to serve the interests of firms and regulators, global competition can mean that regulatory states may well act to serve local interests against other regions. For example, the European Union revoked the patent claim held by US biotech firm Myriad on the genes associated with breast cancer (BRCAI and II genes) on the basis of the claim failing to demonstrate 'inventiveness'. Not only was this a reflection of differences in patent law between the European Union and the United States, it also reflected powerful lobbying within Europe of the European Patent Office by EU-based scientists concerned about the constraints and costs on their research that the patent imposed.

This tension between regulatory regions is paralleled by differences in the interpretation of the potential risks of existing and new medicines. Detailed and systematic analysis of the drug approval and licensing processes for drugs has been conducted over by Abraham and his co-researchers over recent years (see Abraham and Lewis, 2000; Abraham and Lawton-Smith, 2003; Abraham and Davis, 2005; Martin et al., 2006). Among other results, this body of work has shown how the same drug has met with quite different responses either side of the Atlantic. In the European Union there has been a tendency to withdraw unsafe drugs from the market more quickly than in the United States; but rather than this reflecting a more robust system in Europe, on the contrary Abraham shows that the US agency, the Food and Drug Administration (FDA) were *less* likely to approve such drugs and release them on to the market in the first place. Pressures to speeden up approval in Europe in part reflects the fact that agencies compete for pharmaceutical business since their income derives from fees paid for by the industry itself. This arrangement has been criticised inasmuch as it is highly likely to generate too industry friendly a relationship and potential conflicts of interest.

Abraham and colleagues also challenge the claim made by regulators that patients benefit from speedier approval process that foster and enable greater innovation by industry. Neither the United States nor the European Union regulatory agencies require new drugs to demonstrate efficacy compared to existing products or therapies, such that there is no basis on which regulators can show approvals provide increasing real gains to patient medication. As the Select Committee observed, fewer than half of new drugs approved by the US FDA offer any therapeutic gain (p. 47).

Abraham argues for a regulatory system that would foster both innovation and real gains in public health (see Abraham and Reed, 2002; Carpenter, 2003). Regulation is supposed to be designed to reduce risks associated with uncertainty over the quality and safety of medicines, and while thereby providing industry with a more stable and profitable market, should ensure consumers' welfare. In sum, such a system can only be built through greater transparency of the regulatory process itself, allowing much greater access to information about drug trials than is currently the case. The principal recommendations by the Select Committee (HoC, p. 94) with respect to the United States (see Box 3.1) provide further guidance on what other changes could be sought.

Box 3.1 Changing the regulatory oversight of corporate health

Recommendations

- The influence of the pharmaceutical industry is such that it dominates clinical practice, to an extent that deprives it of independent and constructively critical feedback; this is a discipline it needs and which can help it to improve.
- The industry's complaints of excessive regulation are understandable but self-regulation is not at present effective. It could take on greater responsibility for regulation when its activities are fully transparent and effectively audited.
- The regulatory authority, which is responsible for controlling much of the behaviour of the industry has significant failings. Lack of transparency has played a major part in allowing failings to continue. The traditional secrecy in the drug regulatory process has insulated regulators from the feedback that would otherwise check, test and stimulate their policies and performance. Failure can be measured by the MHRA's poor history in recognising drug risks, poor communication and lack of public trust. Regulatory secrecy also underpins publication bias, and other unacceptable practices. The closeness that has developed between regulators and companies has deprived the industry of rigorous quality control and audit.
- Other bodies are in a position to provide feedback and quality control. They include academic, research, clinical and professional institutions, as well as the media and patient groups. However, representatives of these interests have had only limited success in containing excessive industry influence. This can be partly attributed to lack of transparency, limited resources, significant dependency on industry funding, and some conflicts of interest.

(Continued)

- The Government and the European Union appear to believe that trade imperatives and health priorities are as one. The evidence received from the Department of Health was remarkable for its denial that any significant conflict between commercial and health objectives might arise that was not properly addressed through existing process and systems. We do not doubt the legitimacy of commercial objectives, the contributions of the pharmaceutical industry to health and the overlap of commercial and health interests, but this inquiry left us in no doubt that the scope for conflict between health and trade interests is huge.

Conclusion

In this chapter I have described the ways in which what I have called 'corporate health' shapes health innovation in the fields of genetics, informatics and tissue engineering/stem cells. I have argued that these fields provide important markets for novel technologies that have been critically dependent on the socio-technical resources of corporate health. The commodification of body tissue, what Waldby (2002) has called 'biovalue', and of health information through the processes associated with biocapitalism and info-capitalism has been particularly effective to date in the genetics and informatics fields but much more uneven and uncertain with respect to tissue engineering. In turn, these commodifying processes, which seek to reproduce and intensify the value of embodied and disembodied information, have been subject to challenge and countervailing processes as a result of the empowering of consumer and patient, especially in the virtual word of e-health.

Regulatory agencies in turn play both an enabling and constraining role, seeking to balance their support (on behalf of national polities and economies) for private capital with their role as custodians of patient safety and the management of risk. However, there is considerable evidence to suggest that the MIC is alive and well and that national regulatory agencies, as the UK House of Commons observed, appear to be failing to get the balance between trade and patient needs right. Indeed, as Abraham and Lewis (2000) have argued, drug regulatory agencies increasingly see pharmaceutical companies as their customers and compete for their fees, resulting in a shift away from government's independent policing of the industry towards a trusting partnership with industry.

Some have argued that a 'consumer-driven health care' system will be the most effective way of reigning-in the power of corporate heath by putting patient needs first (see Herzlinger, 2004). Such systems are based on employees' buying into different types of health insurance package and determining how to deploy the resource it provides. Critics have argued that this simply passes the burden of health care insurance onto the sicker and poorer sections of society. Against this, there have been calls to replace the consumerism of contemporary medicine with something more actively geared towards public health needs (see e.g. Mackintosh and Koivusalo, 2005). As the Royal College of General Practitioners argued in its evidence to the House of Commons, 'more money is now invested in research into the prevention of disease, such as drugs to reduce cholesterol, than into its treatment, which serves to divert investment away from the sick towards the well, away from the old towards the young and away from the poor towards the rich' (HoC, 2005, p. 45). However, the bulk of the evidence presented in this chapter suggests that such a change in policy is highly unlikely. Corporate health will, allied to a deepening within the public health sector of the discourse of health as consumption and choice, remain the primary determinant of the priorities of the state at national and international levels.

In the following chapter I focus attention on the body, the site where clinicians, the state and corporate health converge to define its meaning, its pathologies, its rights and its limits. It is also the site where individual meaning and identity play their most important role in fending off, accommodating, translating and interpreting these externally generated classifications of health and illness. The sociology of the body is not about corporate health but about corporeal health and how we experience and make sense of it.

Body, Identity and the Meaning of Health

Introduction

So far in this book I have discussed the factors influencing the adoption of health technologies and critically reviewed the principal ways in which it is evaluated. I have also discussed the role of the clinical professions, the state and its agencies, and corporate health in developing new health technologies and defining and managing health care. These three also influence the ways in which patients frame and experience their embodied health and illness. We have also seen how, as a result of the play of genetics, informatics and tissue engineering, the boundaries of the body become more permeable and more plastic. Indeed, within the field of science and technology studies (STS), sociologists regard the body not as a single physical and bounded object, but one that figures quite differently in biomedical models, patients' experience of their bodies, in the datasets of the bio-informatician, in an electronic patient record, and so on (Berg and Mol, 1998). Indeed, as Waldby (2000) emphasises, biomedicine itself depends on this 'malleability' of the body in order to accommodate the vast range of biomedical interventions that medics deploy. While the text book portrayal of the body is of a coherent and stable object, biomedical practice only works precisely by forgetting or neglecting this representation.

But, of course, it is not solely as a result of (old or new) medical technologies that the body gains this plasticity. Cultural anthropologies of the body show how it performs multiple roles in communicating status, wealth, gender and sexuality, power and social privilege and so on (see e.g. Strathern and Stewart, 1999). Cultural diversity across countries and communities produces very different understandings of what it is to be ill, and how to communicate this to others, demonstrated especially effectively in studies on interethnic medical consultations that are often the source of confusion and misunderstanding: Pliskin's (1987) analysis of consultations between Israeli doctors and Iranian patients in Israel is an excellent early example, while a much more recent study relating to ethnicity and communication is that of Hirst and Hewison (2006).

Feminist analyses of the body have drawn on both anthropological and STS approaches to develop a radical critique of the patriarchal framing of the body, and especially the woman's body within the arena of biomedical reproduction and sexuality (e.g. Hausman, 1995; Witz, 2000; Moore and Adele, 2001). Moreover, it is not merely the social analyst who declares the plasticity of the body: social actors routinely do so through cosmetic surgery, or more dramatically through seeking a sex-change, where the social and hormonal body must co-construct a new gender.

The diversity in the form that bodies take is also expressed at a more structural level, in the unequal distribution of health and illness that bodies understood in more collective terms share; here we encounter the more direct relationship between health and social class. Indeed, much of the path-breaking work in the sociology of health was concerned with these material inequalities and the ways they were reproduced over generations of different occupational, ethnic and gendered groups.

Bodies are then simultaneously carriers of physical and social life, are shaped by structural, cultural and discursive orderings, which in turn shape the ways in which health and illness are framed and experienced. In this chapter I discuss how these processes have been explored by those working in medical sociology and its more recent engagement with STS. I begin with a general commentary on work on the body before turning attention to 'unequal bodies', the socio-economic structuring of health and illness, going on to consider the body in the medical encounter as framed by doctor–patient interaction, and the 'sick role'. I then explore the notion of 'narratives' of health and illness through which the embodiment of both is expressed – in the way we talk about, understand and make sense of our health problems. I shall discuss the ways in which technology has influenced notions of health and illness before turning to three case studies illustrating how health technologies foster new forms of identity yet disturb others, especially in regard to our conception of personhood, body and the social relations of belonging. For the body is not only a site for interaction but social anchorage too. Through our bodies we reconfirm each day a sense of belonging to others, to place, to culture and to our own embodied identity and selfhood. As we shall see, as we approach the end of our lives, the end of our bodies, these anchorage points are in danger of coming adrift.

The body and sociological analysis

The body has only relatively recently become a major area of socio-logical research. Some 20 years ago, it was primarily a site that was the preserve of feminist analysis (e.g. Gallagher and Laqueur, 1987; Jaggar and Bordo, 1989) and historical work (Elias, 1984). Much of the time, sociology has conceived of the individual as a social actor rather than one whose action is embodied. Even the contributions of those working in the field of interactionism, such as Goffman (1956), focused attention on meaning and behaviour, without thereby tying these to the physicality and viscerality of the body. The body was con-ceived as a vehicle through which meaning could be conveyed through facial movements and bodily gestures rather than being of interest in its own right.

Today, there is a wealth of research on the body. Much of this work has, in a sociological move been akin to the dismantling of the body by biomedicine, sought in parallel to deconstruct the biomedical body and render it as a particularly social object. This has been driven by a critique of biomedicine and its reductionist tendencies, yet in doing so, as Williams (2006) has recently argued, it has lost touch with the body's 'biological' reality. The Foucauldian perspective on which much of this deconstruction – and social reconstruction – has been based recasts the body primarily as an object of discourse, and thereby subject to discursive regulation and the 'medical gaze' (as we saw in Chapter 2). The disciplining of the body through discourses of control over sexuality, hygiene, and the meaning of ab/normality became defining features of the culture of surveillance in modernity. Bodies become objects for others as we cede control to professional expertise, state agencies and the technologies they deploy – whether the elec-tronic patient record or the national census – that locate each of us in a compendium of disembodied time and space. Classification of bodies at both the individual and collective level is therefore an inherently political act, and expression of what Foucault called 'anatomo-politics'. This form of politics of the body superseded the role of 'sovereign' power in the control of national populations during the nineteenth century industrialisation of Western Europe. Populations became administered as a social body through regulatory controls rather than through subordination to the discourse of royalty, lineage and blood ties (139–40).

Fox (1999) extends the Foucauldian analysis in a strongly post-modern way in his claim that 'the body', as such, as a body-with-organs, is a creation of modernist science and 'constrains and closes down other more promising options, possibilities, choices, rendering us, in effect, (fixed) bodies with organs vis-a-vis other more nomadic, deterritorialised, postmodern forms of subjectivity and embodiment' (Fox, 1999, p. 9[S2]).

But as Williams argues by way of critique, of this Foucauldian line, *what* is left of the body, what is it, when so thoroughly deconstructed? As he puts it,

> the body on offer here, or perhaps more correctly the *bodies* on offer here (for there are as many as we care to construct), are peculiar bodies indeed: disembodied, disembowelled, disincarnated, dematerialized, deracinated, ethereal bodies, based on a 'surface' theory that is only 'skin deep'. (Ibid[S3])

In contrast, Williams explores the contribution made by those working with a very different perspective within the sociology of the body that adopts a phenomenological approach. Here the body is both a biological and social entity that is mutually constitutive. Thereby enables, as I discuss below, links to be made between physiological illness or disability and wider social structures that reproduce this over time. Pain, suffering and the emotions through which these are lived and expressed become core concerns for this approach, as recent writings on cancer (Frank, 1995), disability (Woods and Watson, 2005) and impairment (Parr et al., 2006) have shown.

Building on their much earlier contributions, more recent feminist analyses of the body have much in common with and indeed have drawn on this phenomenological tradition. Interest in autobiography and drama as sociological methods through which lived experience and its troubles and complexity can be recounted, has been an especially important feminist route through which subjectivity and embodiment have been explored (see e.g Coslett et al., 2000)

Much of this recent work on the body has, perhaps inevitably, been driven by the need to understand its pathologies as lived, physically complex and debilitating experiences. But there has also been a growing interest in the body which has opened up other perspectives on the body/culture relationship through consideration of *the senses* the very means through which the body engages with and apprehends its world and itself. Urry (2000) has made a particularly important contribution to this and speaks of the 'cooperation' between the senses, the way they tend to play in sequence, the degree to which one sense comes to a 'threshold' before another kicks in, and a reciprocal yet hierarchical relationship between them, with vision taking primacy. Through our eyes we see others and are seen face to face: 'in contrast the ear does not reciprocate – it takes but does not give' (p. 81). Each of the senses is extended and given other representational forms through which we know and understand the world: maps and photographs extend and distill visuality, while at the same time each sense has its limitations and can as such be rendered in more negative, stigmatised forms, such as the shallowness attributed to the 'sightseer'. The sense of smell, Urry argues, is a much less mediated, much more direct means through which our body engages with the environment, one that cannot easily be 'turned on and off' (p. 96) and the more foul, stagnant and wretched the smell, is the more evidently this is the case. Smells evoke embodied biographies and places through the memories they recreate, as well as reproduce social hierarchies across bodies, as can be seen in the stigmatising of smells linked to subordinate ethnic or class groups. Smells are also markers of bodily health, sexuality, decline and death.

The action of senses is then, as is the body they help bring to life, both physically and socially performative. They are empowering not merely in a sensual sense but also a political one – sight enables a doctor to see but with a 'clinical gaze'. Bodies and their senses perform and are acted upon by others in sexual, brutal, emotional and spiritual ways. As such, when we answer the question 'what is the body' we should not get tied up in debates about whether it has any 'real' existence or is simply discursive, but attend to the way it acts, performs and creates its reality in time and space. 'Constructivist-realism' might get close to being a convenient term we could use to try to capture both the constructed and the physical nature of the body. Shilling (2005) has suggested the term 'corporeal realism' to achieve much the same end.

This seems especially sensible if, as we saw in earlier chapters, sociologists are keen to talk about the ways in which the body is broken up, fragmented and made mobile through the socio-technical dissections of genetics and informatics. For without such a position, what, one would be right to ask, precisely *is it* that is moving through databases, curated in banks, re-engineered in tissue scaffolds and a source of 'biovalue'? There is just so much biovalue that can be created by discourse – though certainly the hype in biotechnology attracts considerable venture capital. In the case studies that appear later in this chapter, therefore, I will adopt this constructivist-realism that enables me to see how the body, technology and experience intersect with respect to the meaning of health and illness. Before doing so, there is more ground to be covered, first with regard to the ways in which social structures generate major health inequalities across bodies at a more collective level.

Unequal bodies

Social stratification has been a core focus for sociologists since the classic contributions of theorists of modernity and industrial capitalism – Marx, Weber and Durkheim. Notions of social class, status, political power, life chances, occupational hierarchies and the division of labour are key dimensions of social stratification. Whereas before industrial capitalism inequality was based on access to religious, political or hereditary rights rather than primarily how people related to the system of production (as wage workers, peasants, seasonal or subsistence labourers, etc.), inequalities of capitalism are heavily based on one's occupation, income and ownership of private productive property (or wealth). However, while these inequalities have been important, many have argued that we have seen the decomposition of class reflecting the decline of strong occupational communities (such as have been found in coal and steel towns), the fragmentation of the labour process especially with the growth of the part-time sector, the decline of trades unionism, and the growth of a consumer market through credit which has flattened out social differences based on consumption goods and lifestyles. Rather than classes, it has been suggested that consumption markets have produced highly fluid status groupings which people choose to buy into (literally) rather than being constrained by the old-class hierarchies and conventions (Pakulski and Waters, 1996). Moreover, greater social mobility and opportunity for women in the labour market has transformed the ways in which gender and social class have been related.

The 'wealthied' upper class is weakened by the arrival of a transnational global capitalist class driven by the interests of international investment than the fading glories of family estates, and the depersonalisation of private capital through the gradual disassociation of major wealth holding from private individuals and their families (Scott, 1997).

Despite these changes, the concept of social class refuses to lie down, as Scott (2000) has shown, and indeed, with regard to its relationship to the pattern and so experience of social disadvantage, continues to structure our lives even if it does so in less palpable ways than before. As Scott argues:

> There remain sharp inequalities of life chances around the distribution of property and employment opportunities. These inequalities of income and assets are reflected in a wide range of material life chances: birth weight, infant mortality, life expectancy, disability, serious illness, housing, education, victimisation in crime, and many other areas are shaped, overwhelmingly, by class situation. These are not simply economic inequalities, they are socially structured differences in life chances that often have their effects 'behind the backs' of the people involved. (p. 13)

Scott's reference to a number of health-related life chances as indicators of the continuing significance of class has been emphasised by Freund (1990), and in such a way as to make more explicit their impact on bodies. Freund puts it this way:

> 'External' social structural factors such as one's position in different systems of hierarchy or various forms of social control can influence the conditions of our existence, how we respond and apprehend these conditions of existence and our sense of embodied self. These conditions can also affect our physical functioning. (p. 461)

And as Blane et al., (1999) have argued, health inequalities 'tend to cluster cross-sectionally and accumulate longitudinally' (p. 69), that is to say, people in a similar social position tend to share similar health disadvantages or advantages and these build over time. Blaxter (2003) speaks of the synthesis of biology, social class and health inequality explaining thereby people's differential access to and holding of what she calls 'health capital', analogous to notions such as economic or social capital used elsewhere. Social capital typically is a term used to describe the resources that can be mobilised through the networks and social relationships that a person enjoys (see e.g. Fukuyama, 1995). This concept can, as Turner (2003) has argued, be seen to be closely linked to Durkheimian notions of social ('organic') solidarity and the networks on which this depends. As research based in Boston (USA) by Kawachi et al. (1997) has shown, loss or lack of social capital is strongly correlated with increases in morbidity and mortality: social isolation is (literally) unhealthy for you. At the same time, the 'value' of social capital is dependent on the ways in which it is tied to other forms of resource a person, household or community enjoys. As Wakefield and Poland (2005) have said: 'social capital cannot be conceived in isolation from economic and political structures, since social connections are contingent on, and structured by, access to material resources' (p. 2819)

So, while the traditional manifestations of social class hierarchies may be less apparent today, access to material resources through social networks remains central to people's life chances both in the Weberian social sense with respect to social standing and in the biophysical sense with respect to health and longevity. Indeed, though it is the case that epidemiology is concerned with the social distribution of morbidity and mortality, this field has been criticised for developing public health models that explain this distribution through reference solely to individual risk behaviours, rather than through reference to socially structured disadvantage.

Those with physical impairment or disability perhaps most acutely experience the relationship between health and social inequality, and are further evidence of 'unequal bodies'. The source of the disability is both physical and social – if we are to accept the constructivist-realism I advocated above; that is to say, disability cannot be seen to be simply a social construct or produced by a disabling environment and no more. While disability activists are right to challenge the way impairment is created and worsened by the physical and social environment that they contend with, it has real physical expression that is chronic, often painful, and wearying.

Often, of course, as we saw with the cochlear implant, technologies designed to address disabilities can simply become vehicles literally in the case of wheel chairs – that reinforce and imprison a person in a disabled status. As Woods and Watson (2005) have shown, wheelchair users have often responded to this narrowing of their identity by actively rebuilding or customising chairs to meet their needs, which has eventually led to many different models – powered, folding, ultra-light designs – being developed for leisure, sports or transport purposes. However, they also show how new designs have quickly become a site for corporate health, and thereby, as we saw with respect to genetics, informatics and tissue engineering in the previous chapter, subject to the process of commodification.

One final area that we should consider with respect to the social stratification of health is that of infectious diseases. Infectious diseases have been brought under control through antibiotics and antiviral drugs, such that the most common causes of death in Europe are not infectious, but diseases such as cancer, heart disease, stroke and diabetes and as a reflection of the ageing population over half of those who die are over the age of 75. The principal infectious diseases in Europe today are pneumonia, AIDS and influenza. Globally, however, the situation is rather different. Of the total annual deaths worldwide, approximately 56 million, about 14 million are caused by infectious diseases, especially among children and the aged. While all infectious diseases relate directly to the degree to which people come into contact with each other by virtue of community, lifestyle, occupation and so on, as elsewhere with health inequality, actual patterns of infection reflect broader social structures that determine whether there is access to food, sanitation, good housing, health services and so on. This is key to explaining the global differences in the spread and impact of infectious diseases between – and within – richer and poorer countries. The 'postcode lottery' shaping provision of health at a national level might well be said to be paralleled by a 'country code' equivalent. Drawing on his research in Russia, Peru and Haiti, the anthropologist and physician Paul Farmer has provided a rich and compelling critical analysis of the way in which the distribution of infectious diseases such as HIV and tuberculosis is directly related to the patterns of poverty, violence and social dislocation experienced by the world's poor (Farmer, 2003).

However, globalisation carries a sting – an infectious sting – in its tail, as the recent outbreaks of SARS and avian (bird) flu bear witness. Increases in global movement for both work and leisure, the deepening of global food chains across diverse and unregulated suppliers, the growing resistance of bacteria (such as MRSA now rampant in hospitals), and the social dislocation caused by war and famine, mean that affluent states cannot presume they are safe from major infections in the future. As Fidler (2004) has noted in regard to SARS, infectious diseases have become a major site for state regulation and the management of risk, though one that nation states find impossible to cope with on their own (see also Dogdson et al., 2002), and indeed, as the SARS story showed, states are *required* to act in concert according to the demands of international regulatory agencies, notably the WHO.

The state, as we saw earlier, plays an important ongoing role in mitigating health inequality through various forms of social insurance that in principle should even-out major social differences. However, in relative terms, poverty is growing throughout all advanced industrial states, and health demand increasing through the demographic shift and the prevalence of chronic illnesses among the aged. As a consequence, socialised insurance systems are becoming under increasing financial pressure and resorting to means-testing and other fiscal devices to control demand. Moreover, in practice, health services are unevenly provided on the ground: in the United Kingdom for example, there is a large body of evidence demonstrating the so-called postcode prescribing, as well as significant geographical differences in policy on admissions and discharge from hospital and so on. Moreover, recent studies (e.g. Hirst et al., 2004) of access to health and social services among ethnic communities indicate that members are less likely to consult local services because they have a strong culture of self-help. This in turn serves to reproduce low expectations among them *and service providers* that they should seek or need outside help. This is clearly a dangerous assumption to make, especially among service providers, if the social capital within such communities decays, especially in inner city areas, and local (self-) support networks are not available.

Patterns of health inequality are, then, structured globally and locally. While the state mitigates these, and social capital helps cope with them in more informal ways, health-related life chances are unevenly, and non-randomly, distributed within and between societies. How might new medical technologies affect these patterns of inequality; how do they, as I asked in Chapter 1, work to ameliorate or exacerbate inequalities in health and access to health care itself?

For new medical technologies to have any significant effect on the distribution of life-chances, they would need to bring about one or more of the following: a redistribution of socio-economic (including health) resources on a more equitable basis; the provision of new resources such that previously disadvantaged groups might be empowered to improve their life chances; pose a challenge to the existing socio-economic distribution of resources; and do one or all of the above in such a way that the outcome had systemic rather than random effects.

Vaccination programmes sponsored by public health agencies are perhaps a good example of medical technology having both a broad clinical and socio-economic benefit for those receiving the vaccine. In developing countries, innovative AIDS vaccines currently under clinical trial could have a major impact on public health, the security and sustainability of families, and so provide a collective and personal health resource that would help stabilise communities currently devastated by a chronic and widespread incidence of AIDS. As such they could make an important contribution to improving the life-chances of poorer people.

As in the AIDS case, the socio-economic benefits of new health technologies are most likely to be broadly based where they are rooted in public health programmes that have strong state, professional and local community support. In more affluent countries where health care systems are characterised by a much stronger market and private health insurance the adoption of medical innovation is much more uneven, and in nationalised health care systems with complex organisational structures is likely to be, as Greenhalgh et al. (2005) observe, 'ambiguous, non-linear and disorderly' (p. 15). Given this, it is clear that we should not expect medical technologies to have any singular, determinant effect on those they are supposed to benefit. Moreover, it is crucial to ask how medical technologies are made available and mobilised, through markets, the state, informal networks and so on, for this will affect the pattern and cost of take-up for those relatively disadvantaged as a result of class, gender, ethnicity or status (such as age). Are new resources associated with the new technologies or is it the case that existing resources are distributed differently, and the responsibility for their use similarly so? For example, in the United Kingdom, the government is keen to reduce the numbers in residential care over the next 20 years through the use of telehealth care services in the home. But questions such as who will pay for this and what new burdens will be placed on the frail elderly and their carers remain unanswered (Barlow et al., 2006). For those with chronic conditions, such as heart disorders, telecare can pose new demands inasmuch as patients using telemedicine in their own homes have to act as 'diagnostic agents' (Ousdhoorn, 2007): wiring up their own ECGs (electrocardiograms) patients must be able to 'read' both their bodies ('what's my heart doing now?') and the technology ('how do I get the best out of this?'). In short, while medical innovations such as telehealth care may be empowering for some, they can create new burdens and risks.

Other forms of medical innovation have been seen to both reinforce as well as create new forms of inequality or exclusion. Genetics may provide for better screening of potential genetic mutation and disorder but thereby works to stigmatise those who are already disabled. Pharmacogenetics may lead to a situation in which those patients who do not metabolise drugs effectively are excluded from certain medicines and become 'orphan patients' (Webster et al., 2006); genetic screening has also been used to determine whether workers have a susceptibility or resistance to specific toxins, but, rather than making working conditions clean to accommodate all, those with least susceptibility have been hired. If pre-employment testing (or less transparently, pre-existing information about an earlier test) for a range of susceptibilities were to become the norm (more likely in the private than in the public sector) those with higher levels of susceptibility could become effectively unemployable (Human Genetics Commission, 2002) creating a new form of inequality based on one's *genetic* capital.

Overall, then, most new health technologies have a limited impact on the broad distribution of social advantages and disadvantages, even when they can be shown to have positive clinical outcomes at the level of the patient. At the level of the individual, health problems that are linked to social inequality may not be seen to result from wider (and rather abstract) social processes, but experienced instead in a more direct, tangible sense; by simply the feeling of being unwell or ill. It is this issue that has been a key area of debate from the earliest writing on medical sociology, and one to which I now turn.

The sick role

One thing that infectious diseases do is make you sick. But 'being sick' is not, again, simply a physical matter, though those who have experienced the discomfort of vomiting may beg to differ. It was the US sociologist Talcott Parsons who first developed the notion of 'the sick role' in his book *The Social System* (1951). There he says, 'illness is a state of disturbance in the "normal" functioning of the total human individual, including both the state of the organism as a biological system and of his personal and social adjustments. It is thus partly biologically and partly socially defined' (p. 431). This restates what has been already argued above, but Parsons' insight was to claim that the sick role is socially sanctioned, a role that can be accepted so long as the person performs that role according to the appropriate conventions, the correct social script and crucially displays a motivation to get better. In the sick role, the body becomes an object of attention for others – doctors, nurses, carers, friends, relatives, partners, and so on – who form part of this social drama. Indeed, the sick role sanctions what otherwise would be socially unacceptable behaviour, such as the probing, intimate inspection of the doctor. The encounter involves what Parsons called 'a set of institutionalised expectations and the corresponding sentiments and sanctions' (p. 436), rewards for 'doing well', coping behaviour, and where necessary, withdrawal of support (at least temporarily) if the patient is seen to demand too much attention or seen to be feigning illness. There are, in other words, various rights and responsibilities that patients and those around them enjoy and must observe.

Parsons' theorisation of the sick role sought to explain why sickness – form of social deviance – could be tolerated and ultimately resolved through the social performances of all concerned. As such, it made an important contribution to the field of medical sociology on which others built, especially with regard to the now extensive research on doctor–patient relations.

Parsons' notion of the sick role has been both embellished, applied and criticised by others. A number of empirical studies have examined how the role is played out in different circumstances, including by poorer mothers seeking to secure welfare benefit (Cole and Lejeune, 1972). Others have suggested that it cannot be performed in some clinical settings as in intensive care units or on the operating table (e.g. Rier, 2000), though a recent analysis of the patient–technology–clinician relationship with respect to surgery suggests how the patient might play an active role even when anaesthetised (Goodwin et al., 2005).

Most critics have stressed the need to explore the negotiated and contested nature of the doctor–patient relation (e.g. Strong, 1979), one that displays highly unequal positions of power (Silverman, 1987). More recently, Bloor (2001) has argued for a better understanding of the 'alternative expertise' that the patient brings to the consulting room based on an understanding of illness as embodied experience, accompanied, perhaps by other sources of information secured from friends, the Web, and other sufferers, what Friedson (1970a, b) called the 'lay-referral system'. These criticisms have shifted the focus away from the doctor-centred model of the clinical encounter to one that has given voice to patient expertise.

Parsons' model was clearly a product of its time, a time when compliance with medical expertise went, for the most part, unquestioned. Over the past 20 years or so, medicine itself has been under pressure from the state to adopt a more patient-centred approach as part of a move towards greater professional accountability (Moran, 1999). At the same time, medical expertise has become much more open to challenge. As a result, as May et al., (2002) argue, the shift towards patient-centred relations has occurred '. . . because within medicine itself there was a move towards *enrolling* the patient into the consultation in ways that reduced the growing strain on the epistemological authority of medical knowledge' (p. 137). Sharing responsibility for diagnosis has become an important means through which, paradoxically, medical authority can be re-established, and sign-off from the encounter successfully achieved.

Despite its limitations, it is important not to lose sight of one of the central elements of Parsons' model, namely the trust that patients invest in medical authority. His model describes not simply the performance of roles, but also the trust invested in that performance. Trust has been framed as the need not to calculate (see Callon and Rabeharisoa, 2002) whether someone is to be trusted in what they say, and provides for a willingness to place oneself in their hands, and to enable the doctor to manage uncertainty (Lupton, 1996). Much has been made of the ways in which the Internet has undermined medical authority and so patients' trust but as we shall see in Chapter 6 this claim can be challenged through more recent evidence.

Despite the criticisms of his work, as Shilling (2002) points out, Parsons' notion of the sick role was underpinned by the claim that people are driven to seek help when experiencing illness. This instrumental action is even more evident today inasmuch as the body has become a 'project' that demands attention, effort and management, especially among a new 'body conscious segment of the middle class' (p. 628).

Why and in what circumstances people – whether middle class or not – present themselves to the doctor depends on what Zola (1973) called a series of 'triggers'. None of these are simply physical symptoms of discomfort but symptoms that disturb a person's wider social relations and so push them to seek medical help. Zola described these five triggers as 'an interpersonal crisis'; the 'interference of an illness with social relations'; 'sanctioning' by others that a doctor's attention was needed; 'perceived interference with physical activities'; and what he called the 'temporalising' of symptoms, how long one is prepared to tolerate symptoms before seeing the doctor. The implication one can draw from Zola's model (confirmed by a variety of studies), is that the vast majority of illness symptoms, perhaps as much as 75 percent (ref) are dealt with by people themselves, with the support of others, outside of the clinic. This pattern of self-medication and treatment is crucial to the continued functioning of most health care systems that would be unable to cope with the demand were this to be shifted to the clinic. At the same time, non-reporting of symptoms can be seen to be dysfunctional to health care systems: the so-called clinical iceberg (Last, 1963) describes how serious illnesses, such as heart disease or angina, may go unreported, and in the longer term generate much higher costs for the state.

While Zola's work is important in telling us about symptoms that trigger moves along the 'pathway to the doctor', they relate primarily to the onset of disorders of a more acute nature. Those who suffer chronic illness are well and truly embedded in a clinical biography that works out the pace and rhythm of everyday life. Chronic illness disturbs a person's life in ways that require new forms of coping with a body that simply won't get better. The sick role becomes pervasive and the 'body project' a task requiring extraordinary courage and support. This was an issue that Parsons model failed to address, but it is one which has become of central concern to medical sociology, and led to sustained interest in how people make sense of such sickness. Patient 'narratives' are especially compelling in accounting for what it means to be chronically sick. It is to this issue that I now turn, as well as what it is understood to be 'healthy'.

Narratives of health and illness

A narrative is an account used to tell a story or to build a picture, that makes sense to its author and those who see or hear it. Such stories deploy facts and incidents, emotions and experiences to weave a moral tale that can explain and attribute responsibility for the way things have turned out. Biographical narratives are structured in a similar way, helping to confirm self-image and account for the path someone has taken over time and how recent events and future plans fit into that story. Bodies are part of these narratives – keeping fit, looking one's age, becoming a parent and so on – and they provide ongoing confirmation of a person's 'somatic subjectivity' (Lock, 2002). Illness, whether acute or chronic, disrupts both the body and the taken for granted assumption of being healthy.

Being 'healthy' has typically been defined in negative terms as the absence of disease. In 1946, the WHO sought to define health more positively as 'a state of complete physical, mental and social wellbeing, and not merely the absence of disease or infirmity (WHO, 1946, p. 1). Yet, as a recent comprehensive attempt to explore health from this more positive perspective, analysts found it extremely difficult not to write about health as the absence of disease (Levin and Browner, 2005), or 'as a kind of "default" condition that inheres when an individual manifests neither symptoms nor clinically measurable abnormalities' (p. 746). Perhaps not surprisingly, Parsons never considered what might constitute a 'healthy role', for he was more interested in explaining how deviant roles, here, being sick, were managed functionally by the unwell and those around them. Health as such seems to lack any specific role, and lends itself more to either a circular and rather unconvincing definition of, say, a properly functioning body, or a more abstract notion of 'wellness' or the WHO's 'well-being'.

Health is more often perceived in terms of culturally specific notions of the body, such as having a good tan, being slim, being athletic, well-nourished and so on; notions that predominate in Western affluent society. Elsewhere, quite the opposite may define well-being, and over time such definitions change. In addition, health might be defined in spiritual and emotional terms, or broader social attributes such as coming from a 'healthy family background'. While one cannot perform a 'health role' being healthy seems to be a state that reflects social expectations about the body, its appearance, and its relationship to other bodies (such as family). It is, like sickness, more than simply a reflection or expression of the biophysical state of the body, and indeed those who suffer impairment or chronic disorders can proclaim how healthy they feel. Health in this sense is anchored in socio-psychological beliefs and emotions and thereby dependent, as is the sick role, for its affirmation and confirmation by others. Health-confirming behaviour is evident in the ways in which social actors in late modern societies engage in public displays of the 'body-project', through jogging, joining a gym, running a marathon, dieting and eating 'sensibly', and so on. These help individuals to construct a narrative of 'being well' that others help to confirm. Ageing complicates this narrative and reframes health in terms of retained mental agility and being physically active, crucially reflected in the notion of being 'independent into old age'. Ageing framed in this way allows illnesses and aches and pains to crop up more often without that then indicating poor health.

There are institutionalised definitions of health underpinning the 'quality of life' measures that were discussed in Chapter 2, most of which refer to the ability to lead as 'normal' a life as possible. Those working in the field of 'public health' see their role in terms of both health promotion and disease prevention. Promoting health implies clear targets and a range of measurable outcomes of 'health' that can be used to justify state investment in the area. However, even though there are many health promotion programmes geared towards disease prevention and health education, uncertainty over the very definition of health has meant that those employed in the field find their claims to professional expertise difficult to secure; a key requirement for any occupational group seeking professional status is monopoly of a set of knowledge claims on which expert-lay relations can be built. Most of the time, the field of health promotion establishes its credentials to expertise through deploying traditional evidence-based approaches, such as health technology assessment, to measure the effect of various health care interventions.

Sociological critique of health promotion (see e.g. Burrows et al., 1995) has generally welcomed the way in which it has turned attention away from a biomedical to a more social model of health. However, it has also argued that the field is shot through with a fundamental contradiction that involves a language of choice – that individuals have control over their health choices – yet a language of constraint, that is that only certain choices are healthy. This second line underpins the development of compulsory health education or health counselling classes in schools. As Thorogood (1996) argues 'If health promotion were truly to accept all choices as equally valid, the role of health promotion would be reduced to promoting access to and decision making about services and the dominance of the rational, medico-scientific paradigm would be challenged' (p. 61). That it does not do so indicates the strength of the paradigm, a strength anchored in the role of health promotion to discipline the individual, part of what Rose (1999) calls the advent of 'self-governing' dominating the politics of contemporary society. Such a paradigm also distracts attention away from the structural (as opposed to individual or behavioural) determinants of health and health inequalities.

These institutionalised discourses of health, public health and health promotion, do not depend on narratives of being 'healthy' that individuals may or could provide were they asked, but rather on prescriptive models of 'being healthy' and the sort of skills people need to live up to them. In contrast, illness narratives, to which I now turn, have become of increasing importance precisely because they have provided a rich source of sociological data about the way in which people manage illness in practice, rather than as a result of professional prescriptions. Such narratives, as I shall argue, also provide glimpses of wider structural dynamics shaping the social distribution of illness.

Patients have always sought to make sense of their illnesses through constructing accounts of them, but until relatively recently, these were treated by medicine as of secondary importance, at worst misleading and potentially dangerous, at best lay commentary about symptoms that can be drawn on to provide a more formal diagnosis. This bracketing of the patient's voice is still commonplace, and simply reflects the dominance of the medic in the clinical encounter such that in the encounter the patient is often unable to relate his or her illness narrative.

Even so, work on illness narratives in sociology demonstrates how important these can be for patients in coping with illness, and as such how they may have important clinical outcomes through the way illness is experienced and perceived. Some areas of medicine, notably mental health, see patient narratives as core to the framing of the clinical problem and its resolution. Elsewhere, narratives about illness have become important in evaluating medical interventions with respect to their impact on quality of life. Indeed, drugs companies seek this type of information from patients recruited for clinical trials when submitting new drugs for approval by regulatory agencies.

One of the key reasons for the strength of interest in narrative was the recognition that the notion of the sick role paid little or no attention to the prolonged suffering that patients experience with chronic illness (see Kleinman, 1988). And, as Frank (1995) has suggested, such suffering may be associated with three different types of narrative: a 'restitutive' one whereby illness is fought off successfully and 'normal life' resumes; a 'chaos' narrative which relates an illness with no clear trajectory, resolution or sense of whether one is becoming more or less ill; and finally, a 'quest' narrative through which the patient gets better but in doing so discovers new meaning to their life.

The relationship between these personal narratives and the wider social structural factors noted above that shape the distribution and consequence of illness is important though relatively under-researched. It is important precisely because the same clinical condition may well produce very different subjective narratives precisely because of the relative socio-economic position a patient is in. In short, the ways in which illnesses disrupt a person's somatic subjectivity will in part reflect what we might call their 'somatic objectivity'. Zinn (2005) argues that the structural and the biographical are 'loosely coupled' (p. 3.) and provides a useful discussion of how they might be explored through a focus on risk. He argues that, 'Illnesses do not begin with a *tabula rasa*. Instead people possess biographical resources as a mortgage of the past and these resources pattern the way people manage an illness'(p. 5). One key resource here is how people have managed the risks that they have faced before, and how this can be deployed in the adverse circumstances of the present.

What sort of challenges or risks does chronic illness pose? Bury (1982) provided the first detailed discussion of chronic illness in his study of the effect of rheumatoid arthritis on patients' lives. Much more recently, Lowton and Gabe (2003) have built on this and other work (Charmaz, 1983) in order to examine the effect of cystic fibrosis on the lives of those suffering from this, ultimately fatal, disorder. These accounts show how chronic illness leads to biographical

Table 4. 1 The challenge of and patient responses to chronic illness

Biographical disruption (M.Bury, 1982)	Loss of self (K. Charmaz, 1983)	Narrative reconstructions (G.Williams 1984)
New awareness of the body	Former self is lost without creation of valuable new one	How people try to recreate identity
Abnormal life 'trajectory'	Social isolation	Realign past and present self
Growing physical dependency: breaches norms of social reciprocity	Spiral of loss: disease stigma; low selfesteem; withdrawal; further loss of self	Normalisation (e.g. arthritis among the elderly)

disruption and a loss of self-identity, but also to the attempt to build narrative reconstructions through which to make sense of the disorder and also to cope with it more effectively.

Table 4.1 below summarises a range of key studies that have explored these three processes, and the way they figure in lay accounts of illness.

While both Bury and Charmaz describe how patients may find it difficult if not impossible to create illness narratives that enable a positive rebuilding of their somatic subjectivity, William's study of older people suffering from arthritis indicates how this is possible, not least through normalising the disorder as simply part of the ageing process. At the same time, the potential to normalise such relations will depend in part on the ways in which patients can negotiate this narrative and secure its confirmation not only by family, kin and friends but by medics too. A recent comparative study by May et al., (2002) shows how different chronic illnesses (menorrhagia; depression; and chronic low back pain) create very different contexts within which patients and doctors negotiate the status of each illness, and indeed whether the clinician frames a disorder as one that can be 'disposed of'. Disposal here refers to a doctor's and patient's coming to agreement as to the origin, nature and resolution of symptoms. Each of the three illnesses and their symptoms are framed in different ways and agreement unevenly secured such that their disposal may be only partly achieved.

The physical impairment associated with chronic disability is another area that has been explored by medical sociologists. Galvin (2005) in her comparative study of the 'disabled identity' gathered data from 92 respondents located in Australia, New Zealand, the United States and the United Kingdom who had a diverse range of impairments, and sought their views on the ways in which these affected their self-image and how they thought others viewed them. Many had experienced the stigmatising or patronising gaze of others and while they had developed a range of coping strategies against this – such as regarding others as foolish – also commonly experienced a sense of increased dependency and need for support which was difficult to reconcile, unless they could afford to pay for personal care rather than relying on kin. Here again, we can see how coping with the risk of disability depends in part on the material circumstances of the disabled person. This is echoed in the way in which disability affected their ability to work or to retain their jobs, though the material need not to work could be important, work was more about providing a sense of identity than income.

Hiding or trying to conceal a chronic illness from others in the workplace is a common form of coping with long-term disorders. Other coping strategies involve the redefining of an illness from being biographically disruptive to one that might have been anticipated; older people might well regard a stroke as part of the ageing process, a crisis yes, but one that could be expected after a certain age. Others who have had a chronic disorder for some time may be much less likely to regard yet another disease as highly disruptive, as Carricaburu and Pierret's (1995) study of the onset of HIV among haemophiliacs demonstrated. For them, their lives were already organised around a 'trajectory of illness' (p. 32). Similarly, some illnesses or crises can simply be part of a wider, and perhaps more serious long-term disorder, such as a stroke within the context of advanced diabetes (Faircloth et al., 2004).

Other coping strategies involve the individual and/or collective use of knowledge sources and technologies to seek a solution to the problem. Patients suffering long-term disorders have often established self-help groups to respond to stigmatisation, provide forms of mutual support, and resources through which to seek new forms of treatment (such as alternative medicine) or lobby for state support for research in the disease area. This has happened, for example, in areas such as cystic fibrosis and neurogenic disorders such as Parkinsons disease, where large patient charities have been established across Europe, the United States, Canada and Australia, acting as powerful social actors shaping the research agenda. Rabeharisoa and Callon (2004) have explored the role of patient-driven research, what they call the work of 'researchers in the wild' who 'stick their noses into science and technology'. They describe these as '*concerned groups* [who] want to intervene in the process of the production and diffusion of knowledge. And in order to do that they develop new practices and procedures, they invent and experiment new forms of organization' (p. 16). Illustrating this argument, they describe the role of the French Muscular Dystrophy Association that has played a key role in determining for themselves what the problems are that need to be addressed, especially in respect to the gradual deterioration of muscle capacity. Like 'real researchers' in what Rabeharisoa and Callon, call 'confined research', the wild researchers mobilise information, seek relevant data and amass evidence that can be deployed to produce credible results that will require action by others, notably 'real scientists', clinicians and the state. Patient activist groups have in effect politicised chronic illness, creating what has been called 'the politics of vitality' (Landzelius, 2006).

Beyond mobilising science and technology in novel ways at a collective level, patients can also use technology to redefine the meaning of their chronic condition at a more personal one. Cohn, for example, has shown how those suffering from psychiatric disorders, notably schizophrenia, have found some sense of solace from new brain imaging techniques that can be interpreted to help account for the disorder. These new techniques hope to map not simply the structure of the brain but its action as a functioning organ, a demanding and extremely complex task, that makes the link between brain and psychiatric disorders difficult to determine. Even so, the promise of the technology has led some patients to see this as a basis on which they can redefine their disorder as being akin to a broken bone. As Cohn argues (in Cullen and Cohn, 2006), 'the faith in material explanation, told through images of the living brain, is used to imagine a single plane of biological explanation that places illnesses such as schizophrenia alongside, say, a limb fracture' (p. xxx).

Coping with chronic illness involves, therefore, a range of strategies that help to build a narrative enabling patients to face the risks and challenges health disorders bring. These in turn have to be set in the patient's wider context with respect to the resources that they can mobilise on their own behalf to secure the support they need. Drawing on various studies from within medical sociology and elsewhere, I want to conclude this part of the argument by emphasising that it is crucial to link the personal with the structural if we are to avoid either, on the one hand, an overly deterministic reading of the distribution and impact of illness among 'unequal bodies', or, on the other, a focus on narrative that presumes illness can be framed as a social construction at the level of the individual. Clearly both dimensions need to be articulated even if we agree with Zinn that they are 'loosely coupled'. This will help to explain why the 'same' illness, shaped by wider structural factors such as poverty or occupational risk, meets with differing degrees of resilience among social actors. Such differences are also expressed in distinctive ways throughout the life course, and as Williams (2003) has argued, the link between 'individual biography and life course is a new and important dimension of research on the connections between social structure and health' (p. 148).

Technology, health and illness

In considering the ways in which narratives of health and illness are constructed, it is important to ask how medical technologies figure in this process. These technologies may, like medicines or drugs, be part of a patient's ongoing or occasional treatment, or function as assistive devices such as the near-patient technologies that diabetics use. They might be implant technologies such as prosthetic hips, or specific techniques and instruments used in diagnosis such as ultra sound scans or the remote monitoring of patients via telehealth care and so on. Some technologies manage and alleviate illness, others determine its extent. The most 'heroic' technology, surgery, intervenes directly to remove, repair or replace body tissue itself. In doing so, these technologies are designed (by bioengineers, clinicians, drugs companies, etc.) with a specific understanding of what the problem is and how it can be measured, addressed, and dealt with to produce the desired outcome. And as we saw in Chapter 2, technologies also play an important part in defining professional expertise and skill in different branches of medicine having developed within and between medical specialties and express and enable different 'ways of knowing'.

Patients confront these technologies in a series of staged levels of sophistication, initially through the gate-keeping role of the primary practitioner. In the European context, primary care carries a limited range of technologies: these include prescription drugs, syringes, basic optical and hearing tests, devices to perform blood or urine tests, perhaps X-ray technology and some basic surgical devices, and increasingly e-health systems such as electronic patient records to log and relay patient data. Beyond this patients are referred to the more technologically complex world of secondary, hospital care. In the United States this distinction between primary and secondary care is much less pronounced given the role of specialist practitioners in primary care.

Within medical sociology and STS, an important area of interest has been how these technologies mediate the doctor–patient relationship, whether that be in routine (such as prescription drugs) or high-tech medicine (such as found in intensive care units). Some (e.g. Conrad, 1979) have stressed how technologies not only serve an immediate biomedical function but also carry within them the politics of medical control to secure patient compliance. Similarly, radical feminist analysis emphasises how reproductive technologies work precisely by making women invisible to the reproductive process (Corea, 1985). More recent work (e.g. Berg and Mol, 1998) adopts a more nuanced perspective on medical technologies that is more attentive to the context of use, and thereby how they perform and the degree to which they are *given* utility and value by both practitioner and patient. This is a much less deterministic reading of technology and one borne out by the detailed studies published within STS.

Timmermans and Berg (2003) have provided a useful classification of these distinctive perspectives characterising the role of technology in medicine. These fall into three principal types: 'deterministic', 'social essentialist' and a third that focuses on 'technology-in-practice'. The deterministic reading, as above, is a highly reductionist approach that presumes that technologies have specific effects as a result of their intrinsic properties, design and use. Apart from the early work of radical feminists noted earlier, more recent examples include Nelkin and Andrew's (1999) critique of DNA technologies that can serve to act as agencies of surveillance (through forensic DNA databanks deployed by the police, for example). Much of the deterministic position is, as Timmermans and Berg say, less to do with examining technology and more about developing a critique of the power of biomedicine especially in the medical encounter. While this is an important objective, its description of the way technology performs and directly expresses economic or professional interests is an oversimplification that cannot be sustained. Both Chapters 2 and 3 examined the role of professional and economic interests in shaping technology, but in doing so argued that these are subject to challenge, critique and even refashioning by patients, users and consumers of health care. I also argued that different technology domains have more, or less, prospect of being captured to serve the interests of biocapital, noting in particular the problems posed by tissue engineering. It seems that both at the wider, macro and the more narrowly defined micro level of doctor–patient interaction, the deterministic reading has little to offer. Before we move on though, it is worth noting that while such a reading can be challenged on analytical grounds as being overly simplistic, in many health policy contexts we see that the deterministic reading of the effects of technology is alive and well. Government health agencies evaluate and approve new technologies on the basis of their utility to patients or services in such a way that they are typically abstracted from their context. This is based on the assumption that the clinical or managerial utility of an intervention can be assessed – and priced – on a uniform basis precisely because it will have a specific impact, rather than a diverse range of effects depending on its context of use. A deterministic reading of technology clearly has advantages for the policy-maker.

The second reading, that of 'social essentialism' is in a sense the complete opposite to determinism. It refers to the view that technology can be seen as a more neutral medium through which the social interaction of the medical encounter and the process of illness management occur. Technology is a 'blank slate' to be 'interpreted and rendered meaningful by culture' (ibid, p. 101). In some ways, this perspective is characteristic of a more general indifference or neglect within sociology of 'the technological' that stretches back many years, a neglect that has been evident too in the work undertaken within medical sociology, until fairly recently. Timmermans and Berg illustrate the social essentialist perspective with various studies, including that of Daly who explored the use of echocardiography tests in determining the severity of heart disorders. Such tests are supposed to provide reassurance to patients, but serve more importantly to manage the relationships between practitioners and patients. While this second approach avoids the oversimplification of determinism, it fails to unpack technologies and crucially to explore how their meaning varies from one setting to another.

This takes us to the third tradition, that of 'technology-in-practice'. This adopts a much more complex approach towards the role of technology, and seeks to understand how medical technologies are implicated in the dance of the medical encounter, where medic, patient, body, illness and device are choreographed, 'perform' in ways that are dynamic, never fully scripted, but provisional and open-ended. Moreover, this approach shows that technologies 'work' only because of a much broader range of factors beyond the clinical encounter itself. These are organisational, regulatory, political and economic. This configuration of both the macro and the contextual is given meaning in the encounter, never stable or uniform, but to be practised and brought to life. In the singularity of the diagnosis, the disposal of the patient, all elements are at work: citing Mol and Elsman's study of diseased blood vessels in the leg, '[the diagnosis] draws together vessels, surgeons, research designs, hospital organisations, patients, apparatus, general practitioners, dye, buttons, interview questions, catheters, gel, blood, and many other elements. All of them interrelated. Yet each irreducible to the other' (1996, p. 628).

It is this latter perspective that I shall use to shape my discussion of a number of examples, drawn from recent case studies, of innovative health technologies. I hope to show how health technologies mediate and are mediated by conceptions of the body, identity, illness and the meaning of the clinical encounter. This is a non-reductionist position that philosophically is rooted in what I termed earlier in the Chapter 'constructivist realism', and explores the play of elements in three very distinct areas, genetic risk assessment in a cancer clinic, the use of drugs in the management of HIV and the 'end-of-life' technologies linked to palliative care.

Case studies: the body–technology nexus

The use of genetic tests to determine whether a person is a carrier of a particular genetic or chromosomal disorder (such as, respectively, Huntingdon's Disease [HD] or Downs syndrome) has been of central importance in clinical genetics for many years. Such tests determine the hereditability of genetic disease and have thereby become commonly deployed in prenatal testing where a family history warrants this. Parents and new borns may be screened as 'carriers' of a defective gene, as in cystic fibrosis. This form of screening – used for example on over four million babies in the United States each year – produces results that are quite definite: someone who carries the HD disorder will die of the disease. There are however a range of other types of genetic test which are much more provisional and relate to non-inherited disorders, such as cancer. These are the 'pre-symptomatic' (or 'predictive') tests and 'susceptibility' tests that have been developed to identify individuals 'at risk', likely to fall ill in the future.

In the United Kingdom, there are approximately 300 tests for rare single gene disorders available. Such disorders affect between 1 and 5 per cent of the population and cost the NHS in the region of £2 billion each year. In 2003, the government's White Paper on genetics (DoH, 2003) opened up the possibility that all newly born would not only be tested for a specific disorder, but would have their DNA profile taken to be held on a new national database. Eventually, the proposal was abandoned, not least because of the huge costs involved as well as the limited clinical value it would offer in regard to more effective treatment.

I want to focus the discussion here on predictive tests associated with cancer, drawing on recent research by Prior and his colleagues (see Prior et al., 2002; Scott et al., 2005). Prior explores the ways in which the criteria used to determine whether someone is at risk of developing breast (and other forms of) cancer are deployed in the clinical setting. Such estimates are based on population-wide markers that have been developed over the years to determine whether a specific individual should be followed up and monitored. Criteria include whether there has been a history of cancer in the family, where that history is located (in close or distant relatives, in near or distant generations), the age of the patient and various lifestyle factors. These general markers have then to be 'translated' into the actual clinical setting and discussed with patients. This is a process that involves negotiation around the initial risk estimate. As Prior points out, the threshold between being 'at risk' or not, that is falling on the 'right side' of the threshold, is highly malleable and depends on the deployment and interpretation of the risk criteria. In addition, it is important to note that the eventual risk diagnosis (or 'risk profile') will determine whether or not an individual receives treatment, support and ongoing monitoring or not.

In interviews with patients it was clear that many were unclear about their condition, whether indeed their risk profiles meant they were ill or not: 'people often expressed uncertain feelings about the fact that they were not fully recognised as cancer patients whilst, on the other hand, were not perhaps entirely 'healthy'. Those who had received a genetic risk estimate as moderate or high often saw themselves as entering . . . a state betwixt two worlds where they waited either to develop a disease and be treated accordingly or to be reassured from screening results that they were in good health' (Bharawadj et al., 2006, p. 17). One of the respondents (P34) who had been reviewed for possible colorectoral cancer describes his position as follows:

P34: It's understandable that they need to see the higher risk people, rather than people like me . . . But who am I?

FW: Well you are important.

P34: But I am not even a patient. That's another way of looking at it, I am not //

FW: Of course you are.

P34: I'm not, I'm not. I do not feel like a patient. Because to be a patient there has got to be something wrong with you. And there is nothing wrong with me. I am just somebody who filled in a bit of paper. That is how I feel. And I would have felt like that even if I talked to somebody. I am still not a patient.

(P34: Clinical assessment: moderate risk, colorectal cancer) (ibid., pp. 17–8).

Here the relationship between the body, patient-identity, and technology (in the form of the risk calculus) combine in such a way as to generate uncertainties across all three: is my body diseased, is the risk estimate telling me so or not, should I claim status as a patient and seek further clinical surveillance or intervention or not? Indeed, these concerns led many who had been 'signed-off' as on the 'right' side of the threshold to ask that their risk assessment be *increased* such that they could secure monitoring and the reassurance this provided. Patient-clients brought to the clinic their own sense of being at risk based on their interpretation of family history, which when discordant with the clinician's assessment, led to these attempts to renegotiate, and so stabilise their patient status in relation to their bodies, their kin, their biographies and health delivery itself. As Prior et al. (2002) put it 'patient-clients are not simply giving voice to 'representations' or health beliefs, but seeking ways of organising health care resources around their specific and particular needs and lifeworlds' (p. 555).

This study provides an excellent illustration of the way in which the technologies of diagnosis and disposal mediates the interplay of biological and social elements found within the clinic. There is no simple biomedical algorithm or calculus at work here that is stable for each patient-client who is referred for testing. Predictive testing is highly provisional and negotiated, and so thereby is the status of being sick, being a patient, being a carrier of a genetic disorder. Conceiving risk calculation in these terms is not merely of analytical interest but has important implications for health care systems, for it points to the ways in which, as predictive and pre-symptomatic tests increase, so will the demand for monitoring, paradoxically even from those supposedly told they have a low risk. Moreover, in broader terms, as the relationship between genetic diagnoses and disease deepens, in the sense that diseases are redefined according to new genetics-based classifications, a person's illness may move from one class to another in something of a diagnostic maze. As a recent study reports, 'individual biographies are inserted into changing classification systems, and patients are ruled into or out of disease categories in unexpected ways' (Miller et al., 2005, p. 2543).

The second case I want to discuss relates to HIV and its management through the use of a cocktail of drugs known as 'Highly Active

Anti-Retroviral Treatment' (HAART). This case is interesting both for its focus on medicine as technology, and for its lessons with respect to treatment that creates new risks for patients suffering from HIV. These risks are both biophysical and social and are co-produced as a result of the effects of the drugs. The study also shows how drug regimes become a defining feature of a patient's lifeworld, illness narratives and so identity.

The case study draws on the recent research in the United Kingdom (based primarily in Glasgow and London) by Flowers and his colleagues (see Flowers et al., 2003; Rosengarten et al., 2004). Whereas HIV had virtually always been a disease leading to AIDS and so death, the development of HAART and associated monitoring of the 'viral load' in a patient's blood, transformed what had, as Flowers et al., (2006) put it, been a 'death sentence' into a 'life sentence'; the intervention meant that patients could now live longer yet only do so with HIV as a chronic companion. HIV carriers need to monitor their viral loading and to adopt a rigorous daily regime of compliance with prescribed drugs.

The drugs that comprise HAART carry significant side effects because of their toxicity, with specific dosage levels key to managing these adverse effects. Patients are required to work hard at maintaining self-care on a daily basis, but find that in doing so their illness is defined by clinicians in terms of their status against a predefined pattern of biological markers, rather than their experience of the disease itself. Prior to HAART, clinicians had little at their disposal that could help alleviate the disease and as a result there was a much greater emphasis given to managing the debilitating experience of the illness, through counselling and palliative care. The new drug regime has weakened and effectively displaced this approach, redefining HIV in exclusively biomedical terms. As Flowers et al. note, 'HIV treatments require trust in a medical model in which health was no longer somatic (part of embodied experience) but delivered by means of monitoring test results in the space of clinical interactions (clinical markers took precedence over subjective well being)' (2006, p. 3).

While HIV has long been a target of social stigma through its association with AIDS, the arrival of HAART has created new forms of stigmatisation as a result of the side effects it produces: not only does a patient suffer from increased risk of diabetes and heart failure, but more publicly and visibly facial disfigurement caused by the drugs' effect of redistributing body fat. These effects simply serve to announce one's HIV status to the wider world. As one female respondent observed: 'You know the way a woman move [sic], a woman is proud of the way she looks, you know a small waist, nice bum, nice legs and suddenly all that's taken away from you. And in a case where you haven't disclosed your status and people start seeing the body changing – that alone is enough to disclose your status' (p. 107).

More pernicious still, other side effects of the drugs are similar to the very effects of the disease itself, so patients may be completely unsure whether the treatment is 'working'. As one patient said:

> You can't actually feel any immediate results, when you take you can't actually feel any immediate results, when you take the drugs you know. They're kind of like silent bombs, I the drugs you know. They're kind of like silent bombs, I suppose that go off inside you, and you know it's not really suppose that go off inside you, and you know it's not really reported to your own senses, you know. So you rely on the reported to your own senses, you know. So you rely on the doctors in fact, to tell you that these things are working, or doctors in fact, to tell you that these things are working, or have an effect. (Flowers, 2003)

Yet, take them they must, and for life. The drug regime becomes part of the patient's identity, indeed, it is like a marriage:

> People don't understand the full implications of what it is to live on drugs. I mean it's a relationship, it's a marriage, you know. People don't realise that there's no cure yet you know. Yes, the treatments are there but they don't work for everybody. You're just negotiating around it every day of your life. (Ibid.)

Flowers' study demonstrates how medical technologies can have a pervasive effect on the patient, but at the same time, and partly as a result, patients have sought other remedies and resisted the imposition of HAART or endeavoured to complement it with other forms of understanding and shared knowledge about HIV. The very experience of the biomedical intervention generates new forms of patient expertise based not simply on a struggle for survival but also hopes for the future. These are creating patient narratives that can be shared with other sufferers, and provide a basis for a renewed politics of advocacy on behalf of patients to which clinicians are being asked to respond (Rosengarten et al., 2004).

The third and final case I want to consider relates to a number of technologies deployed to either delay death or to ease the pain of terminal illness, typically of cancer, in both hospice and domestic settings. Collaborative work by Seymour et al., (2006); Graham and Clark (2005) has researched the development of 'life-prolonging technologies (such as chemotherapy and resuscitation) and pain-relief involving syringe pump drivers or other devices (such as dermal patches) that deliver measured doses of morphine to those who are terminally ill'. Death, as illness, is socially shaped and defined, as is the onset of what Mulkay and Ernst (1991) called the 'social death sequence' whereby a person gradually withdraws from full engagement with society, through retirement, widowhood and ageing. The clinical diagnosis of death has become a site for medical controversy over the necessary and sufficient physical markers that signify actual death (Lock, 2002). The availability of artificial systems to keep people 'alive' (such as ventilators) simply serves to give greater impetus to such debates and the reconstruction of death into a complex pattern of symptoms and indeed 'types' of death. These in turn are caught up in the social definition of how to manage a 'dignified' death, or what is to be regarded as a 'good' or 'natural' death (Sandman, 2004). Given the curative discourse of biomedicine, death creates something of a problem for clinicians inasmuch as it needs to be explained in such a way as to not compromise the authority of medicine itself. As Timmermans (2005) says: 'When death occurs, [doctors] help negotiate a culturally acceptable passing, and after death they rationalise the inevitability of its occurrence with a classification of its causes' (p. 993). So powerful has the medicalisation of death become that as Bauman (1992) says, 'we no longer hear people dying of mortality' (p. 5).

Within this context, end-of-life technologies are not simply about serving the dying but thereby providing information that may be of use to the living. Death in this way is an important arena for biomedical innovation that stretches back now into the ageing process itself and the hunt for the gene that begins the body's terminal decline (see Collins et al., 2003) Those who find themselves in hospices are immediately thrown into a world where narratives of illness are replaced by narratives of death and dying. However, while this defines a subjective identity that is looking to the past than the future, it is one that in physical terms is collapsing in the present, as the body succumbs to the pathological effects of cancer. In part this explains what Mellor and Shilling (1993) called the 'sequestration' or hiding away of death from society.

As Seymour et al., (2006) show, palliative care in these circumstances is welcomed by hospice residents for it allows them to relieve family and kin of the responsibility for their care. The sick role is no longer an option for 'getting better', is itself no longer possible. Moreover, the patient and the family are spared the mutual embarrassment that comes with the decay of the body – the emissions, fluids and smells of a body out of control: as Gott et al., (2003, p. 15) argue, 'there is a strong belief that suffering, and evidence of bodily "unboundedness" should be contained within institutions', that is, within hospices or hospitals. As one of Seymour's respondents observed See, and if it happened to me I wouldn't want my family to endure seeing me there like that, I would want the [feeding] tube removed'.

Narratives of dying are, as of illness, as much about the implications of the disorder for others as they are for the self. The residents in the hospices saw their dying as a process that gradually redefined, and in some sense threatened not only their identity and self-respect through loss of control, but also their relationships with their families and the obligations each had to the other. The technologies helped to mediate this process and provide for a more graduated and 'natural' death sequence that enabled residents, family and staff to move towards sedation and a 'good time' to die. This helps to construct a coherent death narrative for those involved, and one that re-anchors a patient's biography and identity in the broader narrative of the family itself. As Seymour argues, we can see the play between palliative technologies and the body as one that is 'attended by a complex mixture of beliefs about care, personhood, family and obligation' (2006, p. 144).

These three cases reported here (and there is much more rich sociological material within each that is worth exploring) show how technologies cannot be read as being either deterministic nor simply neutral media through which medicine is delivered or experienced. Rather they illustrate the ways in which they perform, and are given performativity, in specific contexts, and how patients, clinicians and others bring life even in death – to the body/technology drama.

Conclusion

I have argued in this chapter that the body is both physically and socially constructed at the same time. The notion of constructivist-realism seeks to capture this, and was drawn on to explore three sites where the technology–health–illness nexus plays out in different ways. The cases also point to ways in which the notion of the sick role has to be understood in rather different ways from that originally conceived by Parsons, inasmuch as there are more 'actors involved, including technology, and in the context of chronic illnesses, such as HIV, 'being a patient' is both a fraught and uncertain status.

At the same time, we have also seen how the chances of becoming ill are unequally distributed in society as a result of social structural processes. These are neither random nor short-lived, and typically intergenerational. Even so, I discussed a research that showed how, especially in the case of chronic illness, people can draw on differing degrees of social support (or social capital) via networks within which they are embedded and this, along with personal biographies of risk coping, influences the ways in which health risks, and illnesses are seen as being more, or less serious. This in part explains why, as I suggested, some people may perceive themselves to be relatively 'healthy' despite carrying the burden of chronic illness.

The significance of the sociological work and recent research reported in this chapter relates not only to how we theorise the body–technology–health nexus, but also how the currently favoured notion of 'patient-centred' or 'patient-led' medicine might be criticised. Much political weight is placed on such discourse in Europe and the United Kingdom especially, a point touched on in Chapter 2. In light of the analysis above, what would 'patient-centred' actually mean, whether this be someone suffering from HIV, in need of palliative care, or genetic risk counselling. Individualising risk, choice of care and consent through patient-centred medicine would appear to ignore the complex dynamics at work through which illness is defined and managed by the coming together of an array of actors. Diagnoses and disposals are, as May et al. (2002) showed, patient-centred in quite distinctive ways depending on the context through which all involved seek to negotiate some sort of consensus about the meaning of the illness itself. Patient-centred care also suggests considerable freedom for the patient in making decisions about managing their illness, whereas this may be far from the truth, not least as professional and regulatory controls limit such freedom: assisted suicide and euthanasia are typically not options open to those in hospices. In the next chapter I shall explore this question of patient-centred medicine in more detail as part of a wider examination of the social organisation and management of health care delivery itself.

Managing and Governing New Health Technologies

5

Introduction

New health technologies are already having a major impact on the health care provider and health care manager, not only in the specific context of primary and secondary clinical care, but in the wider private and public arenas. This chapter will explore the changing ways in which health technologies shape, and are in turn shaped by, the broad social management of health. There are various questions that arise: for example, in earlier chapters we saw how, in the clinical context, health technologies can lead to the creation of new disease categories, new categories of patients, so one can ask what effect this will have on the patterning of health service delivery? Might this result in the development of new criteria for determining eligibility for treatment and the exclusion of some people as patients?

There is also a need to explore the social organisation of health care systems and the relationship between policy made at the centre and how this translates down through lower levels of the system. This is rarely a linear or straightforward process, and when coupled with major technological investments, such as national health information systems, can, as I describe here, be a recipe for confusion rather than coherence in delivery. Health care is also delivered through an increasing range of professional groups who in turn relate to each other quite differently from the past, while new non-medical actors in social services and social care are being asked to shoulder more responsibility, especially for the aged and chronically unwell. How should we understand these changes and how do technologies relate to them, to change or reproduce existing professional hierarchies and practices?

One of the major developments in recent years has been the formalisation by the state of more explicit procedures relating to the governance of medical practice and research. In this chapter, I also explore three distinct but related forms of governance and then ask whether these are jeopardised by moves in the United Kingdom and elsewhere towards the privatisation of health care and the embrace by many governments of the notion of patient-led self-care. One last point is that I do not propose to deal with the extensive debate over the new 'managerialism' that has been said to characterise health systems today, except in so far as this touches on professional–technology relations and matters relating to clinical governance. For those interested in the area, and debates over performance indicators, budgets, performance-based pay and so on, see Ferlie et al. (1996) and Germov's (2005) critical analysis of the 'hyper-rationalisation' driving an intensification of managerialism in the Australian public health care sector.

I begin though by discussing the processes through which innovation in health technologies is translated from the policy domain to the clinical setting, and do so through two examples, that of health information systems, and of current embryonic stem cell research. These two are useful examples because with respect to the first, we can see how the introduction of large-scale innovation systems rubs up against and is mediated by existing organisational structures; the second case, stem cells, illustrates a rather different process whereby translation has involved the establishing of *new* institutional structures in the hope that the research in the field will be of use in the clinic.

Translating innovation: from policy to practice

Innovation in e-health is one of the major priorities of the state, promising faster, remote, and in theory more cost-effective care. Many national health care systems are now implementing hugely expensive health information management systems as national 'spines' along which data about patients and their treatment will flow while others are developing such systems in a more incremental way. For example, in the United Kingdom the English NHS 'Connecting for Health' programme (not to be confused with a private-based system of the same name being developed in the United States) is expected to cost in the region of between £12–20 billion by 2010 while the Australian system, 'Health *Connect*' is developing more modestly over a three year period (2006–09) with funding around £70 million (this does not include upgrading existing equipment). This huge difference, reflects a number of things: the differences in political systems (nationally based compared with a loose federal structure with local state autonomy for health policy), in the structure and funding of health care (state-funded verses. more private, insurance based), in the size of the populations (c. 59 million compared with 20 million) and consequent number and range of clinical sites and facilities, and in the political investment in a *nationally co-ordinated* system of e-health as a medium through which standardised, cost-effective, and flexible care can be delivered (rhetorically powerful in the United Kingdom, much less evident in Australia where there is less investment in 'building an entire electronic health environment' [Dearne, 2005]). Even so, the level of investment in the NHS is disproportionately high compared to virtually all other countries introducing such systems. The potential risk is thereby that much greater.

As one of the most extensive of systems, and therefore one which is of international interest, what are the main features of the NHS Connecting for Health programme? Much of the cost will be incurred putting in place the national electronic and telecommunications infrastructure that will be the platform on which national facilities will be based and through which localised aspects of the system can function. At a national level, the most important component will be the electronic patient record or 'NHS Care record' that will be accessible to health practitioners wherever (e.g. on holiday) the patient might be. Second, the system will support electronic prescribing (informed by the care record), and facility for patients to 'choose and book' hospital appointments on line in liaison with their local doctors. More specialist elements include a national broadband network for transfer of data including imaging, such as the 'Picture Archiving and Communications Systems (PACS)', effectively digitised X-rays or photographic images that can be electronically archived and relayed when needed. Other aspects of the system include using the data in anonymised form for public health (epidemiological) purposes, for example tracking the pattern or incidence of disease. According to the claims made on behalf of the programme, 'Once installed, the new IT infrastructure and systems will connect more than 100,000 doctors, 380,000 nurses and 50,000 other healthcare professionals; benefiting more than 50 million patients in England' (NHS, 2005; DoH, 2003).

Given the level of government investment, not surprisingly IT companies have been keen to secure contracts to provide these systems, and some of the major firms under contract are Oracle, Sun Microsystems, iSOFT and BT among others. Most firms operate globally and secure contracts in other countries introducing similar systems (Sun Microsystems has, for example, been involved in the US programme).

Putting such a systems as Connecting for Health in place is a complex process, whereby a range of technologies, social actors, their networks and organisations have to be enrolled and recruited to make the system in any way workable, akin to what Law (1987) and Mackenzie (1990) have described elsewhere as a process that involves 'heterogeneous engineering', 'the engineering of the social as well as the physical world' (Mackenzie, 1990, p. 28). Not surprisingly, the dreams of state policy-makers, have become something of an organisational nightmare for those charged with implementing this system on the ground. One of the most significant problems has been introducing a national platform across a health care system that is 'national' only in name, inasmuch as the NHS is made up of Trusts numbering in many hundreds, each with degrees of autonomy, funding levels, and different ICT needs, such as acute compared with community-based Trusts. As a House of Commons Health Committee of Inquiry observed, '[t]he diversity across NHS Trusts has resulted in incompatible and inconsistent procurement policies' (2005, p. 14).

At the same time, as is often the case with government departments, changes made elsewhere in the management and direction of services provide a new context within which ICT systems and their heterogeneous engineers must operate. For example, the United Kingdom government established in 2005 a new 'Strategic Implementation Group' to translate the recommendations of a quite separate inquiry into the use of health technologies in the NHS. This has introduced new institutional routes for managing innovation including new 'Collaborative Procurement Hubs' and an 'Innovation Institute'. In addition, stronger links between health and social services are envisaged as a way of managing the introduction of ICT systems for the aged in community care settings. In theory these initiatives are supposed to reduce the barriers to effective implementation of all technologies. A key issue that remains to be addressed, however, is how the expansion of work in the health technology assessment field that will inevitably be associated with these developments be properly informed by a more sophisticated understanding of changing social context of use (as I argued in Chapter 2).

Beyond this changing organisational and evaluative landscape, software and hardware suppliers have to comply with specific standards requirements and costs established nationally, while dealing regionally or locally with legacy systems that need to be made interoperable with the national programme or replaced. As local service providers supply hard- and software on an incremental and fragmented basis across the NHS, so adjustments are made along the way to cope with delays and cost overruns. In January 2005, the government public accounts agency, the National Audit Office, criticised implementation of key parts of the system, notably the 'Choose and Book' facility, as unreliable (NAO, 2005).

The physical and social 'engineering' of this system means that its stability is always under threat and is illustrated by major problems experienced in the functioning of the information 'spine' in December 2005 when a series of crashes occurred related to 'intermittent failure updating patient demographic information', 'failure to automatically generate a patient password' and 'occasional slower searches for patients' (NHS 2005). These problems were in turn generated by system managers recognising that only those doctors with a direct or 'legitimate' link to patients should be able to access their records. Here issues relating to consent, anonymity and accountability feed back onto the technical design of the system. This is a chronic feature of all IT systems (see Williams and Hartswood, 2001) and echoes and confirms Suchman's (2003) critique of the rationalist assumptions on which ICT design and implementation is typically based, neglecting the 'labour' involved that makes things 'work'. As she says,

> [My] critique starts from the observation that discourses of ICT have tended to erase the human labor that continues to be involved in techno-logical production, implementation, maintenance and the like (p. 34)

Those making things 'work' are not only the designers of the systems, but the clinicians, nurses, finance managers, in-house IT technicians and patients and carers who are being recruited as users of the system. This co-construction of ICT systems by a range of actors and technologies echoes my argument advanced at the start of Chapter 2 with respect to the need to see such processes as creating a social matrix that is only as strong as the network of relations that holds it together. When things go wrong this is the same as saying that the network has lost some of its socio-technical ties, or that they have become more precarious and fragile.

Indeed, the notion of network underpins the state's characterisation of the future e-health system: the functionality of the system is seen in terms of tiered areas of activity each carrying its own more or less formalized networks, deploying different forms of ICT to manage and deliver care. Figure 5.1, provided by the Department of Health, captures this layering,

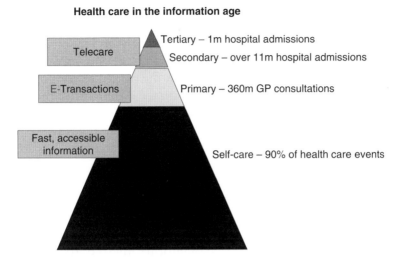

Figure 5.1   Location and function of different e-health systems in the United Kingdom
Source: Royston, DoH

a system of triage in which most health needs are met informally by individuals and the social and digital (Internet) networks that they can draw on outside of formal clinical care.

This is, of course, an overly tidy image of how e-health systems function and fails to address how people engage with e-health systems, the networks they enable, and what intended or unintended effects they might have. This raises a range of sociological issues that need consideration.

First, e-health does not function as discretely bounded arenas of activity but bleeds across them, where, for example, patients access both Connecting for Health and connect to their own favoured Internet health sites for advice and information. The effect is to create competing network dynamics, patients, on the one hand, incorporated and embedded within the system (through their 'care records') while, on the other, increasingly seeking information about their care needs outside the orbit of medicine, performing and occupying an 'e-scape' beyond the clinic (see Nettleton 2004; Nettleton and Hanlon, 2006). This could even have legal implications inasmuch as patients may discover through the Internet certain forms of treatment that are denied to them by the state healthc are system on the basis that they are clinically inappropriate: if there is little or no evidence-base for this refusal, patients could take legal action against the health agency.

Second, while these systems are supposed to enhance patient choice and autonomy, they can be seen to have quite the opposite effect.

Autonomy implies some degree of independence and control over information about one's personal record, but as a record becomes distributed across a range of clinicians for assessment and monitoring purposes, autonomy and control are compromised. Moreover, national information spines require compliance on the part of patients to accept incorporation within and cooperation with the system, while the advent of remote monitoring (through telehealthcare) of the chronically sick in their homes, typically requires 'work' on the part of carers as intermediaries between clinician and patient in the system. Paradoxically, perhaps, anonymity has often depended on the fact that ICTs are *not* integrated: if government databases are more integrated the capacity for surveillance grows and autonomy thereby comes under threat.

Third, the massive increase in the flow and volume of data that such systems produce generates a range of risks connected to confidentiality, safety, clinical governance, sale of information to third parties, and possible system failure. Focusing simply on clinical governance, for example, as information and treatment is distributed across ever-wider networks where does clinical governance, risk and responsibility reside, with which medic and why? ICT systems tend to lead to the distribution and fragmentation of delivery, such that the meaning of who is accountable for that and even what 'treatment' itself means becomes an open and potentially contentious question. One related possibility is that clinical errors become digitally embedded within the system and so amplified over time (akin to the same phenomenon commonly experienced in regard to financial credit).

Fourth, these systems, whether in the United Kingdom, Australia or elsewhere, are premised on the assumption that they will enable a more preventative approach to medicine inasmuch as early and ongoing monitoring of patients, especially the ageing chronically ill, will allow speedier and more timely treatment to be delivered. But this begs the question whether the clinical system will be able to respond to the likely huge and time-sensitive growth in demand for monitoring. Patients too may well expect higher and more frequent IT-based exchange (through Web-based services for example) than the economic threshold for these predicts or allows, so either increasing costs to health care suppliers or creating new forms of resentment among frustrated patients, or, as is likely both.

Finally, as Berg and Goorman (1999) have argued, information is always 'entangled' with its context of production (how, where and by whom it was produced and for what purpose) and can only be used by others if some work is put in to disentangle it from its original context. Indeed, they have gone so far as to propose a 'law of medical

information', viz. ' . . . the further information has to be able to circulate (i.e. the more diverse contexts it has to be usable in), the more
work is required to disentangle the information from the context of its
production' (1999, p. 59). May and his colleagues have similarly
shown through their detailed examination of telemedicine, that 'work'
is also required to normalise such systems within the existing clinical
landscape (May et al., 2003). They also show (Finch et al., 2006) that
what counts *as* a 'working system' is one that will *complement* and not
displace more traditional forms of health care delivery. As they say,
'where telehealthcare systems are seen by their users to 'work', they are
characterised as *alternatives* rather than substitutes for conventional
services' (2006, 91). Much of the state rhetoric accompanying ICT
systems tends to focus on substitution rather than complementarity.

There are, then, a range of sociological issues that attend the implementation of ICT systems, that highlight the difficulties of translating
state policy into practice, as well as pointing to the unintended effects
of new technologies which can work against patient interests, and generate new risks with regard to the governance and economics of delivery, precisely the two areas that initiatives like 'Connecting for Health'
are supposed to address. I also described in brief how these systems
have to articulate with existing organisational structures and policy
changes elsewhere if they are to 'work' effectively. In the next example,
I describe how UK policy designed to support the emergent field of
embryonic stem cell research (touched on at the end of Chapter 2), has
required the building of *new* regulatory and enabling institutions.

Research on stem cells is not in itself a recent development, for
work on 'adult' or somatic stem cells goes back almost 30 years. One
area which has had a long history of clinical application relates to the
use of haematopoietic (blood-derived) cells that have been grown in
lab conditions and used to treat, through transplant, cancers of the
blood (such as leukaemia). Embryonic stem cells, in contrast have a
fairly recent origin based on work originally conducted in the United
States (principally at the University of Wisconsin Madison in the late
1990s) but now global in its spread, with major research centres in the
United Kingdom, Japan, Singapore, China and Canada. It has, as I
discussed in the closing section of Chapter 2, been met with considerable political and public hostility in a number of countries, which have
restricted or banned the use of embryos as a source of stem cell lines.
This is clearly a powerful socio-political barrier to its implementation,
but even in those countries that champion its cause, there has been a
range of regulatory, ethical and organisational issues that have meant
new institutional structures have had to be socially 'engineered'.

There was considerable hype about the promise of embryonic stem cells both from within the science community (Brown et al., 2006) and appearing in the press (Petersen, 2001). Yet developing the science base has proved especially problematic, not least because defining and characterising stem cells has required negotiation over different biological 'markers' that everyone in the field can agree to (Eriksson and Webster, 2007). This itself has prompted the establishing of an 'international stem cell initiative' through which agreement might be reached in the near future. Without this, it will be difficult for different groups of scientists to be sure that they are working to the same scientific protocols when undertaking their experiments and therefore whether progress across the network is actually being made.

The cell lines are also highly unstable and cannot be reproduced easily to the quality that is deemed desirable – perhaps only 5 per cent of lines cloned in any one lab might be regarded as high quality. Many lines, for example, carry contamination or are affected by the medium within which they are grown, or fail to develop properly in the first few days. Even with 'quality' lines, controlled differentiation into different types of cell–tissue is itself extremely difficult and the use of animal models to test this has been regarded as of limited value with regard to eventual human applications, not least as regulatory bodies will be reluctant to approve trials on such a basis. Even were this last aspect successfully resolved, clinical scientists then have to address the problem of the body's immune response to the introduction of cells from (literally) other bodies.

Despite these problems, the field has secured considerable public and some private sector support on the assumption that it will generate biovalue return on their investment. In regard to the private sector, venture capital investors (such as Intercytex, Avlar, Renovo) have put relatively few funds into the area, approximately £ 30 million in 2005 from a total of £ 600 million, worldwide. The majority of patents are held by US firms, such as Incyte. The risk on investment is higher than, say the pharmaceutical industry, for a number of reasons: stem cells is about cure not management of disorders (and therefore generative of limited funds over the long term); it is also unclear whether the costs incurred in developing the technologies will be eligible for reimbursement (as drugs are) nor are there equivalent 'blockbuster' products envisaged. Moreover, even if products, especially therapeutic products which are likely to have a higher return, were developed in the near future, corporations face uncertainty with respect to their intellectual property holdings, for the European Patent Office decided in June 2005 that there would be no new intellectual property (IP) granted until the ethical issues surrounding stem cells were resolved. Public health care markets are also seen to be clinically volatile and fragmented.

Given both the technical and commercial uncertainties sketched out above, it is not surprising that there has been considerable effort expended on establishing stability where possible, especially in regard to regulation, and providing some framework for the translation of basic research into therapies that have clinical (and commercial) utility. Among a number of institutional and organisational developments, three are especially important in the UK context, and each has led to similar forms of 'heterogeneous engineering' elsewhere. These are the UK *Code of Practice for the use of Human Stem Cell Lines* relating to the procurement, development, deposit and access to stem cell lines, developed by the UK Stem Cell Bank Steering Committee (under the auspices of the Medical Research Council) (MRC, 2005); the UK Stem Cell Bank itself established in 2002 charged with responsibility for overseeing the quality of lines and ensuring good practice across the UK stem cell community; and the much more broadly based 'UK Stem Cell Initiative' announced in March 2005 by the government that sketched out its 'ten year vision' for the field (DoH, 2005). Included in the last, are proposals for new types of 'translational research centres', co-funded by the state and the private consortium, the Stem Cells Foundation. The 'development' gap, between science and its application has long been a site for organisational innovation in many fields (such as Faraday Centres, Technology Transfer units, and so on). The stem cell centres are supposed to be developed in such a way that the basic science, the industrial interests, and the clinical application are combined and the 'gap' between these three narrowed.

Again, however, there has been much hype associated with the SC Initiative and pressure placed on bioscientists to deliver the technical goods in a timeframe that has been seen by many to be unrealistic (Dunnett, 2005). Yet such hype and the organisational innovation are both crucial to mobilising the field, indeed to mobilising the future on its behalf (Brown and Kraft, 2006). Expectations about a new field play a key role in recruiting social actors and building networks, and they provide a policy and investment niche that protects emergent fields from wider competitive pressures (van Lente and Rip, 1998). Even so, we should expect that the social matrix of stem cells will remain highly unstable over coming years. Incidents such as the discovery that the lead researcher in South Korea, Hwang, had fraudulently reported breakthrough in creating human stem cells from a cloned embryo (see Chong, 2006) had not only a local but also global impact on the reputation of the field, and led to rapid closing of ranks. Yet, as Gottweis and Triendl (2006) have argued, the Hwang case reflects not only the ambition and corruption of a particular research group but more importantly underdeveloped governance networks – the regulatory institutions that, precisely as they constrain, are also enabling of fields of research, as we noted in the discussion of corporate health in Chapter 3.

Both the e-health and the stem cell cases illustrate some of the common problems experienced by the state, private corporations and scientists in trying to translate the broad policy priorities of government and the ambitions of both industry and career scientists into clinically useful products. During this discussion, I have very briefly touched on the organisational context within which health technologies are to be made to 'work', such as in the case of telehealthcare, the NHS Trusts in the United Kingdom. We need to look in more detail now at the social organisation of health care and how this is changing, and as a result effecting the management of health. In turn, how might new technologies impinge upon this process?

Social organisation of health care delivery

Health care delivery is a complex and highly diverse social process, that varies from country to country, that can be defined in formal and informal terms, and that involves a vast range of professional practitioners (doctors, nurses, technicians etc.) and managers and administrators who are required to respond to national and increasingly international requirements. While there are clear differences between health care systems based on the private market (such as in the United States), socialised care (as in the United Kingdom)more mixed forms, (such as found in Australia and the Netherlands), during recent years we can see each of these systems being shaped by a number of common dynamics. To some degree, therefore, we might expect these differences between health regimes to become less pronounced.

Most important has been the attempt by the government to check the power of the medical profession and control costs. This has been broadly achieved through the introduction of stronger health management and controls on expenditure through audit, rationing or budget-capping, 'payment by results', the introduction of 'internal markets', organisations (such as NICE in the United Kingdom) that determine the 'cost-effectiveness of medical interventions and so on (see Harrison 1996; Harrison and Moran, 2000). Managed health care in the United States, discussed briefly in Chapter 2, encapsulates many of these features.

How far the medical profession has been weakened by such developments is, however, a matter of some debate, illustrated by Salter's (2004) exploration of the 'new politics of medicine'. He suggests that while it may be true to say that state intervention has circumscribed the power of the profession and that much greater political investment has been accorded to patient and public participation in shaping the delivery of care, the profession has itself responded to these challenges and in such a way as to retain control over professional practice. Most importantly, he argues, professional bodies still control the certification and registration of doctors to practice. Elsewhere (Salter, 2002), he also argues that it is in the political interests of the state not to be overly critical of medicine for this would damage public trust, nor to take up regulation itself, which would create new political problems. As he says,

> what no state wants to do is to reduce, rather than restore, the public's faith in the profession by adopting an over-aggressive stance towards doctors, since this would limit medicine's ability to implement official policy. Nor, if it is wise, does a state wish to assume direct responsibility for the governance of medicine since it, rather than the profession, would then become the immediate target for citizen discontent with the standards of health care. The advantage of self-regulation to any government is the distance it places between itself and its citizens. (2002, p. 63)

This argument that political pragmatism plays a decisive role in actual regulation is important, but should not lead us to conclude that there have been no significant changes in the delivery of health care on the ground, especially through challenges to lines of professional demarcation by the emergence of new practitioner roles and sites where care is delivered. Nursing in particular has experienced some significant changes over the past decade with respect to its own professional role and jurisdiction within both care (its traditional role) and treatment. This has been given greater impetus in primary care by the growing role of nurses within GP practices to assist with acute clinical work, and the employment of more junior health care staff to provide general assistance to the practice. As a result, as Charles-Jones et al., (2003) have shown, this more complex division of labour is redefining the role of GPs from that of the generalist who will see all patients to a biomedical specialist, dealing with those who need more expert-based attention. Though changing the pattern of clinical jurisdiction in the doctor's clinic, this retains the professional hierarchy found therein: 'Patients are thus disposed of according to an extended hierarchy of expertise' (p. 88).

Changes in the division of clinical labour accompanied by new technologies (such as computerised decision support tools) have also led to new working practices and posed a challenge to professional hierarchies. I return to this below. The reallocation of certain forms of health care to social services gives further momentum to the reshaping of health delivery. Stacey (2005) for example, reports on the growth of the 'home care industry' in the United States in response to an ageing population with fewer younger relatives inclined to look after chronically ill kin. She points out, however, that the vast majority of those taking up such jobs, such 'dirty work', are likely, even if they find aspects of it rewarding, to be 'unskilled, untrained, and underpaid' (p. 832). In the United Kingdom, it is estimated that home care will grow by 60per cent in the next 30 years and cost in the order of £15 billion per annum (Karlsson et al., 2006).

Two of the most important shifts in the social organisation of health care relate to the move towards patient-centred, or 'patient-led' health care, and, in parallel, a much greater emphasis on exploiting the potential of 'self-care'. Both discourses dominate health policy circles in Europe and beyond.

It might come as a surprise to read that the notion of patient-centred care is relatively recent, since an assumption might be that health care is and has always been centred on meeting patient needs. So what explains this move to identify it as a novel and valuable shift in health delivery? There are a number of factors that have led to the new discourse about patient-centred medicine. First, the state's push towards evidence-based medicine accompanied by extensive guidelines for clinical practice, requires the enrolment of patients to ensure that they fall in line with protocols medics are asked to deliver. Second, it relates to the move to de-hospitalise care and repeat attendance, and relocate delivery in the home setting, or the wider community, where appropriate. This can reduce the costs of care, and, as some evidence from the world of HTA suggests, provide clinical benefit for patients, effectively by de-medicalising some aspects of treatment and placing this in the patient's control (Wolpert and Anderson, 2001) Third, it relates to the emergence of the notion of the 'expert patient' whose experience givens them an understanding of their (especially chronic) illness that should be drawn on in partnership with the medic. Such programmes have been initiated in many countries, including Australia, the United

Kingdom and the United States. Finally, and relatedly, it focuses on increasing patient 'choice': in the United Kingdom for example, from 2006 patients will be offered a choice of up to four hospitals if they need 'planned hospital care'. (This might, of course, indirectly increase the costs of secondary care.)

The move towards patient-centred care would appear to encourage a more equal relationship between medics and patients and empower the latter to take greater control over the meaning and management of illness. Indeed, as noted in Chapter 4, medical sociologists such as Bloor (2001, 2001a) have advocated the introduction of alternative lay expertise into the medical consultation. At the same time it is important to recognise the clinical and economic drivers noted above and not lose sight of the ways in which patient-centred care enables new forms of both compliance over individuals in terms of conforming to a medical agenda and control over resources. In terms of the former, Opie's (1998) New Zealand-based study of doctor–patient consultations showed how medics assumed that their agenda and understanding of how best to handle the problem was one shared by patients. Similarly, Patterson's (2001) Canadian study of consultations involving diabetic patients concludes that '[medics] discounted the experiential knowledge of people who have lived with the disease over time and they did not provide the resources necessary for someone with chronic illness to make informed decisions' (p. 577). In addition, patient-centred care presumes consensus between doctors and patients and an increasing responsibility placed on patients' shoulders to manage their illness. As Lupton (1997) has argued, however, patients' desire and ability to do this will vary according to context and over time, often preferring practitioners rather than they themselves take on the primary responsibility for their care.

This means that the 'centre' of care may well move as circumstances change, and indeed according to the ways in which the anxieties and risks associated with illness are made sense of: this will in turn reflect a biography of 'the self' that is always developing, and never static. A key aspect of this biography is whether social networks can be drawn on to help share the burden of care. In practice, patient-centred care will rely as much on informal carers, family, relatives, friends, in home settings especially for the growing number of older and infirm numbers in society. A recent assessment suggests that in the United Kingdom, 2.3 million people rely on informal care, and this will grow to around 3 million by 2050 (Karlsson, 2006). The burden of responsibility can be very high: for example, it has been estimated that over 1 million carers are providing up to 50 hours unpaid care per week.

Indeed, it has been estimated that the efforts of unpaid carers is, in economic terms, equivalent to the annual NHS budget (Carers UK, 2002). The capacity to care is, of course, unequally distributed, creating new forms of social inequity in the health system. Carers are expected to make a trade-off between caring and sacrificing – meeting their own needs, including their need to work.

In short, the degree to which the move towards patient-centred care will affect the delivery of care is less likely to be felt in practice in the clinic than in the increase loading it places on patients and informal carers. This will vary by the nature of the illness to, with high loads being placed on cares of patients diagnosed with mental illness, such as forms of dementia associated with the ageing process (Henderson, 2005). The compliance of informal carers can be seen in Foucauldian terms as a form of social self-regulation and disciplining of *both* the patient and the carer (Heaton, 1999). While this may be the case, this should not preclude the possibility in practice of carers and patients disagreeing about the sort of care that should prevail, and who between them has the priority to make the 'right choices' in that regard.

Apart from the pattern of care itself, a distinction also needs to be drawn between the needs of someone as a patient and expectations that he or she may have of health delivery as a *citizen*. A recent Healthcare Commission (2005a) national survey of 117,000 people in the United Kingdom found that respondents most valued communication, access to practitioners, and advice and information about medication, especially with regard to its side effects. But these expectations formed part of a more broadly based expectation of care that would be free at the point of use, the cornerstone of the NHS since its formation in 1948. How far the restructuring of health care through marketisation and privatisation will change this is discussed later in the chapter. It is always the case of course that in the attempt to save money government will deploy what legitimatory rhetoric it can. For example, in mid-2005 the UK government sought to reduce the overall costs of the Primary Care Trusts (which account for about 80% of the NHS annual expenditure) through proposals entitled 'Commissioning a *Patient-Led* NHS' (DoH 2005d, emphasis added). The intent is to relocate commissioning from Trusts to GP practices, that are seen as being 'closer' to their patients. But far from being 'patient-led', as the House of Commons Health Committee report on the proposals observed,

The Government has downplayed the financial motivation for its reforms, concentrating instead on its aim of strengthening commissioning. However, cost savings seem to have been the key consideration in the reconfiguration proposals – In fact, it is doubtful whether the reconfiguration will yield the £250 m savings the Government is hoping for if the costs of restructuring including those incurred by redundancies and by establishing new structures to secure local engagement are taken into account. (HoC, 2005)

The scale and range of the related but distinct discourse of *self-care* is currently of major interest in the United Kingdom following the publication of the Wanless Inquiry in 2002 (Wanless, 2002) and subsequent government documents on the matter (DoH, 2004, 2005b, c). The NHS Plan of 2000 (NHS 2000), among a variety of other issues, captured much of the UK government's aspirations for self-care when it observed:

> The frontline in healthcare is the home. Most healthcare starts with people looking after themselves and their families at home. The NHS will become a resource which people routinely use every day to help look after themselves. (p. 4)

A recent review of types of self-care by the Department of Health is summarised in Table 5.1 This describes how such care is seen to cut across prevention, diagnosis, treatment and monitoring by patients themselves. A more compendious account of the notions of the body-as-project, and self-disciplining would be difficult to imagine.

Here one can see a number of ongoing tasks associated with health care and various sources of support that can help achieve them within the twin context of self-treatment and self-management. Different sources of information, networks and 'equipment' are identified that make this possible.

It is tempting to say that to be able to achieve the level of social competence required to complete these tasks the individual will have to be fairly fit in the first place. One of the problems of self-care is that those for whom it might be possible are those that enjoy more advantaged life chances and social capital. The UK's NHSDirect, telephone helpline has been shown to be used more frequently by more prosperous middle-class callers than poorer, especially ethnic minority groups (Hanlon, et al., 2005). It is clear too that the equipment noted here – the personal portals, household aids, monitors and so on – are envisaged as home-based rather than located in clinical settings. Again, households vary dramatically in regard to access to and uptake of such technologies, especially where these are to be secured through the market. It is quite likely,

Table 5.1   Forms of self-care support

Support	Information and knowledge	Training and networking	Facilities and equipment
CARE			
Prevention/ promotion	Interactive online courses, information on health TV	Lifestyle courses Personal trainers	Gyms Personal portals
Diagnosis	Home health care literature	Training in self-diagnosis	Home pregnancy test Blood and urine tests
Action to take	Telephone help line/interactive video on treatment decisions	Decision support; patient peer groups; Internet discussion groups	Personal portals; decision algorithms
Treatment/ medication	First aid manuals; software tools for mental health self-health	First aid courses; self-care courses	First aid kit; OTC medication; home dialysis
Maintenance	Self-management in post-hospital care	Self-care community groups	Mobility and household aids
Monitoring	Self-maintained medical records	Supermarket MOTs	Home or public access; BP monitors

Source: Department of Health, 2003

however, that the broad levels of self-care (at around 70–80%) will continue to be met by people themselves, and unlikely that failure to adopt the recommendations outlined in Figure 5.1 will lead to a drop in self-management. What will be crucial, however, in shaping future experience and access to care, is the degree to which state agencies in the United Kingdom, Europe and beyond *presume* that these tasks can be accomplished across the board, and in light of that, restructure and manage health care *as though it were the case*. For this would institutionalise a new form of inequality lost in the rhetoric of 'self-care'.

One of the ways in which self-care is being promoted is through the use of devices that can be used directly by patients outside of the clinical setting, in the home or elsewhere. There are examples of such technologies in use for many years, such as the pregnancy test kits, blood glucose level monitors that diabetics use, or the remote monitors used by asthma sufferers. More recent developments include bioimplants and 'smart clothes' that using inbuilt sensors can monitor blood pressure, heart rate, breathing and other parameters, and these and other devices that relay information through telecare systems (linked to the Web) to a central database for clinical monitoring. At a more holistic level, 'smart homes' have been devised to enable those who would otherwise have been in sheltered care (such as those suffering mild forms of dementia) to remain in their own residence by providing automated lighting, gas cooker monitors, electronic calendars, medicine reminders and so on.

As I have noted earlier in the book, understanding the context of use is key to any discussion of the utility of such devices. But beyond the issue of utility, these devices act in a number of ways: as substitutes or as prosthetics for loss of physical or mental function; as devices that enable clinical surveillance at a distance; as systems that provide generic epidemiological information for public health purposes. They also provide corporate health with new opportunities for product development. These technologies give further momentum to the twin process of greater capacity for surveillance by 'the centre' allied to, and dependent on the decentralisation and spread of monitoring through free-standing and/or integrated systems. The management of health is more broadly distributed as a result, among a more heterogenous population made up of health and social service professions, patients and informal carers. Just as in the context of ICT systems, so here too the social distribution of care across these groups raises questions about the locus and meaning of clinical governance; where and with whom does it lie, not simply in any jurisdictional sense (for this could in principle be clarified legally) but more importantly in a practical sense. Boundaries of responsibility, the locus of decision-making become both more complex and possibly thereby more clinically difficult to evaluate in terms of outcomes. This was demonstrated in the analysis by Heaton, et al., (2005) of the home-based use of technologies supporting chronically ill children (such as the use ventilators etc.). In contrast to a hospital setting, a more heterogenous group of professionals and kin were involved in managing the child-as-patient within a family setting: health visitors, nurse practitioners, paramedics–ambulance staff–taxi drivers (who might ferry the child to a hospital appointment), parents, siblings, grandparents and so on. The distribution of care was seen to open the child to much greater risk not least in regard to improper use or maintenance of the technology, such that ultimately, parents felt more comfortable if they took on the overall burden of care and oversight of the devices in the home. The effect was, as one might expect, that parents spent long hours caring for the child, including through the night, and found little opportunity for respite lest an accident occurred or mistake was made. Despite the perceived benefits of patient-centred care, the case illustrates how the decentring of technology regimes from hospital to home settings *without* considering the impact on the social management of care can produce adverse effects.

This last point raises the wider question of the relationship between technologies and the management and delivery of health care more generally. Here it is important to consider the impact technologies have on professional practice and hierarchies. Medical technologies have always been central to the diagnosis and treatment of clinical symptoms and clinicians in different disciplinary fields routinely deploy generic or more specialist equipment in managing patient disposals. As we saw in Chapter 4, new technologies continually extend the range of medial provenance and intervention, while at the same time create new uncertainties with respect to diagnosis and the classification of disease. In regard to the social management of health, they can also create uncertainty with respect to the relationships between practitioners as specific skills are 'black-boxed' in technologies, as is, thereby, the performance and meaning of expertise. This in turn can raise doubts over the locus of medical authority over care and the pattern of decision-making with respect to diagnosis, prescription and disposal.

One area that best illustrates this is the widespread introduction of computerised decision-support systems (CDSS) now used routinely in hospitals to manage patients and the interventions they receive. These systems are supposed to improve decision-making by staff, especially in terms of practitioner compliance with guidelines. For example, CDSS systems are used in intensive care to ensure nursing staff keep to time in say delivering drugs to, or monitoring glucose levels of patients. If a blood sample is taken too late or a dose given at the wrong time, the effect on the patient could be serious. CDSS is supposed to reduce the chances of this happening. In fact, the few evaluative studies on the actual clinical value of CDSS in such settings produce mixed or neutral results (see Ansari, et al., 2003; Richards, et al., 2004; Rood et al., 2005).

A recent study by Mason, et al. (reported in Seymour, 2006) of the introduction of CDSS into a maternity clinic to help decision-making with respect to monitoring fetal well-being provides important sociological insight into the impact of such systems. The system was introduced to try to reduce avoidable infant mortality that might be linked to professional misjudgement by midwives or medics. In part, this might result from an incorrect reading of the existing technologies that monitor heart and intrauterine markers. CDSS could, it was proposed, address this by providing much clearer decision-support guidance for the maternity staff. Among a number of findings, one is especially worth noting, namely that the CDSS presumed decision-making was an individual affair rather than, as was the case, a jointly produced outcome. It was 'a complex social process drawing on formal patterns of supervision and hierarchy, informal modes of communication and consultation, tacit knowledge and experience, and taken for granted 'ways of doing things' (2006, p. 134). Rather than improving clinical outcomes, new risks may be created as a result of individualising responsibility, while at the same time, inter-professional cooperation could be undermined. It is often, quite rightly, theorised that contemporary ICT systems dissolve traditional boundaries or borders and thereby create new fears and risks (see Sandywell, 2006); in this case, the new individualised boundaries of care are quite antithetical to the mutual reciprocity that informed the clinic. It is clear that context of use is again key in designing CDSS in such a way that it is made sense of and optimised rather than ignored and compromised.

This study, as well as the more HTA-based reviews mentioned above, provides good grounds for adopting a more cautious and critical approach to CDSS and its widespread adoption into health care. Moreover, some have argued that while it might have little or no significant effect on clinical outcomes, it does improve clinical processes; Mason's study suggests that even this is open to doubt.

Moreover, there is evidence that such systems disturb professional hierarchies. This relates in particular to the way systems depend for their interoperability, functionality and (claimed) efficiency gains on the introduction of common standards that users must adopt. As a result, professional discretion is threatened by the protocols laid down in advance. Doctors and nurses in particular can feel under threat. However, as I noted above, professional hierarchies are quite resilient to changing working practices and where technologies are implicated in this process, evidence indicates that such resilience is put to good effect – at least with respect to serving existing professional interests. Greatbatch et al. (2005) explored the role of standardised 'expert systems' upon which NHS Direct in England has been based. These provide a series of solutions to callers' queries made to the telenurse, who is expected to draw on different pre-defined algorithms in responding to the caller. Through using conversation analysis of over 100 exchanges and follow-up interviews with NHS Direct staff who had used the 'clinical assessment tool' (CAS) the research showed that nurses were able to work around (by 'over-riding or under-riding') the standardised protocols, and by departing from the CAS-based guidance when dealing with callers. Rather than adopting a uniform approach, the nurses may 'reorder, conflate, decline to ask and supplement CAS's algorithmic questions . . . Moreover, they sometimes initiative their own lines of symptom-based questioning independently of CAS . . . or they explore candidate diagnoses offered by patients, which may or may not be consistent with the dispositions and advice that CAS recommends' (p. 826).

The principal point of the study, confirmed by others elsewhere (e.g. Berg, 1997), is that the managerialism that seeks to codify and standardise the indeterminacy of expert systems and knowledge will have limited effect in practice. Even if management were to insist on and police telenurses (or health practitioners in other settings where ICT systems are introduced) it is clear that formalised rules would still be subject to localised interpretive meaning and judgements that will determine their implementation. Just as in the case of CDSS so with CAS, context of use is not simply about the practices that one finds therein but also the knowledge and understanding that informs them. More successful systems will be based on an understanding of both and how they articulate with each other, for the trust and dependability invested in ICTs mirrors the way they enable and confirm the trust invested in the relationships on which their 'workability' will depend.

This matter of trust is one that is central to all health systems, whether mediated by ICTs or not, and it is the main theme to which I now turn in a discussion of the governance of health care and delivery.

Governance of health

Trust in health practitioners has typically centred on the doctor–patient relationship and the display of trust and confidence seen within the sick role (Lupton, 1996). Trust is based on the tacit acceptance and confidence in others' ability to understand problems and how best they might be addressed, and to do so without recourse neither to formalised contractual procedures nor to calculation. Trust informs many types of relationships beyond health, of course: the trust invested in shared risk-taking (such as may be involved in sexual relationships); the trust on which cooperation of a political or occupational nature is based (as in activist groups, dangerous workplaces and so on); the more abstract trust in social systems (as placed in online banking); or the trust embedded in and helping to reproduce social capital found in neighbourhood communities. Trust may be affective (closely tied to emotional or kin ties), knowledge-based (linked to expertise) or institutionally based (such as tied to religion, education, the state etc.), and is often linked to forms of charismatic leadership (O'Neill, 2002).

Much of the writing on trust has been concerned with the trust at the level of the individual in relation to others, the presentation of the self as trustworthy, where trust acts as a form of social capital that can be mobilised and reciprocated by others (see e.g. Luhmann, 1979). Extending this a little further, Garfinkle (1963) argued that the basis of trust lies in shared expectations that can be taken for granted in everyday life. Such routines provide what Giddens (1990) has called ontological security and indeed, for Simmel trust is crucial to society at large, for without it, it would 'disintegrate' since 'very few relationships are based entirely upon what is known with certainty about another person' (1978, pp. 178–179). Trust also can be conceived of as being expressed at a more macro level, characterising normative coherence, a general stability to the social order, transparency in and legitimacy of political institutions and so on, and crucially that these will be sustained into the future. At this institutional level, trust in complex, differentiated social systems depends on the mobilisation of more reflexive, more codified forms of trust that can provide the reassurance and accountability demanded from and accorded to the state and its agencies, and thereby manage as well as take new risks that attend complex systems. This however requires investment in forms of *governance* than simply are found at the level of (inter) personal trust, forms of social accountability and responsibility that are more procedural, codified and subject to scrutiny if need be. Governance in this sense is a highly reflexive set of procedures and expectations that mark out contemporary society, and its subsystems, such as health.

The claim that there is a loss of trust in science associated with a growing distrust in expertise (Giddens, 1994) and expert systems is based on the argument that as expertise becomes more distant and both more abstract and abstracted from people's everyday experience, so people are more challenging of expertise (and monitor and report on it through the Web as exemplified by 'Genewatch'), and when it fails, the effects spread far beyond any local setting. We can see this in the example of Hwang and the South Korean stem cell case, where the fallout from the collapse of his reputation engulfed the global stem cell community and the biotechnology sector. It is clearly the case that expertise is now globally subject to challenge, not least in court through claims of malpractice and negligence.

However, it is equally important to recognise as Irwin and Michael (2003) do that the relationship between expert science and lay publics in regard to trust is a complex affair. They point to 'contradictory patterns of trust' across these groups: on the one hand, the non-expert is chronically dependent on expertise in ensuring safety and the management of risk (such as in maintaining and operating an aircraft); at other times there may be very strong mistrust in and disillusionment with science, as has happened in the collapse of support for the nuclear energy industry; or again, a provisional trust can be rebuilt over time as issues are seen to be effectively addressed by experts. In other words, lay people display an 'integrated ambivalence towards expert systems' (p. 74), and may combine and draw on both reflexive critiques as well as modernist faith in scientific expertise as circumstances change.

Within and in part as a response to this more volatile engagement with science, government has in recent years typically sought to manage expertise and the risk–trust relationship through a series of more formalised measures. In broad terms this has meant moves away from the self-regulatory culture of expertise to forms of institutionalised regulation, often through state agencies. In medicine there are three principal forms of governance that we can see at work today; *jurisdictional, moral, and administrative.* Let me take each in turn.

One of the defining features of a profession is its claim to regulate its members' professional practice through a code of conduct to which all members must subscribe. The British Medical Association has a range of guidelines relating to ethical matters – such as what to do when offered inducements by medical suppliers to prescribe certain products – that GPs are expected to conform to, while the General Medical Council is authorised to register doctors for medical practice in the United Kingdom, and at the same time sets certain standards for medical practice and has legal powers (which stretch back to 1858) to protect patient interests, and will handle patient complaints when required to do so. Doctors can be suspended or removed completely from the GMC register for 'serious professional misconduct' and prevented from practising in the United Kingdom (though not abroad). Similar bodies can be found throughout Europe, the United States, Canada, Australia, indeed all countries with formally recognised professional associations.

While these professional bodies retain and deploy powers of self-regulation of their professional members, their jurisdiction over clinical self-regulation has been subject to increasing challenge through action taken by patients on both an individual and collective basis (Allsop and Saks, 2002). Such has been the force of this that government has had to introduce much more formalised scrutiny of the medical profession. This has led to the shift from a reliance simply on 'self-regulation' to more top-down scrutiny by the state. One of the best examples of this relates to the controversy surrounding the removal of tissue from hundreds of children's dead bodies at the Alder Hey hospital in Liverpool. A senior pathologist, Professor Dick van Velzen, was, in 2005, 'struck off' the register and banned from practising by the GMC for removing organs over a six year period without the parents' or relatives' permission. While the GMC was still central to the resolution of this specific case, the Department of Health came under political pressure from patient groups to tighten up on medics' practices, and the NHS itself was criticised as being negligent by a public inquiry into the case for failing to monitor organ removal. The UK government, driven also by new regulations emerging from the European Union, introduced the UK's Human Tissue Act (2004) which requires all doctors to secure consent before organs are removal: failure to do so could lead to a three year prison sentence. Key to the Act was the meaning of 'tissue' and the circumstances under which it might be removed, and the purposes it might serve. 'Tissue' would include all human organs but also specimens of blood, urine, faeces, sputum and cerebrospinal, joint and other body fluids. This was a considerable tightening up of what medics could and could not do and made all human cells legally of equivalent status. Moreover, the procedure through which medics sought approval for research was also made much more rigorous and transparent through tighter control over ethical and research governance approval made at Trust level (DoH 2004). Such developments relocate and redefine the authority to practise – what I term 'jurisdictional governance' – away from a self-governing profession to a more state-regulated one, what Gray and Harrison (2004) call a shift from a 'communal' to a 'command' form of governance, as medicine becomes increasingly subject to the practices and discourse of managerialism and a risk averse culture. Of course, as Salter (2004) has argued, we should not assume that these developments create a more coherent or necessarily better form of governance of medicine. In regard to the first, he points to the fact that professional bodies have responded to this situation through renewed and greater investment in self-regulation to try to retain as much authority over members' practice, while the government moves are in the opposite direction towards ever-greater bureaucratic control of medical practice and research.

In regard to better governance per se, these developments may have paradoxical effects: as Rothstein et al., (2006) have argued we need to distinguish between 'societal risks' relating to risks to society at large, and institutional risks referring to risks to regulatory organisation. They observe that the 'pressures towards greater coherence, transparency, and accountability of the regulation of societal risks can *create* institutional risks by exposing the inevitable limitations of regulation' (p. 91, emphasis added). In other words, greater regulation both creates risk as well as responds to it and in doing so generates an ever increasing spiral of need for risk management and regulation. Where proper governance sits, where responsibilities lie become more rather than less difficult to determine. Trust, far from being enhanced, becomes defined in terms of procedures associated with audit, scrutiny and performance indicators. The result is that the health service is much less likely to be 'glued together by a bond of trust between staff and patients' (NHS, 2000, para 6.1). Instead, as Dibben and Lean argue, '[a] clear gap is apparent between macro-level policy incentives calling for a trusting and trusted health service and micro-level practical initiatives that could engender it' (2003, p. 255).

While jurisdictional governance relates to the oversight, codification and management of medical practice and research, a linked but discrete notion of *moral* governance works to manage the ethical implications of existing or future medical science and clinical practice. This is very much the realm of bioethics, especially as found in the arena of genomics and the biosciences (stem cells, cloning, genetic testing etc.) more generally. The bioethical specialist has become an important figure in government policy circles, especially in the United States through the so-called ELSI (ethical, legal and social implications of research) programmes attached to most publicly funded science, providing advice on issues relating to moral, legal and 'social' implications of developments in bioscience (including medicine). Bioethical governance focuses on the abstract, philosophical aspects of biotechnology/medicine especially in regard to their impact on questions such as informed consent, risk/benefit balance, rights of and obligations towards research subjects or patients and so on.

As elsewhere, this discursive turn to bioethics has led to an institutionalisation of good bioethical governance through the establishing of a range of intermediary bodies whose role is to advise government on the broad social and ethical implications of new developments in science. There are both international and national bodies that perform this role. Internationally, in the field of bioscience and stem cells research for example, the European Commission (EC) that funds research across Europe through its 'Framework Programmes' requires all those seeking funding for research relating to human Embryonic stem cells to secure not only national but also EC ethics approval. In Australia, the Australian Law Reform Commission, in the United Kingdom, the Human Genetics Commission (HGC), and in the United States, the President's Council on Bioethics serve this role. In the United Kingdom, for example, the HGC has provided advice and made recommendations with respect to a wide range of issues, including genetic testing, pre-implantation genetic diagnostics, genetics and age-related disorders and so on. In the United States, similar issues as well as ongoing concern over high-risk areas such as gene-therapy have been central to the agenda of the Council on Bioethics. Such bodies play an important political role in shaping public debate and legitimising eventual policy decisions taken by government.

However, just as the move towards more bureaucratic modes of governance has been criticised, so social scientists have questioned the role played by this 'moral' governance with respect to managing the implications of new technologies (see e.g. Haimes, 2002; Corrigan, 2003). Typically, bioethics focuses on individual rights rather than how new developments might have a wider, more collective impact or the broader societal directions they may point towards. While ethics committees or review boards can play a role in advising and overseeing research such that risk to individuals is minimised, they are often based on a biomedical model that assumes risk can be measured in terms of the possible harm or injury to a person. New technologies pose risks of a more complex and contextualised nature: for example, the risks relating to the use of computerised decision support tools are not just about managing the accuracy of medical decisions and the responsibility of those making them, but also about the ways in which, as we saw earlier, such tools undermine inter-professional relationships among medical and support staff. This secondary effect can feedback on the quality and so efficacy of the medical treatment or intervention a patient receives. It is also, of course, an effect about which 'informed consent' is not sought! Beyond the level of the individual, questions can be asked about the broad direction that medical research takes, and whether this accords with or follows the grain of public sentiment – has, if you like, *social consent*. Here though we are moving towards the level of political priorities and definitions of the public good, beyond more specific questions of good governance. Challenges to the new genetics as a form of social eugenics exemplify this more political level of debate.

Matters of governance have also taken on what we can regard as a more *administrative* form in recent years. Here the focus is on the management of patients and clinical performance according to predefined standards that both define good practice and ostensibly reduce risks, while defining, often in law, who takes responsibility for such risks. In respect to the management of patients the most notable development has been the arrival of 'care-pathways' through which to handle a patient from first clinical encounter to their disposal as treated, or as in need of ongoing care. Pathways criss-cross the health care systems of many countries like footpaths that guide the patient and attending practitioners across the clinical landscape. Unlike public footpaths, however, where the direction taken is relatively open-ended, care pathways presume a specific route that should be taken to manage a condition most effectively. They originated in the United States in the 1980s and were taken up by the United Kingdom and Western Europe in the 1990s. They encapsulate various forms of efficiency and efficacy: as Pinder et al. (2005) note,

> From almost nowhere, apparently, they appear to have become the tool of choice for ensuring (or so it is claimed) quality of care, equity of treatment, optimal allocation of resources and a rational division of labour between healthcare professionals. Simultaneously, it is claimed that they respond even-handedly to concerns for patient safety, variable healthcare quality and spiralling health costs. (p. 760)

These pathways are supposed to integrate and co-ordinate clinical care from across a range of specialties appropriate to the condition, and in this co-ordinative role are distinct from clinical practice guidelines at the level of the individual practitioner.

There are now in the United Kingdom almost 300 such pathways covering a wide range of disorders, such as cancer, diabetes, heart disease, mental health and so on. Their strength is said to lie in their standardising of (multi-) clinical delivery, but as Piner et al., show in their analysis of care-pathways for cataracts in the field of ophthalmology, there are in practice quite different, competing routes for the treatment of patients that can be mapped. Yet it is precisely conditions such as cataracts – apparently a common and easily managed condition – that pathways and their maps were designed for. However, this precision can be highly misleading and potentially unhelpful:

> The more the maps aimed to furnish a precise, systematic representation of reality, the less true to life they became. Paradoxically it was knowing the detail, not eliminating it, that allowed the practitioner to find his/her way around, and avoid the pitfalls. (Ibid., p. 762)

And typically it was those relationships that are central to managing conditions in practice that often failed to appear on the map:

> What had started out as a one-size-fits-all model of professionally-delivered care turned out to be dependent for its success upon a complex (and unmapped) network of relatives, friends and informal carers in the community. (Piner et al., p. 776)

It may well be impossible to map this diversity without producing something of a confusing therapeutic maze, far from the tidiness of a linear route down which the patient is supposed to travel. Governance of a condition and its treatment in this way affords only a limited form of accountability to the patient, and one that has to accommodate quite different possible routes, all, apparently, subsumed within a single pathway. Pinder et al. point out that the medical practitioners they observed were aware of the limitations of pathways as descriptors of what they did (especially for example in cases of chronic illness where no end-point was achievable). Despite this they have come to play an important, not merely rhetorical, role in the coordination of health resources (both human and technical). Pathways are themselves a form of socio-technology inasmuch as they act as tools (even if somewhat insensitive ones) to orchestrate and shape the social management of clinical delivery.

These three forms of governance that in turn regulate medical risk, ethics and delivery reflect a political context within which the social management of health has become increasingly bureaucratised and standardised. Professional practitioners have been able, for the most part, to accommodate these new demands for greater rationalisation of their work and accountability to regulatory agencies. It is perhaps ironic that these developments have occurred at the same time as public health care systems have become increasingly entangled with private sector, commercial interests, whether to build hospitals, provide infrastructure (such as Connecting for Health) or subcontracted services sought by health Trusts. Paralleled by a growth in the consumer market for medicine and the 'marketisation' of services, the growing privatisation of health raises new concerns over the degree to which formal governance procedures can effectively manage hybridised public/private interests.

Restructuring care: charging, privatisation and self-care

While health may be seen as an individual 'good', valued in our personal lives as something upon which all else – family life, work, sexuality etc. – depend, it is also in more formal terms both a public good and appropriable as a private good. As a public good, health depends on access to collectively provided health care resources (including clinical expertise, hospitals, ambulatory care etc.), public health programmes such as vaccination, and broader environmental provisions relating to food, clothing, sanitation, energy and so on. As a private good, access to health resources is secured through an exchange relationship between suppliers and consumers, and, in theory, extends the market choice for health goods, what Strong (1979, p. 207) called the high level of 'product differentiation' found in fee-based systems. The relative balance between the two depends on the economic support government makes available to public health through national insurance/tax systems, the role of the private sector in enabling personalised medical care, and the political priorities of the state in defining public health as part of a broadly based system of welfare or simply a safety-net that catches most (if not all) of the poorest sectors of a population. The US system is primarily based on the latter, and until recently, the UK's health system was based on the former.

In fact this binary classification needs to be differentiated further; Hall (2001) has suggested a six-way division between state, municipal and corporatised public health, and not-for-profit (such as charities), public–private partnerships and fully commercial organizations making up the private health sector. He also points out that globalising processes add further momentum to the privatisation of health, including the ways in which the World Bank (along with the International Monetary Fund) and even the WHO have favoured privatisation as a core objective that their funding is to support (see also, Waitzkin and Iriart, 2001; Kolko, 1999). Legal directives associated with the General Agreement in Trade and Tariffs favour the establishing of open markets for all goods and services, including health, so much so, that collectivised risk-sharing (as in the UK's NHS) could, in the future, be deemed 'anti-competitive' and so subject to legal sanction.

Indeed, in many countries that have had nationalised health care systems funded principally through taxation (such as the United Kingdom, Sweden or Norway), there has been a growing shift towards defining health as a private good beyond a certain basic threshold of provision, and at the same time increasing resort to charging patients for services which are not directly 'clinical' in themselves, such as ambulances, hospital car parking, or which require co-payment to match the cost the government will meet, as in dental or ophthalmic services. These charges can of course hit those who support or visit long-term chronically ill patients, or those who need to access services away from their home (see House of Commons, 2006). In addition, organisational changes through the restructuring of delivery provide opportunities to redefine the public/private boundary, as has been true of the move towards 'Foundation Trusts' (now 48) in the United Kingdom which, though within the NHS, do not fall under the direct control of the Minister for Health. Such Trusts, managed by elected governors from staff, patients and the local community, can raise capital, sell assets and bank surpluses for local use year-on-year. This putative 'liberalisation' of health delivery adds more weight to the growing private market in health. Finally, there has been growing political interest in a mix of public/private insurance provision through so-called 'social insurance' schemes (already in place in Germany and France).

These changes are typically presented as providing better use of resource in what will always be a limited state budget (and hence one that has to be rationed), and opening up opportunities for paying 'customers' to access more expensive forms of health care if they wish so. Critics of these moves argue that the likely outcome is an increasingly inequitable distribution of and so access to health care unless the state is prepared to take direct action to prevent this (see e.g. Harrison and Moran, 2000). Such inequities characterise the US system (Buchanan, 1995).

At the same time, care must be taken not to assume that large multinational firms are moving in to take over public health provision, or integrating their activities across a number of markets (such as pharmaceuticals and insurance) to control provision more extensively. In fact, direct ownership over clinical services, notably hospitals, has not been a major source of profit for the major European firms involved in this area, such as Vivendi or Parkway Holdings; instead more investment is being made either in new-build hospitals through public-private finance initiatives, ancillary services such as catering, or in diagnostic and therapeutic technologies sold into and maintained for primary and secondary levels of care. Some firms have also seen new opportunities to develop diagnostic monitoring and therapeutic products for the home as patients with chronic illness are relocated from a fully medicalised clinical setting to a domestic environment. Whatever the specific form of investment, it is clear that in the United Kingdom, the government has adopted the view that public *ownership* of health resources (such as hospitals) is no longer important simply public *funding* to ensure universal access to health care (provided by public and private agencies) is what matters. Paralleling this is a move away from the NHS as the sole provider of clinical services, and instead it acting as the primary commissioner of services, sourced from public *and* private sectors.

While the impetus behind such changes is driven by a belief in the greater efficiency of the private sector to meet 'customers' (i.e. patients) needs, there is however, evidence from the United States to suggest that commercial health care may not be of a higher quality than that provided by the public sector (see e.g. Duckett, 2001). Moreover, how government would manage failing private hospitals without simply continuing to bail them out raises not simply economic but also wider political issues in respect to accountability and social equity. The move in the United Kingdom towards Foundation Trusts suggest no immediate or noticeable improvement relative to other Trusts in the quality of care either (see Healthcare Commission, 2005b).

These changes also raise questions about the location of and responsibility for the governance of health delivery. Not surprisingly, perhaps, in the United Kingdom the move towards liberalisation of the health market and the basis on which health is delivered has required a closer examination of formal governance requirements than might otherwise have been the case. Indeed, though this may be temporary till they 'mature', Foundation Trusts have been on a somewhat tighter rein compared with conventional Trusts: unlike the latter, for example, Trusts cannot charge private patients beyond what their fees were before they assumed their new status, whereas ordinary Trusts have no such 'cap'. This bears out Rothstein's (2006) argument noted above, that innovation in social institutions creates new risks that need to be regulated through audit and close scrutiny, paradoxically those designed with liberalisation in mind.

Where public and private sectors are more closely linked in hybrid relations such as the PFI or social insurance schemes, the three forms of governance noted above are made more complex, for they need to manage not only the clinical oversight of professional practice but also the contractual requirements that can be placed on commercial organisations. The conventional hierarchical management structures that underpin these forms of governance in single organisational setting such as a hospital trust are confounded by two competing or at least discrete regimes of control that are supposed to be managed through a 'partnership' rather than sole source of authority.

It is highly unlikely that the mixed economy of the UK's NHS will lead to its full privatisation. Even the Foundation Trusts will be heavily dependent on ongoing public finances to operate, and experience elsewhere, notably in New Zealand, of this more 'corporate' form of public health management (Barnett et al., 2001) has not presaged the wholesale commercialisation of health delivery. Firms much prefer the cocoon that state underwriting provides.

But beyond the issue of charging for and the relation between public and private sectors in the provision of services, a third dynamic – the promotion of patient 'self-care' on the back of the rhetoric of patient-centred and patient – chosen medicine – is opening up health systems to the discourse not only of 'choice' but also 'consumption'. Technologies are playing an important part in this re-orientation, as was suggested in my earlier discussion of ICTs. Patients and their carers can already choose to buy into alarm and monitoring systems, or diagnostic kits of differing degrees of sophistication. The use of health vouchers which people can decide to cash in different ways will encourage this still further. The social management of health here is perhaps no different to that long-associated with over-the-counter drugs, which are primarily biochemical technologies.

There are however a number of risks associated with self-care: increasing social inequality or exclusion as those who cannot afford to purchase high-quality services suffer; the increasing likelihood of clinical risk as inappropriate choices are made; and the possibility that as a result of the latter, increased demand for remedial treatment is placed on the state services. The inauguration of telehealth information services, such as NHSDirect/Online in England, are devised in part to mitigate this by providing self-carers with informed advice acting to triage demand in cost-effective ways. But there is a more important question that needs to be raised as a result of this fostering of private choice and the individualisation of health, one that runs to the core of the social management of health: to what extent do the policies driving these changes compromise the epidemiological and broader social calculus underpinning the concept of a *public* health? Does the move away from an emphasis on a modernist version of the welfare state towards a more post modern, heterogenous health care system matter in respect to the broad quality of health in a country? Clearly, such a question could only be asked within the context of a developed, relatively affluent context, and would be the height of insult in poorer societies struggling to find water never mind choosing which pill to buy over the counter. But, given that poverty and inequality in advanced states is as extensive (at least in relative terms) as ever (see Chapter 4), the capacity to choose health is not equally distributed. As Bauman (1998, p. 86) has argued, 'All of us are doomed to the life of choices, but not all of us have the means to be choosers.' This is precisely what health as a public good seeks to ameliorate and as such requires quite specific administrative, political and professional structures if it is to be delivered effectively. Of course, there is a more informal sense to 'public health' that we find in the informal networks of social support that people mobilise when they are ill or need advice. This informal social management of health is probably more important in terms of enabling the state-based system to function than is realised.

Conclusion

In this chapter I have examined some of the key features that characterise the health care system in advanced states with respect to its management and regulation. I have sought to do so through reference to the ways both are shaped by and in turn affect the advent of new medical technologies, such as telemedicine and stem cell technologies used in regenerative medicine. The introduction of new technologies into social contexts requires forms of socio-technical 'engineering' that is often thwarted by both unintended effects, and by local institutional structures whose boundaries are more or less permeable to socio-technical innovation.

The wider move towards a more managed health care system is fed by and feeds back on the introduction of new technologies, while the changes in the clinical division of labour and the discourse of 'patient-centred care' and major responsibility taken by informal carers have marked a growing heterogeneity in the meaning, site and provision of health information, support, diagnosis and treatment. This in turn has led to a redefinition and to some degree a compromising of the meaning of clinical governance and trust, sometimes aggravated by the deployment of e-health technologies that distribute responsibilities and risks across different practitioners. At the same time, the evidence discussed here also points to the ongoing resilience of professional structures to accommodate and withstand the disruptive affect of new technologies. Yet even this resilience is under ever greater pressure from new forms of regulation and governance that the state has introduced partly in response to the risks generated by new technologies and partly as a way of requiring greater accountability from practitioners in both their medical research and practice.

The relationships between health innovation, practice and governance is also complicated by the advent of marketisation of health services and a hybrid public/private health care system. Again, technologies must be seen as being in part enabling of this shift and in part the very site where commercial investment will be made as health care becomes more a consumption item, one that is, as noted, not equally available to all.

The social management of health can in one sense be seen to be about the social management of the 'sick role', for as Parsons noted, illness has to be managed if it is to be both accommodated and, ultimately, successfully resolved. But just as we have seen how the more formalised (state) management of health care is undergoing significant changes, in part dependent on new technology, so the meaning and management of the sick role is itself undergoing significant change. This forms the focus of the next chapter.

The Contested
Sick Role

6

Introduction

In Chapter 4, I discussed the long-established debate on 'the sick role' and 'illness behaviour' from the initial contributions of Parsons and beyond. This work has been central to much of medical sociology but has not only tended to neglect the role of technologies as was noted, it has, understandably, also tended to be confined to conventional doctor–patient relations and narratives found therein. These narratives are about how to interpret ill-health itself, though we saw too that the discourse of 'patient-centred' medicine and the formalisation of expert-patient programmes moved the focus of an illness narrative from one that is based on a specific individual to one that is more abstract and collectively defined. Such wider discursive moves are encouraged by health care agencies that are keen to enrol 'the patient's voice' as part of the policy-making process. In the United Kingdom, the National Institute for Clinical Excellence (NICE) has an extensive range of policy mechanisms that it deploys to achieve this end.

In this chapter, in contrast, I want to move away from the way the sick role is *performed and defined* within a conventional medical arena to explore the ways in which the sick role can be *mobilised* by individuals or groups *outside* of or located on the boundaries of the orbit of medicine and health care agencies. Here, the sick role is a contested site where claims are made in respect to what a particular condition means for those who experience it. Patient groups are typical of the social actors found here, but others might include more informal support networks, or activist groups challenging the conventional framing of a pathological condition. In this chapter I focus on four senses in which the sick role is contested: as a collectively defined and shared identity used to leverage additional health care resources; as a site through which an illness seeks to be acknowledged *as such* by medicine itself; as a site for debate over the very meaning of an illness itself; and as a site for the denial of a medicalised version of an illness. Many of these contested sites are mediated by and dependent upon certain technologies – notably the Internet – that can be used to define the meaning and boundaries of the sick role itself. These are sites that are not found in the conventional medical textbook, indeed are more, as Nettleton et al. (2003) note, an 'e-scape' from medicine – in both its digital and liberational senses. An 'escape' from medicine has its most obvious expression in the turn towards alternative or complementary medicine that has marked western societies over the past 20 years or so. In the closing part of the chapter, I discuss some of the sociological literature on this and what lessons we can draw in respect to the role of alternative health technologies today. Let me first turn to a consideration of patient groups and their importance in shaping the meaning of the sick role.

The sick role as a collectively defined activity

Patient groups have mushroomed over recent years, the majority being formed in the *United Kingdom*, for example, after 1980 (Wood, 2000). They have often been associated with rare diseases, and sometimes a group's membership may comprise virtually all those who have the disorder: for example, of the 1000 or so patients diagnosed with progressive supranuclear palsy (PSP) in the United Kingdom 776 are members of the PSP Association.

While some groups may be quite small, a large minority (almost one third) have funds in excess of £2 million (Wood, 2000) similar in scale to interest groups elsewhere, such as trade unions and business associations. Some, such as the Genetics Interest Group, act as umbrella organisations for many (perhaps over a hundred) smaller charities, others are single-disease focused, large organisations that have extensive research capability in their own right and much larger funds to draw on, such as Cancer Research UK which deploys over £200 million per annum. to support clinical research and practice. As Rangnekar and Duckenfield, (2002) have shown, these larger bodies (which include other major national charities such as those for diabetes, Alzheimers, Parkinsons, cystic fibrosis and muscular dystrophy) engage in a range of activities that include funding biomedical research, engaging with the clinical trial process, participation in regulatory debates, running campaigns and supporting social services. Similar evidence is found on groups in other countries – HIV/AIDS in the United States (Epstein, 1996), breast cancer in the United States and the United Kingdom (Anglin, 1997; Klawiter, 1999; Parthasarathy, 2005) and muscular dystrophy in France (Callon and Rabeharisoa, 2003; 2004). These groups have been successful in lobbying for legislative change, additional resources for treatment (including insurance provisions) and revisions to informed consent procedures.

In his classic study of HIV/AIDS groups in the United States, Epstein (1996, p. 9) argued that as patients 'begin to organise and exchange information, the breadth and durability of their lay expertise is enhanced'. The mobilisation of this lay expertise in framing the meaning and experience of an illness is often most apparent where patients consider existing medical research to be failing them, failing to address the 'unmet needs' of patient members (Gross et al., 1999). Callon and Rabeharisoa (2003) contrast the conventional or tamed research of clinical science with 'research in the wild' undertaken directly by those suffering from a condition neglected by conventional science. While sometimes this failing is attributed to the ways in which medicine is heavily dependent on the priorities of 'corporate health' (see Chapter 3), we should note that is often the case that charities depend on major contributions from drugs companies to continue their work. Indeed, such companies regard this support as of great value to their own research and commercial interests, for it not only provides access to patients, but also valuable public relations.

Patient groups regard their knowledge as expertise-through-shared-experience, but link this experiential epistemology to a collective moral position. That is, patient groups are driven by an obligation to secure accessible and assessable (O'Neill, 2002) information for their members which is not only effective but also committed to members' rights and interests as builders of a shared consent about clinical priorities and practice, as carriers of a duty of care and obligation to patient members, and as agencies within which trust can be invested.

In both the Callon and Rabeharisoa's (2003, 2004) study and that of Epstein (1996) one sees how the patient groups were not only key to the definition of the 'problem' and its treatment, but gradually built links with medics who in turn came to share the patients' problems. Callon and Rabeharisoa studied the role of the AFM (Association Francais contre les Myopathies) in France in shaping the medical agenda on muscular dystrophy. The group mobilised what resources they could to understand the disease and how it could be managed, doing so in ways that contrasted markedly with the conventional clinical approach. For example, parents used family photos of their children as visual markers and a basis for comparison of the severity of the disease:

Photos play a special role in this comparative evaluation because they act as tools for visualization, which make it possible to compare children's abilities to act. The patients and their parents are never without their photo albums, which they exchange and comment on at every opportunity. (2003, p. 197)

In building up their understanding of the disease, they gradually recruited specialists to their cause who in turn found their professional role change as a result:

Symmetrically, specialists who engage in this collaboration are forced to consider the disease 'from the bench to the patient's bed,' ... This manifests itself in new professional identities and careers: some specialists circulate back and forth between clinics and laboratories. (2003, p. 199)

Epstein's work on those with HIV tells a similar story, notably in regard to those who were sick drawing on their experience to explain the illness itself. They had to come out of the sick role, to contest it, in order to refine and so re-enter it on terms that they saw as acceptable (see Davis et al., 2002). They did so only by becoming researchers in their own right:

To engage fully with the project of biomedical research, treatment activists needed to undergo a metamorphosis, to become a species of expert that could speak credibly in the language of the researcher. This is the agenda that treatment activists pursued over ... several years. (Epstein, 1996, p. 417)

While this has often resulted in a more holistic and less reductionist approach to the clinical management of patients, this is difficult to sustain as new medical technologies or new drugs arrive to re-establish the predominance of a strictly medical approach to the condition. In the case of HIV, as Flowers (2006) has shown, the arrival of a new cocktail of drugs (HAART – Highly Active Anti-Retroviral Treatment) has led to the re-medicalisation of HIV management such that 'the experiential expertise of people with HIV has *less* importance in treatment, which emphasises viral management and medical models of living with HIV.' To the extent this occurs, the sick role no longer becomes a site of contest but rather one of compliance (monitoring viral loading in the blood, taking the pills as required, and reporting any adverse effects to the doctor).

In short, while patient groups may challenge and seek to redefine the meaning of sickness and so the sick role, not least through their own efforts outside of medicine, they find it difficult to withstand the full medicalisation of their condition. At the same time, there is a danger here that patient expertise as experience is overly romanticised as in some sense providing a 'real' understanding of their condition. As the medical sociologist, Prior (2003) has argued, 'experience on its own is rarely sufficient to understand the technical complexities of disease causation, its consequences or its management. This is partly because experiential knowledge is invariably limited, and idiosyncratic . . . lay people can be wrong' (p. 53).

In contrast to those able to mobilise a collective vernacular to describe their illness and translate this into medical support for treatment, there are those who despite experiencing chronic sickness find that they cannot secure a diagnosis and thereby remain marginalised by medical practitioners. Here, people are actively seeking some form of medicalisation of their condition, such that their sickness can be explained and treated.

Seeking the sick role

Medical expertise is based on the assumption that a pathological cause can be identified that explains a set of symptoms such that a diagnosis can be made and the condition treated. If a person has a set of symptoms for which no cause can be found, this means that a sick role is not, in a sociological sense, 'available' to be performed. New medical technologies are developed to screen, test and diagnose for various conditions, and reinforce the notion within medicine that illness must have a core pathological cause. People presenting with symptoms that remain unexplained, despite this technological sophistication, create problems for the successful negotiation of doctor–patient relations, and indeed may in some contexts find that their concerns are dismissed as being 'all in the mind.' Some sociological work has, for example, reported on the ways in which this has been the experience of those suffering from chronic fatigue syndrome (CFS) (Horton-Salway, 2001). Indeed, some evidence suggests that individuals may be allocated explanations (offered in effect specific diagnoses–sick roles) until their symptoms are eventually 'properly' explained. Cowie (2007) cites one of his CFS respondents as saying:

> I first went when I was nineteen, been back ever since in between being diagnosed with rheumatoid arthritis because of the pains, spondylitis because of the neck stiffness, everything to that effect, depression again. It got to where I had to have a nervous breakdown more or less before I finally got a diagnosis, so basically it's taken me over twenty years to get a proper diagnosis.

Similar accounts have been made with respect to other contested sick roles in regard, for example, to syndromes such as repetitive strain injury (Arksey, 1998) or chronic back pain (Rhodes et al., 1999; Ong and Hooper, 2006), which as Nettleton et al. (2004) describe as having 'medically unexplained symptoms'. They suggest too that such accounts resonate with what Frank (1995) describes as 'chaos narratives' of illness, wherein a person's illness narrative is both 'difficult to listen to . . . and difficult to hear', because they remind the person 'of their own vulnerability . . . and the practitioners of their limitations' (p. 50). Not only do patients live in a 'diagnostic limbo' but as a result must try to cope with their disorder through their own devices and will seek information through the Internet, complementary medicine and healing, and seek out others with similar symptoms for mutual support and advice. Even in those cases where GPs and specialists do endeavour to treat an unexplained condition, patients may find themselves having to make sense of a confusing series of diagnoses. Ong and Hooper's study of those suffering back provides good evidence for this when they report: 'while the GP is the main referrer to other clinicians, there is limited continued communication between the various professionals, apart from occasional letters reporting outcomes of treatment. Thus, no multi-professional and co-ordinated approach appears to occur around the management of back pain . . . .The patient emerges, by default, as the 'manager' of a series of dyadic relationships and thus the patient gives meaning to any variation between the different clinicians that are consulted' (p. 219). At least in such circumstances there is a semblance of an emergent sick role, but where no sick role is available, just as Parsons (1951) would have envisaged, people find that they have to struggle on without professional support:

> it's just the frustration of trying to prove it to the outside world . . . I think it's the permission to be ill, because I don't want to be ill, but

I obviously am, and just want permission to get on with that . . . I've got to pretend to be alright. (Nettleton et al., 2004, p. 57)

Ironically, 'pretending to be alright' requires a degree of psychological resilience, when it is quite the opposite that is often seen as the 'real' cause of the problem by medics and other people; hence the frequency with which doctors will prescribe antidepressants for what they see as primarily a psychological problem. Such a label may induce more stress and its own — genuinely psychological – side effects, and perhaps become self-confirming. The difficulties that patients experience in coping with unexplained symptoms reflects the important social and personal function played by the notion of the sick role; where it is not available or contested, individuals remain on the margins of medicine and what they regard as appropriate medical care. The greater medical investment in more precise diagnostic tools, the more unexplained illness becomes increasingly anomalous and subject to question, for how could such tools fail to isolate the cause of the problem? All of which of course depends on how the problem is to be defined, which take us to the third type of contested sick role wherein the deployment of new experimental tools provides an opportunity for patients to re-interpret what their illness means.

Redefining the sick role

As was noted above, technological advances in diagnostics or therapeutics (as in the case of HAART) can play a key role in how an illness or disease is to be defined and managed: in the case of HIV patients the availability of HAART has been met with an ambivalent response inasmuch as while it extends life it demands a high price in terms of compliance, monitoring and coping with side-effects. Technological development can be so dramatic that it might redefine the very meaning of the illness and what sort of role is available to a patient.

An excellent illustration of this is Cohn and Bichard's (2005) study of highly sophisticated but also highly experimental and so unstable, brain imaging technology being used in innovative neuroscience research on mental disorders such as schizophrenia. The imaging system generates pictures of the structure of the brain and can be used to image in real time specific functional areas of the brain that are linked to these disorders. The patients who took part in experimental trials on the imaging system regarded the images as providing an explanation for their schizophrenia that located the disorder entirely in structural terms, as a defect in brain functionality, rather than as had been the case, a psychological disorder 'in the mind'. If a particular definitive feature in the topography of the brain could be identified as being linked to schizophrenia, patients felt this would redefine the whole meaning of the illness for them, even if at this point in time, their treatment would remain the same as before. As such, their sick role as psychiatric patients could be redefined, for they felt that they were in some sense not responsible for the problems they had to contend with, since these are derived from a defective architecture in part of the brain. For many this relieved the burden and to some extent stigma of the illness among family and friends.

However, this response was not uniformly shared by all the patients nor by the psychiatrists that Cohn and Bichard interviewed. Those who were members of patient support groups were much more suspicious of the imaging technology, for they saw it as a threat to the ways in which psychiatric disorders should be understood as being socio-cultural, interactional matters not reducible to biological (dys)functionality. As such, these patients (and their doctors) were highly critical of and did not participate in brain imaging experiments. Cohn and Bichard explain these contrasting perspectives in terms of the high level of investment in the collective identity derived from being a member of the patient support group whose *raison d'etre* depended on the sharing of experience that in itself was part of the performance of their sick role. Professional psychiatrists also saw their definition of the mental disorder being redefined in structural terms.

Here, then, the advent of new technological developments can disturb long-standing definitions of an illness and so how medics and patients negotiate proper role performance. The sick role itself is open to multiple, contested interpretations, and here does so precisely through the ways in which the conventional distinction between body and mind (the body–mind dualism) breaks down as schizophrenia is framed on the one hand as a physical and on the other as a mental disorder.

This redefining of what a chronic condition means and so how it is performed as an embodied role – as 'a process rather than a pre-given biological fact' (Berg and Akrich, 2004, p. 3) – has also been explored in detail in Watson and Woods' (2005) analysis of the contest over the meaning of physical disability and the ways in which the disabled movement has sought to redefine the meaning of 'being disabled'. The condition of being physically impaired is inscribed in the very technology – the wheelchair – that represents a failure of medicine to find a cure. As they observe, 'the technology [of the wheelchair is] synonymous with loss, tragedy, passivity and dependency. Wheelchairs are often viewed with trepidation: as machines that disable, confine, and remove from their occupant a state of independence' (p. 161–2). Not surprisingly, as Shakespeare (2005) has noted, 'disabled people are [seen as] eternal children in need of surveillance' (p. 143), though unlike children who have some prospect for growth and development, the disabled experience a closing off of opportunity, a lowering of social status and stigmatisation producing a 'spoiled identity' (Goffman, 1963).

Countering this, the disabled movement has sought to break the link between having a physical disability and being simply defined *as* disabled, while at the same time, attributing their problem of mobility to the environment rather than to their own inabilities; the environment actively disables by failing to accommodate the needs of the physically impaired. In addition, over the past thirty years wheelchair users have customised chairs, and through the development of powered chairs overcome the dependency of being pushed and the subordination and marginalisation this often meant. The capturing of wheelchair design by users meant the chair could be adapted for a wide range of uses including sports (such as athletics and basketball) and much lighter, mobile designs that enhanced the independence of the users. The powerful political activism of the disability movement ensured that the state had to respond positively to the demands for a more enabling and less discriminating environment.

The shifts described above can be seen as driven by a critique of the conventional medical perspective on the disabled which has tended to define them principally in terms of their impairment alone. The challenge to the disability movement has been to balance the demand that society recognises and responds to the needs of the disabled with the desire to distance themselves from the notion of 'the disabled person', which homogenises and reduces a diverse range of individuals to a marginal and deviant status.

Challenging the medical definition of an illness or chronic condition while demanding the condition be properly acknowledged requires ongoing political engagement with the medical professions and the state. In other contexts, we can find groups who also reject the ways in which they are labelled by medicine but who do not then seek re-incorporation on their own terms, but rather establish a completely separate social world within which the condition can be managed through their own efforts and mutual support. It is to this fourth arena of the contested sick role that I now turn, through a discussion of anorexia.

Denying the sick role

A recent study by Fox et al. (2005) examined the growth of the 'pro-ana' movement, a Web-based extensive network of those with anorectic symptoms that acts as a form of resistant expertise, challenging the orthodox medical definition of anorexia as a pathological condition that needs remedying through hospitalisation and dietary control to 'normalise' food intake. Medical models of anorexia explain it in a variety of ways, principally through biological (an organic deficiency) or psychological explanations (typically explained as a denial of adult sexuality by the desire to retain a 'childlike' figure). More cultural and feminist accounts focus on the pathological effect of a gendered discourse favouring the slim-line body shape that dominates in Western culture (Bordo, 1993; Orbach, 1993).

In contrast, the pro-ana movement (which can be sourced through the website 'Anagrrl') rejects all of these models and sees anorexia as a positive (embodied) statement that affirms a distinctive and outsider identity in modern society that can be successfully managed and sustained. As Fox et al. 2005 observe:

> The pro-ana movement challenges and rejects medical, social and feminist models that regard anorexia as a condition to be 'cured'. In a disturbed life, the 'anti-recovery' stance of the pro-ana movement offers its participants a safe and positive place to share experience and gain further insight into their condition, away from the judgement, gaze and scrutiny of parents, boyfriends, husbands and the medical profession.

The Anagrrl website provides its members (mostly female between the age of 17–20) with information (and 'thinspiration') about anorexia and is said to act as a sort of 'sanctuary' or refuge, and, at first sight rather paradoxically, provides members 'with recipes to promote healthy anorectic eating, and advice on nutritional supplements to sustain well-being' (Fox et al., 2005, p. 953) as well as what pharmaceutical drugs could help to maintain a low body weight. Such drugs (e.g. Xenadrine) are conventionally used to treat obesity and deliver weight loss but only available in the UK by prescription: the pro-ana members bought them online through the Web. The members regard themselves as having a condition but one they deny as a sick role for medical intervention. Instead, the condition itself, while causing considerable pain and anxiety also provides a route to a degree of personal control. As one of Fox's respondents comments:

> I think of my ed [eating disorder] as a sanctuary from the pain that I've lived through. I have control over myself when I restrict, and I have control over my body when I purge and that is what has got me through the hard times in my life, the times when there was no control or stability in sight. (p. 958)

The pro-ana movement provides guidance on how this level of control can be most effectively achieved and managed, that is, 'a space to manage and live with the disease in the safest way, as opposed to eradicating it and forcing the participants into recovery' (p. 956). This echoes the findings of Rich (2006) whose own study of anorectics speaks of the ways in which 'young women were propelled towards contexts and relationships wherein they could construct alternative, more positive self-representations of their anorexic identities.' (p. 302). The pro-ana site provides a virtual safe-haven until those who shelter there decide they want to move towards a more conventional body-weight and so 'recover' and regain the status of being 'normal'.

Apart from its actual role in managing anorexia, Fox et al. 2005, p. 963 emphasise the dependency of the pro-ana movement on the Web as a vehicle through which this 'resistant expertise' can be reproduced, despite many attempts to censor websites for what is seen by regulatory agencies as anti-social or dysfunctional behaviour. This contrasts with the more common sociological exploration of the Internet as a source of medical information that informs without necessarily undermining doctor–lay relationships (Hardey, 1999); here, the pro-ana group actively reject the medicalisation of their disorder and seek to manage it on their own terms. This contrasts too with the collective agency of a patient advocacy group discussed above, for there the typical pattern is one in which lay and medical understandings eventually converge even if subsequently the latter might take precedence as research and therapies develop.

Fox et al. 2005, do not explore how long participation in the pro-ana movement and the denial of the sick role be sustained, for while the redefinition of anorexia as a more positive identity statement is clearly a powerful resource that group members can draw upon, it is clearly the case that they will be under considerable pressure from parents, family and medics to 'normalise' their food intake. This pressure reflects not simply concerns over health but also matters of social status and the need to reintegrate into mainstream society. Anorexia is seen as a condition in which the anorectic is unwilling to take up or neglects social responsibilities; Scott (2006) has suggested the way in which 'shyness' is regarded in similar terms (and indeed has become pathologised and medicalised as a result).

Rich's (2006) study does examine the ways in which anorectics 'reconnect' to the mainstream, and indeed does so through conveying a greater sense of the ambivalence among young girls over their anorectic identity than do Fox et al. 2005. In part this reflected the dual sense of closeness and distance the young women felt towards fellow anorectics, such that while they might be supportive of one another they might, in some contexts, become quite resentful:

> And when this other girl at the school became anorexic, I felt that I had been pushed out of my place and I was furious . . . and how dare she, that was mine, that's who I had been, and who was I going to be now that she was there and now that she was obviously thinner than me? (p. 300)

In this situation, doubts begin to set in over one's status in the anorexic group and the move towards 'reconnection' thereby becomes more likely. Such a move would mean accepting anorexia as an illness and not both as that and as a source of subjective identity as in the pro-ana movement. Thereby, the young woman would re-engage with the sick role and become compliant with the medical regime deployed to treat it, moving fully into the orbit of medicine.

This completes the overview of four ways in which the sick role can be contested between individual patients, professionals and collective groups. The substantive examples were very different (muscular dystrophy/HIV; schizophrenia/disability; CFS; and anorexia), but they have a number of features in common. First, they are all forms of chronic disorder that thereby provide the time, space and motivation for patient engagement with professionals that in each case poses a challenge to orthodox medicine. Second, they open up rather than stabilise the meaning of an illness and so define the sick role as yet to be agreed, yet to be closed down; this leads to ambivalent framing of a condition as at once highly personal and yet also very publicly political in the sense of a commonly shared objective that is not per se about 'getting better' but about carving out a space for recognition (CFS), resource (HIV), or a particular social status (disability/anorexia). Third, because they are on the margins of medical science and practice, on the boundaries of conventional medicine, each of the example illustrates how those with a condition develop localised forms of knowledge and lay understanding that can be mobilised not only in an immediate everyday sense, but also migrate into formal professional practice and become part of the language and practice of medicine, as we saw with the 'research in the wild' undertaken by MS and HIV sufferers.

Technologies are mobilised as part of the opening up of the sick role, in these examples, pharmaceutical drugs, the Internet, wheelchairs, research programmes, and imaging systems. Most are used in ways that their originators had not intended – the drugs were designed as a therapy for obesity, not to enable anorexics to lose weight, the imaging system was developed by neuroscientists to understand brain function not to redefine the meaning of schizophrenia, and so on. Not surprisingly, this has led to moves by orthodox health care and regulatory agencies to control access to technology – as in the attempt to regulate drugs over the Internet and indeed censor websites promoting anorexia. This has had uneven results and indeed often fosters an even stronger movement away from orthodoxy. The turn to complementary and alternative medicine is often pointed to as indicative of the failings of conventional health technologies and therapies (Sharma, 1992) to meet patient needs. It is estimated that in the United Kingdom some 25 per cent million people seek alternative practitioners each year (Andrews, 2003) and in the United States a figure approaching 63 per cent (Astin, 1998; Barnes et al., 2004). Indeed in the United States it is estimated that more alternative than orthodox practitioners are consulted each year (Eisenberg et al., 1998). What characterises alternative medicine and in what sense does it redefine the conventional sick role?

Alternative health and medicine

The growth in the number using complementary or alternative medicine (CAM) has been explained as the result of a number of factors found in society today. First, with respect to medicine itself, many perceive it fails to provide solutions for the growing chronicity of illnesses, and indeed this is accompanied by an increasing anxiety over the side-effects that conventional drug-based medicine generates. Second, there has been a cultural turn towards more holistic belief systems that encourage the re-unification of the mind and body as a singular 'project' rather than the tendency in medicine to seek only biological causes for illness. Third, people regard CAM practitioners as more prepared to listen to patients' experience and help them to manage illness more effectively (Sharma, 1993) as Foote-Ardah (2003) found in her study of US AIDS sufferers. Finally, and in part related to the latter, there has been a move towards a 'therapy culture' (Furedi, 2003) which seeks therapeutic help (through counselling for example) for the body and 'soul', therapies and lifestyles that are less about dealing with symptoms through medical intervention and more about securing a sense of general 'well-being' and coping with the risks and fears of everyday life (Sointu, 2005). Furedi is in fact highly critical of the growth of the counselling industry that produces ever growing numbers of 'victims' that need support to survive, a development he believes reflects the collapse of the more collective culture of the political left that provided a wider anchorage and sense of direction for individuals. The individualisation and commodification of health adds greater momentum to the search for yet more alternatives, possible paths to an individualised (not collective) well-being.

Perhaps not surprisingly, many practitioners are consulted about stress-related disorders, anxiety and problems associated with lifestyle, such as digestive, allergic or dietary disorders. Others consult in their search for solutions to chronic pain– typically neck and back pain – that are merely masked by orthodox drugs such as anti-inflammatories, pain killers or steroids that treat symptoms rather than causes. Others use herbalism and massage as preventative, self-healing techniques that need not depend on alternative practitioners' assistance. Many patients with cancer or other serious illnesses such as HIV look to CAM as an alternative to aggressive chemotherapy or as a way to ameliorate its affects (Foote-Ardah, 2006). The resort to CAM is not then a 'last resort' but best understood as 'help/health seeking behaviour' (Sharma, 1993, p. 139). As such it is also the case that many do not regard it as a replacement for orthodoxy, but as a complement to it.

The presumption is, nevertheless, often made that CAM is marginal to orthodox medicine: clearly in terms of numbers consulting it is not, but it is, within western clinical contexts, marginal to and indeed often in conflict with professional 'allopathic' medicine and often proscribed by the state. The response of orthodox medicine to CAM has been either to reject it (e.g. crystal therapy), incorporate it (osteopathy), marginalise it (homeopathy) or adapt it. In regard to the latter, for example, acupuncture has been taken up by many orthodox medics themselves, but not necessarily in such a way as to presume acceptance of traditional Chinese medicine's model of 'meridian' lines through which energy or 'Chi' flows. Instead, many medics redefine acupuncture as 'transcutaneous nerve stimulation' (TNS), a needling of nerves through the skin to relieve pain symptoms. Often, where there is some clinical integration of CAM with conventional medicine, such as in a hospital setting, practitioners are unlikely to be professionally integrated into clinical teams, and, as Mizrachi et al. (2005) show in their study of Israeli hospitals, CAM practitioners are often 'spatially marginalised', located 'at the end of the corridor . . . [or] in an outside building' (p. 37) with no proper provision for storing their equipment. As such, 'the spatial marginalisation of the alternative medicine team provides a visible expression to their symbolic status as aliens' (p. 37).

Partly in response, in an attempt to enhance its reputation and retain some control over its medical philosophy and practice, Saks (2003) argues that CAM has itself sought to become increasingly profession-alised in Western health care systems. An indication of this in the United Kingdom is the establishing of the Research Council on Complementary Medicine, which is part-funded by the Department of Health, while a recent UK House of Lords (2000) Select Committee recommended that a number of therapies, notably chiropractic, acupuncture and osteopathy should be subject to clinical trials to determine their full effi-cacy. Such a move to de-marginalise CAM, however, clearly comes at a price – namely, how far it can meet the criteria set by evidence-based medicine, discussed earlier in Chapter 5. Many alternative medical sys-tems distance themselves from the reductionist, causative models of dis-ease found in the West, so would be likely to claim that failure to meet EBM criteria could be expected from the outset and would not in itself cast doubt on the validity and utility of CAM. Indeed, whereas EBM presumes a fairly stable object – the patient with a specific set of symp-toms – CAM often declares that the patient is a different person every day and so one has to adjust therapy and measures of its success accord-ingly. The emphasis in CAM is on the interaction between patient and practitioner – especially for example in homeopathy – and this too will change over time and in different contexts. This clearly creates problems for CAM if it seeks to enhance its status through signing up to ran-domised controlled trials (see Welsh et al., 2004).

Of course some of the less complex CAM approaches can them-selves be quite reductionist and lack the holistic aspirations of other modalities; this would be true, for example, of chiropractic. This points to the need to recognise the diversity lying within CAM and that when CAM and orthodoxy meet we should expect quite a diverse set of results. One way of exploring this engagement is through the patients themselves and how they experience CAM and allopathy, especially with regard to the sick role. As patients/clients move from one to another, does the performance of the sick role change? Is it true that what *counts* as 'the sick role' in CAM is clearly quite differ-ent from that found in orthodoxy with the latter's emphasis on patient compliance or – in its more consensual guise – 'concordance' (see Armstrong, 2005) while the former is much more on patient-centred and holistic care?

Chatwin and Tovey (2006) have explored the use of CAM in cancer care in both the UK and Pakistan in order to compare the relationship between alternative techniques and conventional ones and patients' experience of both. What they found does not support a simple dichotomy between a holistic CAM versus. a reductionist orthodox experience. In fact in Pakistan, CAM is part of a more heterogeneous and more market-based system of medical demand and provision: as they put it,

> [I]n Pakistan the divide between CAM and orthodox medicine is far more blurred, and has different dynamics. The choices people make over which one to use are very much more pragmatic – often relating to issues of cost (CAM usually being a cheaper option), and which treatments are perceived to be effective for a given complaint, rather than to issues of holism or patient participation in the treatment process. (p. 228)

Within the United Kingdom, the authors found that there were two main types of CAM user groups in the cancer area, those that were in existence before CAM was deployed and those groups whose networks were developed in response to the therapeutic promise CAM offered. The first are typically found within NHS hospitals or hospices, where CAM is routinely deployed alongside conventional medicine, and done so under the supervision of an orthodox practitioner. No special status is allocated to the CAM approach:

> Therapies are not incorporated as part of a wider holistic agenda, and in this way the utilisation of CAM proceeds very much in terms of the orthodox organisational framework (and by extension, the orthodox medical perspective). While individual therapies and therapists may well benefit from the exposure that involvement brings (particularly in terms of the legitimacy conferred by mainstream sanction), the kind of rich CAM / life-world narrative that can be observed when exploration of therapies proceeds in *ad hoc* and holistic environments is largely absent. (p. 229)

The second type of CAM group do exhibit more holistic and 'alternative' approaches to health delivery and can only do so because they are institutionally and organisationally on the margins of the NHS system. When they seek a close alignment with orthodoxy, their distinctiveness is lost as they become merely another form of intervention, as is CAM's status in the first group above. The Chatwin and Tovey study points to the importance of exploring the relationship between the promise of CAM, patient aspirations towards it, and the organisational setting in which it can be practised. It is not evident then that there is what we might call an unambiguously 'CAM-ful experience' grounded in holistic care and delivery, founded on an alternative sick role that is fully holistic and as much spiritual as it is physical. It seems that though millions of people throughout the world experience the alternative to what is principally Western-derived medicine, they are more likely to do so as part of a health-seeking strategy that is complex but never simply determined by what an individual patient/seeker does: it is hedged about by markets and organisational and professional constraints that shape the actual form and content of CAM practice.

In terms of medical technologies, this state of affairs tends to foster a conceptual and technical hybridisation of allopathic and CAM techniques and tools, such as is illustrated by the development of TNS noted above. Or one finds CAM clinics deploying traditional techniques but in rooms that also sport pieces of equipment more commonly found in orthodox settings; this is done in part to render the clinic more conventionally 'medical' to the newly arriving client. In fact, in light of the argument above with respect to the pro-ana movement, it could well be argued that those, like the anorectics, who use orthodox medicine and digital technologies in what are perceived to be deviant ways are perhaps at least as or more 'alternative' in their determination of illness and its management as CAM groups.

Conclusion

In this chapter I have examined a number of different sites where the conventional notions of the sick role are disturbed, challenged, made different and to a greater or lesser extent captured and used by patients, individuals or groups. In its most developed form this is institutionalised as an entirely distinct, 'alternative' medical universe known as CAM. The orthodox definition and management of the sick role is contested and contestable, often in very public fora. In all cases, dispute centres around the meaning of evidence about health–ill-health and who defines this and on what basis. In almost all cases too, the sort of evidence that is drawn on are the indexical, contingent experiences of those who suffer from a specific condition. Patient advocacy groups mobilise and codify personal experience which is seen to be marginalised or ignored by biomedical knowledge; members of the pro-ana movement protect an anorexic identity precisely through framing their experience in positive rather than negative terms; those with unexplained symptoms fight to get their experience of illness recognised as not simply 'in the mind'; imaging is interpreted in novel ways to secure alternative accounts for mental disorders that are not shared by orthodox psychiatry; CAM users and practitioners adopt a mixture of empiricism and practical epistemology that renders the meaning and treatment of illness highly plastic and contingent on a 'reading' of not just the body but 'the person' as a 'whole'.

The discussion of the contested sick role reveals again the sense in which health and medicine have to be seen as embedded within a biopolitics in which the evidential is entangled with the normative, science with cultural beliefs and choices. Much of the recent work on biopolitics (see e.g. Rose, 2006) has focused attention on developments in contemporary biosciences, such as those relating to genomics, stem cells, and xenotransplantation, emphasising the ways in which these developments redefine 'life itself' where the body as a site to be mined, broken up, exchanged as body parts and tissue to be accorded given biovalue, where the body becomes 'other' to ourselves. The biopolitics of the contested sick roles discussed above reflects a rather different set of processes where there is a strong move towards integrating the body/person/mind in ways that are rooted in experience. This is why such areas are less likely to attract 'corporate health' for the commodification process depends crucially on the capturing and codifying of specific values attributed to health, medicine and the body as a 'speculative' site (Waldby and Mitchell, 2006, p.179) that can be standardised and exchanged on a global basis. There is, of course, an asymmetricality to the biopolitics underwriting contested health and that informing biomedicine, and in all of the cases discussed above, we see pressures to incorporation and eventual closure around a biomedical definition of 'the problem', sometimes reluctantly (as in CAM), sometimes willingly (as in CFS).

Information technologies are especially important in enabling the contestability of sick roles for they enable networks to be built, knowledge to be shared and are difficult to police by the more powerful. We saw how the Internet is a crucial vehicle through which voices on the margins of medicine can be heard and mobilised. CAM techniques and devices are, in contrast to the digital world of ICTs, 'traditional', indeed it is their very link with the past that enables users to anchor a modality in a deeper, more spiritual form of understanding and practice. The Internet and the acupuncture needle facilitate different forms of marginal health using new and old technologies.

The various cases described here also point to more fundamental processes through which social systems define what are to be considered as the proper boundaries of health, illness and therapy, and the ways in which these are to be evaluated. The social management of health and its regulation, as we saw in the previous chapter, produces insiders and outsiders. Moreover, as new governance procedures are introduced, those challenging conventional medicine will find that they have to contend with regulatory structures and procedures that are associated with the wider bureaucratisation of medicine. The 'politics of life' are not then simply about priorities and choices but how these are embedded in and reinforced by governance frameworks that are supposed to enhance accountability and thereby trust. The powerful social reciprocity that underpins many of the contested sites is a form of social trust that is outside of the conventional lay/expert relations found in medicine. The social production and reproduction of health and medical systems are becoming increasingly heterogeneous and opened up to a mix of competing interests and voices, producers and consumers, at a local and global level. The relationship between health, technology and society is then itself open to much greater contest than perhaps ever before. The implications that this has, and in particular the role technology plays in this, provides the focus of the following, concluding chapter.

Conclusion: Novel Technologies, New Social Relations?

7

Introduction

This book has offered an exploration of the relationship between health, technology and society. Throughout I have been especially interested in asking how innovation in biomedical technoscience – such as that found in tissue engineering – opens up the possibility for new social relationships without thereby assuming that these will be uniform or uncontested within and between different societies. I have suggested in the different chapters that contemporary innovations disturb our understanding and experience of the body, medicine, health and illness. This in part reflects much wider social changes that characterise late modern societies in the sense that, as Bauman (2000) has argued, some of the traditional anchorage points upon which we depend are strained or worked loose – perhaps the expertise and trust upon which doctor–patient relationships are founded, for example.

In this chapter, I provide first, a brief summary of the broad arguments of each of the chapters, suggesting how these together lead us to ask whether the shifts they report have created a more complex and heterogeneous social world of health that is thereby both more powerful yet also more precarious, and certainly one that need not always lead to better health care itself. I then go on to explore the meaning of novelty in regard to health innovation and discuss how new technologies can be *both* a source of continuity and of discontinuity, that is, a means through which existing social relationships surrounding health care are both reproduced and yet changed. I conclude by looking forward towards the issues that sociology should consider exploring in the future in its critique of the intersection of health, technology and society.

A synopsis of the argument

Much of sociology had, until the arrival of science and technology studies (STS) from the 1970s onwards, failed to understand technology as a thoroughly social phenomenon. Where it had been a focus of sociological inquiry, this was typically one that was either overly deterministic (as in some versions of Marxist critiques of the role of technology in capitalism) or reductionist (as in some of the earlier attacks made on medicine and medical technology by feminist scholars). The earliest sociological work that treated science as a proper area for inquiry in itself tended to privilege the epistemological status of science as a certified form of knowledge, in contrast to say the vagaries of simple faith of religious belief. Merton (1979), the strongest exponent of this view, argued that there is a functional relationship between the norms of science as a social activity (based on social rules that police the scientific community) and as a technical activity (that was focused on the need for replicable results and their empirical verification). In contrast, current work in STS understands science as a social practice given meaning in different social worlds (Clarke and Leigh Star, 2006), while technology through which science is typically applied has only utility and works precisely because it is accorded value and utility in specific social settings or contexts (Grint and Woolgar, 1997). As such, neither science nor technologies 'speak for themselves' but must be framed, mobilised, given voice and indeed certified, but through complex networks of social relationships. Things could always have been otherwise, and what counts as a replicated experiment is often open to dispute across scientific networks (Collins, 1974). To this extent, STS has been strongly, though not solely, linked to a commitment towards a constructivist position – science and technology as socially constructed. But this has been criticised for its relativism and failure to recognise the material power of science (Hacking, 1999). The position I have adopted in this book – and shared elsewhere by others (Beck, 2000; Wynne, 2002) – is that of a constructivist realism, which recognises that science, here biomedical science, has a capacity to understand, work on and modify the materiality of nature while arguing that what this means and how it is used is negotiated, contested and *always* unfinished. Nature, the body and disease are understood by technoscience with much greater degrees of sophistication, yet thereby with much greater degrees of provisionality, as, for example, the results of the human genome project attest.

If we adopt this position, we are more able to explore the diversity within biomedicine today and its sites of contest as well as closure. It encourages us to look for the ways in which different disciplines and their paradigms or models define and 'know' the body or disease in distinctive ways that are not always commensurable, and why they do so; to see how the contingencies of medical practice and the 'doing' of diagnosis (May, 2005) are lost in the codified and artificial world of evidence-based medicine; to look for gaps in biomedical science and what it means to apply it in clinical settings; to expect different perspectives on evidence and practice across different professional groups such as doctors and nurses (Seymour 2000) and so on.

It is this approach that underpins the broad arguments outlined in the opening chapter (and beyond). There I suggested that we should see medical technologies and the assumptions on which they depend as being part of a wider universe of meaning within which a range of other technologies and social practices can be found. To this extent, the technologies that we are exposed to in a clinical setting, such as an X-ray or endoscope, make sense precisely because they realise – make real – models of the normal and abnormal body found in medicine, confirmed by *other* technologies such as biochemical markers, surgical techniques (such as biopsies) and so on. At the same time, and in part perhaps because of this web of technical instrumentation, compounds, testing devices, monitoring and surveillance systems, it was argued that medical technologies are double-edged: they enable us to penetrate the material layers and functioning of the body and disease, but as they do so they open up new questions that take medicine into more uncharted waters. As a result, the paradox of higher levels of knowledge coupled with higher levels of uncertainty and risk becomes more and more common for medical specialisms. In turn, the social relationships which make the management of illness, whether acute or chronic, socially viable become sites of contest and challenge as patients and carers ask why and how new technologies can both relieve their conditions but create new ones – new side effects. As Beck (1992) notes, 'Because of its success, medicine also discharges people into illness, which it is able to diagnose with its high technology' (p. 205).

This in part reflects the fact that the definitions of health or disease are not simply defined in terms of the symptoms experienced by the person who must deal with them, but also through the play of powerful professional, commercial and institutional interests that must codify and commodify health and illness in order to define, control, exploit or deliver 'it'. Even so, as health becomes a site not simply for biomedical but also lifestyle choices, the market for medicine grows ever wider as the demand for access to health products and services increases. This in turn opens up and makes more starkly apparent the long-standing question of who pays for health, the consumer or the state. Rationing of health care presumes management of health needs and how these are to be met. But the national health care systems on which rationing depends, such as that of the United Kingdom and Australia, are redrawing the boundaries, the thresholds at which private expenditure takes over from public provision. These changes have very real effects on the structuring of health care delivery, effects that new technologies, notably e-health, may influence in both positive and negative ways, shaping the patterns of inequality in morbidity and mortality.

In Chapter 2, I explored what I called the 'social matrix' of medical innovation. This term was used to describe the diverse socio-technical assemblages that make medical technologies successful. The argument was couched in the language of STS for this enabled me to show how innovation is co-constructed across diverse actors and networks. I argued that the spread and take-up of new medical technologies or ideas depends on their being successfully mobilised across such networks, using a number of examples, such as stem cell research to illustrate this. At the same time, those seeking to foster new developments have to attend to the evaluative rigours of the holy trinity of HTA, EBM and QoL measures, and it was this that led to my discussion in Chapter 3 of the broader role of the state's regulatory apparatus in regard to the public health care system (and especially the professions), and that of the private sector in enabling yet constraining the interests of corporate health. The growth of more clinical audit, more managerialist control, and an opening up of the medical market to greater commercialisation may mean that, as Friedson (2001) argued in his last of many texts on the medical profession, the latter could come to play an increasingly important role in maintaining 'public good' medicine. This was a considerable shift from his long-standing critique of the power of the profession, captured in his 1970 examination of 'professional dominance', where he had declared, 'Indeed I now believe expertise is more and more in danger of being used as a mask for power and privilege rather than, as it claims, as a mode of advancing the public interest' (p. 337).

However, beyond the play of state, profession and corporation, I argued (through a discussion of the controversy surrounding stem cell research) that we need to attend to the political cultures of different countries – such as those of the United Kingdom in contrast to Germany – to see how they influence medicine by opening up or closing down research and innovation paths through the regulatory positions they adopt. These differences are not simply about whether, say, a stem cell is mere tissue or a (developing) human being with rights, but more generally about what Rose (2006) calls the politics of 'life itself'. That is to say, such debates reflect the ways in which contemporary societies regard the relationship between bodies, selves, our conduct, and how these are defined and regulated. Biology and the science (especially molecular biology) that informs it are highly charged politically, and require and receive considerable attention within the political machinery of the state.

So too does corporate health, which I considered in some detail in the second half of this chapter. I looked at the ways in which private sector interests have shaped the sort of innovation we have seen in the fields of genetics, informatics and tissue engineering. Despite the constraining influence of the state, we saw how corporate health is very much part of the contemporary global economy and, as the 'medical-industrial complex', has played a key role in the emergence of biotechnology and thereby biovalue, one of the key drivers of contemporary capital investment, growth and profit. As such I argued that corporate health and the state together play key roles in setting health agendas, developing new markets and determining the delivery of care.

In Chapter 4, I explored more recent work related to the sociology of the body that has shown how the body is simultaneously both a physical and social object. This has ramifications for the ways in which illness and health are experienced and for the narratives of medicine that are associated with specific conditions. There is no direct or uniform relationship between having a particular disorder such as cancer or diabetes and the ways in which these are experienced (hence my epistemological position of constructivist realism), a point often overlooked in broad demographic data on patterns of morbidity. At the same time, I also stressed how important it is to investigate the social structuring of illness as a result of differences in access to social resources and material well-being. We noted that the chances of becoming ill are unequally distributed in society as a result of non-random, socially structured processes that are typically reproduced across social divisions (such as class and ethnicity) from one generation to the next. The extent to which the current discourse on patient-centred care individualises and so neglects these chronic patterns of ill health should alert us to the ways in which sociological data on health inequalities needs to be continually brought to the attention of the 'modernising' policy makers within the state.

In Chapter 5, I discussed some of the principal characteristics of the ways in which health care is managed and regulated, primarily in advanced industrial societies. I noted the convergence across many countries towards more 'managed' health care that also sees the advent of hybrid public–private provider/supplier arrangements, which have helped foster increasing investment in medical, paramedical and infrastructural technologies (such as the English 'Connecting for Health' system, despite this seeming to also foster technical, clinical and financial problems for all concerned).

In Chapter 6, I offered a synoptic analysis of the different ways in which we can see the 'sick role' being redefined, opened up, challenged and made thereby much more heterogeneous in its form and effect than Parsons (1951) original version described. Insofar as this reflects a weakening or at least redefinition of the doctor–patient relationship, it points to some degree of empowerment of the patient either at the individual or collective level. Such a strengthening of the patient voice is also a hallmark – at least in a rhetorical sense – of the turn towards complementary medicine, which is much more extensive than is often realised. It marks too, perhaps, a mix of pre- and post-modern moves towards experimenting with our bodies' health, in as much as it reflects a preparedness to embrace 'traditional' medicine while doing so in quite reflexive and ambivalent ways, recognising its limitations compared with orthodoxy (e.g. in dealing with acute medical problems). Traditional medicine is not however insulated from contemporary ('modern') technologies and may indeed depend on them to sustain its vitality, as is true of the use of the Internet for example, which has had a major impact on the spread of CAM in Western societies. What indeed is of interest sociologically is how old and new technologies are to be understood, an issue that was introduced in brief in the opening chapter, and to which I return shortly here.

First, however, it is worth reiterating what I have suggested to be three significant changes in the body/medicine/technology nexus: these are what I have called the *socialisation of medical innovation*, the *socialisation of clinical diagnosis* and the *socialisation of clinical implementation*. In general, all three point to a deepening and broadening of the range and diversity of social actors and organisations that create, reproduce, modify and redefine what is understood to be the universe of health and illness. A socialising process is in this sense one that points to much greater heterogeneity in the cultural, economic and political dynamics that we have to attend to when thinking about health. Innovative health technologies play a role in enabling this much greater heterogeneity not least in terms of opening up the temporal and spatial boundaries of this universe. Sociologically, then, we need to look at a more rapidly changing and expanding locus of activities and discourses associated with health and illness, and their management. But this does not thereby displace the conventional forms and location of professionalised health care, but rather creates a more diverse demographic meaning we need to give to the notion of 'health practitioner' – the member of the 'pro-ana' movement is not thereby marginalised but treated sociologically symmetrically with medics who, from within their therapeutic position, see anorexia as a condition that needs to be treated and overcome. In short, as I noted much earlier in this book, the three forms of socialisation help to explain changes to the spatial, experiential and epistemic boundaries of conventional medicine and the clinic.

Novelty: so what's new?

There is a temptation to regard novelty as primarily an event or process marked by scientific or technological breakthrough (Brown and Michael, 2003). The hype associated with developments in science – be these in genetics (Petersen, 2001), biotechnology (Martin and Nightingale, 2004), telemedicine (May et al., 2003) or elsewhere – typically depends on claims to have found some 'technical fix' or solution to a long-standing problem. That a major step might have been taken – such as therapeutic cloning of embryos to enable the reproduction of stem cell lines, or the development of broadband communications systems to enable the relaying of high definition images from remote communities to clinical centres – reflects the power of expert knowledge systems to shape material reality. But the utility, value and workability of these developments have to be delivered too, and this is not inscribed in the technologies themselves.

Clearly we have two debates to address here: what do we mean by new health technologies, and if we can answer that, is there something specific about the sort of novelty characterising technological developments today? Novelty might be considered in terms of a gradual change over time – what, for example, the so-called next generation of computers might be seen as being – or a disruptive break in existing technology, such as the move from an analogical to a digital signal in telecommunications, or the arrival of 'wifi' systems. Clearly, these apparent breaks do not arrive unexpectedly but depend on the coming together of convergent ideas, techniques and materials that have existed for some time. But even these notable shifts may actually work to reproduce existing social relationships or ways of engaging with the world around us – our TV moves from an analogue to a digital signal, but this does not trigger radically different patterns of viewing of our favourite programmes. What these arguments point towards is the proposition that novelty is perhaps better seen as having a greater social quality of 'newness' when it opens up the possibility – though never determinant of this – of new social relationships. Over time, biomedicine as a science, a set of techniques and practices, has made significant progress in coping with disease, through vaccination, for example. Many of these developments however have a ring of developmental continuity to them, a building on previous ideas and understanding that have improved (public health) without thereby posing radical changes in the way in which we regard our bodies, our health, our selves and our relationships to others. They may enable us to extend existing relations in time and space – vaccination means more people can be more mobile and travel more safely in countries known to host dangerous viruses (a boon to the backpacker). But as such they tend to deepen existing relations rather than disrupt them.

Historians of medicine have indeed shown how shifts in medical understanding have helped to see or 'know' the body and its disorders in different ways. In part, this has depended on the development of more penetrative techniques – from the stethoscope, through the X-ray, to the CAT scan and DNA diagnostic test – that open up and offer new ways of seeing into the body and its pathologies. There has, therefore, always been a strong relationship between models of the body, the technologies used to open it up and the clinical therapies developed to treat patients. As a result, the body itself has become more available or accessible to clinical intervention and through imaging, sampling and testing made more 'mobile' as an object for scrutiny by many. These processes can be traced back through to the earliest days of allopathic medicine and, through increasing sophistication and complexity of technoscience, have continually redrawn or redefined the boundaries of what are to be seen as the 'normal' and the 'abnormal'. In turn, new diagnoses are possible though these can make the closure of diagnosis – and thereby patient 'disposals' – more difficult to achieve quickly and 'cleanly'.

What I want to argue then is that these features above characterise the ongoing innovation within biomedicine; in themselves they may offer new ways of doing routine things, or providing new sorts of information and knowledge that can be deployed to treat the untreatable. This would lead us to suggest that what we mean by a new technology is one which both builds on existing bioscience but does so in ways that enable not merely more precise and (perhaps) effective biomedical interventions, but also creates the conditions within which new socio-technical relationships might emerge. This marks out new technologies today that serve to reproduce continuities from the past while at the same time acting as a source of discontinuity in the possibilities they create within and most importantly *beyond* medicine itself.

This approach means that we avoid attributing novelty and its meaning to some *intrinsic* properties of a technology. Novelty is primarily, as STS would argue, a social rather than technical attribute. As Andrew Barry (2001) has put it,

> inventiveness should not be equated with the development of novel artefacts, or indeed with novelty and innovation in general. Rather, inventiveness can be viewed as an index of the degree to which an object or practice is associated with opening up possibilities . . . . What is inventive is not the novelty of artefacts and devices in themselves, but the novelty of the arrangements with other objects and activities within which artefacts and instruments are situated, and might be situated in the future. (pp. 211–12)

Barry is drawing attention here to the inter-relatedness that defines novelty, one based on both technical objects and 'activities', as well as on context – their 'situatedness'. Context is key if we are to understand what makes socio-technologies perform as new, and/or as reproductive of existing relations, as creative of new possibilities (as well as uncertainties) beyond the formal medical context.

We can illustrate this through considering the characteristics of technologies closely associated with reproduction. Table 7.1 describes both the continuities and discontinuities that characterise socio-technologies such as pre-implantation genetic diagnostics, ultrasound, IVF, screening, and other techniques and devices that are used to manage or enable pregnancy and childbirth. As can be seen, the left-hand column identifies some of the principal ways in which these techniques work to continue what has been characteristic of clinical intervention in the reproductive field (of gynaecology, obstetrics, paediatrics, fertility clinics) for many years. These techniques are used to assist or restore reproductive capacity, and reinforce the pre-eminence and power of the biomedical model and medical professionals. They serve to push back the moment or time when a child is seen as coming into being, right back to the first embryonic cells if parents so wish, and ultimately ensure that children are (albeit through a highly medicalised process) born as 'naturally' as possible.

In contrast, they also open up new possibilities, Barry's 'novel arrangements', that are discontinuous with the practices and priorities that mark out the conventional domain of reproduction. These are

Table 7.1 Continuities and discontinuities in reproductive biomedicine

Continuities	Discontinuities
Assistive/restorative reproduction of children; confirms link between social/bio (role of DNA paternity tests; IVF)	Increasing diversity of reproductive relations ***Breaks the social/biological link***
Consolidation of biomedical model	Locus of control and role of NRTs changes ***Biosciences as driver***
Temporal horizon of the 'pre-born' pushed back (ultra sound, PiGD etc.)	Temporal horizons of reproductive entities multiply ***Breaks link between tissue and identity***
Reproduced bodies/babies	Reproduced tissues (clones/stem cells) ***The creation of biovalue***

summarised in the right-hand column. There we see how the new technologies have led to developments that are not directly to do with the reproduction of children but much more about opening up the site of reproduction to new actors and interests, whether this be in terms of where technologies break the social and biological ties of parent and child, where the clinic becomes a source of tissue for bioscience, where that tissue (as embryonic stem cells) becomes the property of public and private research and so accrues economic 'biovalue' that has absolutely nothing to do with the identity or human value of its source.

Patients, carers, clinicians and regulators confront both of these continuities and discontinuities though not necessarily at the *same* time. As Roberts and Franklin (2005) have shown in their examination of PiGD, the frozen embryo which is selected for pre-implantation in the IVF clinic evokes a sense of reproductive continuity when it is seen as the first step towards paternity, and in spatial and temporal terms encompassed, embraced, by the rhythm and narrative of 'having a child'. Yet, the same prospective parents and clinicians frame a second embryo very differently when donated for embryo research, outside of the reproductive domain. This second embryo occupies a very different spatial and temporal universe that is populated by different social actors and so creative of new arrangements not least through its performing a role in conjunction with, in Barry's phrase, 'other objects and activities', such as research labs, biocapital and the 'tissue economy'.

So, we should look for novelty in this nested sense, a combination of innovation in medicine and a wider innovation in social relations linked to, but perhaps discrete from, medical practice in the strictest sense. This stretching of the novel across different domains stretches too our sense of risk and uncertainty as we move across the two with a mixture of hope and trepidation. These patterns can be found in all fields of biomedical technology, not simply reproduction. Similar tensions are evident at the other end of the life course, in palliative care, which I discussed in brief in Chapter 4. The continuities and discontinuities are co-present but have to be realised – made real – through the social relationships through which they are given expression and made material.

I now want to conclude this final chapter by asking what might be the sociological implications that arise from this understanding of novelty and my earlier discussion of the health, technology and society relation. I want to do so not simply in conceptual terms but also in a more practical way by raising some issues that need to be addressed in health policy.

Sociological prognoses

What then might inform future analysis of health, technology and society? The key aspects of a sociological critique which I outlined in Chapter 1 will be as crucial as ever: how are health technologies introduced, and what drives this process?; what clinical and social value do they have?; how are they made sense of by patients, carers and kin?; how does new technology help open up the domain of health and medicine to non-clinical markets?; what is the relationship between regulatory, economic and political interests especially in determining the growth of a global biocapital?; how do new technologies affect the existing unequal distribution of health care resources across a population?; and how far does new technology have a beneficial impact on public health and how can this be measured? Many of these issues have been explored over the years by those working in the field of medical sociology, providing valuable insight into the factors shaping health and its meaning and delivery. However, future sociological critique should bring such work together with the conceptual tools found within STS, precisely because of the need to interrogate the socio-technical as a singular object of study, rather than speaking of 'social' and 'technical' as though they were separate. It was these tools that helped us identify the co-presence of continuity and discontinuity in contemporary medical innovation.

Theorising the socio-technical relation within health will also need to depend on ongoing work on the body as a site where innovation is most directly experienced and given meaning. The body occupies multiple sites – physical, experiential, virtual, fragmented – and as such is itself to be understood as having a heterogeneous identity and boundaries. Future work will need to focus in particular on the ways in which the clinical gaze encompasses some but not all of these instantiations, how an individual describes her or his sense of embodiment, and how new technologies foster new forms of identity yet disturb others. The extensive research conducted on patient narratives of health, illness and the body should also endeavour to attend more closely to the socio-technologies that are deployed in the management of chronic conditions. Most importantly, we need to understand how the management of such conditions enhances or harms a person's sense of security and confidence in their health care and their personal life. We need to do this by social class, gender, ethnicity and age, for the sense of 'choice' associated with how people manage their health (and body) will differ considerably across these social groups. Indeed, simply being able to speak of and articulate 'choice' as an expression of the reflexive individual is unlikely to be equally available to members of such groups: here narratives and inequalities of power converge in very distinctive ways.

This touches on the meaning and status of knowledge – whose accounts and versions of health and illness are to be accorded more 'truth' than others? – and opens up a key issue for future work, of how knowledge and expertise are being strengthened or challenged by the three forms of socialisation of health I have described in this book The heterogeneity of social actors framing health means that its social disciplining through the clinical gaze and the professional knowledge upon which this depends are weakened and contestable (as we saw in Chapter 6).

There are broader theoretical traditions that will play their part in exploring these issues, especially those that attend to the increasing 'fluidity' or 'liquidity' in social relations (notably Bauman, 1990, 2000), stressing the ambiguities and contingencies of this hybrid modern/postmodern world. Beck's work on risk (1992, 1999) helps make sense of the 'side effects' of medical innovation and the attempts to manage through ever greater audit and calculative techniques – such as health technology assessment and evidence-based medicine. More recent work in STS which has focused on the 'complexities' of the body/health/technology relationship (notably Law and Mol, 2002) provides an important methodological approach that asks us to open up the simplifications – a clinician's diagnosis, for example – that remove the complexity of the array of meanings and experiences of illness and disease. Mol (ibid.) for example, shows how through a careful comparison of two different treatments for arterial disease in the 'lower limbs' – a walking therapy or surgery – the experience/disease classification and intervention are differently defined. Her point is that this makes notions of rigorous comparison – through the language of evidence-based medicine – highly problematic. There is no singularity that can be compared. This does not, however, take Mol into a position of a relativist dead-end, for she argues, in a powerful critique implicitly directed at the conventional clinical trial, 'Here those involved [in such exercises] are invited to spend more time and effort to address questions that involve values: "What do we want?" [rather than the reductionist line of the trial "what is the case?"] .... Such a shift, however, can only be for the good if, and as long as, there is indeed a dispersed *we* in health care, who – were it to pay careful attention to all the simplifications it engages in, addressing the question what *we* want – is likely to come up with better alternatives than those implied in current practice' (p. 249).

This last point leads us to the more applied, political and policy-related matters that future work in sociology should undertake – the move towards a more reflexive policy making that draws on sociology as a contributory expertise (Collins and Evans, 2002) to help shape policy making. There are dangers and pitfalls in this, as I have recently argued (Webster, 2007), but this should not deter practising sociologists from seeking to engage with policy in what Fuller (1993, p. 214) has called 'non-opportunistic criticism'. One of the most valuable of recent contributions to this is Lehoux's (2006) work on health technology assessment written by someone who is both an HTA practitioner yet who has anchored her work in STS. She brings together HTA and STS not simply to open up an analytical dialogue between the two but also for explicitly normative reasons, that is 'to see improvements in the ways medical innovations are designed, disseminated, assessed, and regulated in health care systems' (p. 207).

Those who believe it is important to retain a distance from the policy domain lest the analyst is co-opted and loses the capacity for critique often decry such normativity. I do not share such a view, as I believe I have shown throughout this book, where I have endeavoured to bridge between the analytical and the political, especially in the discussion of the social management of health in Chapter 5. In this regard, a sociological 'prognoses' might be suggested that identifies those areas of work that are likely to become especially important in the future, and when 'non-opportunistic' critique will be key.

The first relates to the moves towards 'self-care' and 'choice'. Moves towards patients making choices and shared decisions about their own health care may well be enhanced by new health technologies, but the invitation for patients to redefine their role in these terms is often, as we have seen, accompanied by doubt and uncertainty, and this questions where risk and responsibility should be allowed to 'settle'. This was an issue I explored in some detail in Chapter 5 in my discussion of developments within ICT systems, but is one that applies across the full range of new health technologies, central as it is to the political and economic agendas of all advanced health care systems. More generally, we should also be prepared to undertake a form of sociological scenario analysis (akin to the approach adopted in Foresight studies [Webster et al., 2002]) that asks what would a health care system look like were it to be primarily orchestrated around self-care?

The second relates to the social dynamics of risk communication in health deliver between doctor and patient (and patients and their kin, carers and friends), and indeed between those in specialist medical research or services who deploy new technologies to probe disease and clinicians who have to treat patients with it. How do medics translate the scientific information they receive through high-tech diagnostic tests into treatment options for patients, especially those who might be seriously or terminally ill? This has important policy implications for ministries of health promoting the adoption of new diagnostic technologies (in cancer, CHD, diabetes etc.) both to identify disease earlier on and, while doing so, to then filter the form and level of intervention that health economics and clinical judgement would regard as sensible. Sociology can explore how these aspirations are mediated by local practices in clinics and so how this cultural context affects 'take-up' of new techniques. More generally, it will be important to track the broad effects of contemporary genetic technologies as they are mobilised across the health system.

The third area that sociology will be able to offer contributory expertise relates to the evaluation of technology. From the argument developed in Chapters 2 and 5, I would suggest that this evaluation should be based on three forms of evidence: experimental (as in RCTs), evidential (in terms of clinical knowledge and practice), and experiential (in terms of the patient's understanding). Can these three be brought together in new social algorithms that might better serve public policy, clinicians and patients more effectively? Moreover, these evaluations should try to explore the continuity/discontinuity relations that characterise new technologies, as well as the advantages and disadvantages they carry. How do technologies re-order and perhaps dis-order existing social relationships found in the clinic and beyond?

These are some of the areas that sociological work could usefully explore. This book has, I hope, provided a conceptual framework on which these future studies might be built.

Bibliography

Abbott, A. (1988) *The System of Professions*, Chicago, IL: University of Chicago Press.

Abraham, J. (1995) *Science, Politics and the Pharmaceutical Industry: Controversy and Bias in Drug Regulation*, London: UCL/St Martins Press.

Abraham, J. (2002) Regulatory science as culture: contested two-dimensional values at the FDA, *Science as Culture*, 11: 309–35.

Abraham, J. (2005) Regulating the drugs industry transparently, *British Medical Journal*, 331: 528–9.

Abraham, J. and Davis, C. (2005) A comparative analysis of drug safety withdrawals in UK and US (1971–92): implications for current regulatory thinking and policy, *Social Science and Medicine*, 61: 881–92.

Abraham, J. and Lawton-Smith, H. (eds) (2003) *Regulation of the Pharmaceutical Industry*, Basingstoke: Palgrave.

Abraham, J. and Lewis, G. (2000) *Regulating Medicines in Europe: Competition, Expertise and Public Health*, London: Routledge.

Abraham, J. and Reed, T. (2002) Progress, innovation and regulatory science, *Social Studies of Science*, 32: 337–69.

Akrich, M. (1992) The de-scription of technical objects, in W. Bijker and J. Law (eds) *Shaping Technology / Building Society: Studies in Sociotechnical Change*, Cambridge, MA: MIT Press, pp. 205–24.

Allsop, J. and Saks, M. (eds) (2002) *Regulating the Health Professions*, London: Sage.

Anderson, J., Williams, N. and Seemungal, D. (1996) Human genetic technologies: exploring the links between science and innovation, *Technology Analysis and Strategic Management*, 8: 135–56.

Anderson, J., Neary, F. and Pickstone, J. (2007) *Surgeons, Engineers and Industry: A Transatlantic History of Hip Replacement Technology*, Basingstoke: Palgrave.

Andrews, G. (2003) Private complementary medicine and older people: service use and user empowerment, *Ageing and Society*, 22: 343–68.

Anglin, M. (1997) Working from the inside out: implications of beast cancer activism for biomedical policies and practices, *Social Science and Medicine*, 44: 1403–15.

Ansari, M., Shlipak, M.G., Heidenreich, P.A., Van Ostaeyen, D., Pohl, E.C., Browner, W.S. et al. (2003) Improving guideline adherence: a randomized trial evaluating strategies to increase beta-blocker use in heart failure, *Circulation*, 107(22): 2799–804.

Arksey, H. (1998) *RSI and the Experts: The Construction of Medical Knowledge*, UCL Press: London.

Armstrong, D. (1995) The rise of surveillance medicine. *Sociology of Health and Illness*, 17: 393–404.

Armstrong, D. (2006) Evaluation as an innovative health technology, in A. Webster (ed.) *New Technologies in Health Care: Challenge, Change and Innovation*, Basingstoke: Palgrave Macmillan, pp. 232–41.

Astin, J.A. (1998) Why patients use alternative medicine: results of a national study, *Journal of the American Medical Society*, 279: 1548–53.

Atkinson, P. (1995) *Medical Talk and Medical Work*, London: Sage.

Australian Productivity Commission (2005) *Impacts of Advances in Medical Technology in Australia*, Melbourne: Productivity Commission.

Ballon, P., Dantuma, L. and Hoving, D. (2003) *Ambient Intelligence in Everyday Life: The Health Application Area*, TNO Strategie, Technologie en Beleid (TNO STB), Delft, The Netherlands.

Barlow, J., Bayer, S. and Curry, R. (2006) Implementing complex innovations in fluid multi-stakeholder environments: experiences of 'telecare', *Technovation*, 26: 396–406.

Barnes, P., Powell-Griner, E., McFann, K. and Nahin, R. (2002) *CDC Advance Data Report #343 Complementary and Alternative Medicine Use Among Adults*, United States, Washington: CDC.

Barnett, P., Perkins, R. and Powell, M. (2001) On a hiding to nothing? Assessing the corporate health governance of hospital and health services in New Zealand, 1993–1998, *International Journal of Health Planning and Management*, 16: 139–54.

Barry, A. (2001) *Political Machines: Governing a Technological Society*, London: The Athlone Press/Continuum Books.

Bartley, M. (2003) Health inequality and societal institutions, *Social Theory and Health*, 1: 108–29.

Bauman, Z. (1990) *Modernity and Ambivalence*, Cambridge: Polity Press.

Bauman, Z. (1992) *Mortality, Immortality, and Other Life Strategies*, Cambridge: Polity Press.

Bauman, Z. (1998) *Work, Consumerism and the New Poor*, Cambridge: Polity Press.

Bauman, Z. (2000) *Liquid Modernity*, Cambridge: Polity Press.

Beck, U. (1992) *Risk Society: Towards a New Modernity*, London: Sage.

Beck, U. (1999) *World Risk Society*, Cambridge: Polity Press.

Beck, U. (2000) Risk society revisited, in B. Adam, U. Beck and J. van Loon (eds) *The Risk Society and Beyond*, London: Sage, pp. 211–29.

Bekelman, J.E., Li, Y. and Gross, C.P. (2003) Scope and impact of financial conflicts of interest in biomedical research, *Journal of the American Medical Association*, 289: 454–65.

Berg, M. (1997) *Rationalising Medical Work. Decision Support Techniques and Medical Practices*, Cambridge, MA: MIT Press.

Berg, M. and Akrich, M. (2004) Introduction – bodies on trial: performances and politics in medicine and biology, *Body and Society*, 10: 1–12.

Berg, M. and Goorman, E. (1999) The contextual nature of medical information, *International Journal of Medical Informatics*, 56(1/3): 51–60.

Berg, M. and Mol, A.M. (eds) (1998) *Differences in Medicine: Unravelling Practices, Techniques and Bodies*, Durham, NC: Duke University Press.

Bharadwaj, A., Prior, P., Atkinson, A., Clarke, A. and Worwood, M. (2006) The genetic iceberg: risk and uncertainty, in A. Webster (ed.) *New Technologies in Health Care: Challenge, Change and Innovation*, Basingstoke: Palgrave Macmillan.

Bijker, W., Hughes, T. and Pinch, T. (eds) (1987) *The Social Construction of Technological Systems*, Cambridge, MA: MIT Press.

Bijker, W.E. and Law, J. (1992) *Shaping Technology/Building Society: Studies in Sociotechnical Change*, Cambridge, MA: MIT Press.

Blane, D., Harding, S. and Rosato, M. (1999) Does social mobility affect the size of the socioeconomic mortality differential? Evidence from the Office for National Statistics Longitudinal Study, *Journal of the Royal Statistical Society*, 162: 59–70.

Blaxter, M. (2003) Biology, social class and inequalities in health: their synthesis in 'health capital', in S.J. Williams, L. Birke and G. Bendelow (eds) *Debating Biology*, London: Routledge.

Bloor, M. (2001) On the consulting room couch with citizen science: a consideration of the sociology of scientific knowledge perspective on practitioner–patient relationships, *Medical Sociology News*, 27(3): 19–40.

Bloor, M. (2001a) The ethnography of health and medicine, in P. Atkinson, A. Coffey and S. Delamont (eds) *Handbook of Ethnography*, London: Sage.

Blume, S. (1992) *Insight and Industry: On the Dynamics of Technological Change in Medicine*, Cambridge, MA: MIT Press.

Blume, S. (1997) The rhetoric and counter-rhetoric of a 'bionic technology', *Science Technology and Human Values*, 22: 31–56.

Blume, S. (2005) HTA: a critical re-appraisal, *Innovative Health Technologies*, International Conference, Rome, June.

Blume, S. (2006) Anti-vaccination movements and their interpretations, *Social Science and Medicine*, 62: 643–53.

Blumenthal, D., Campbell, E.G., Causino, N. and Louis, K.S. (1996) Participation of life-science faculty in research relationships with industry, *New England Journal of Medicine*, 335: 1734–9.

Blumenthal, D., Causino, N. and Campbell, E.G. (1997) Academic industry research relationships in genetics: a field apart, *Nature Genetics*, 16: 104–8.

Bordo, S. (1993) *Unbearable Weight: Feminism Western Culture and the Body*, Berkeley, CA: University of California Press.

Bordo, S. (1993a) Feminism, foucault, and the politics of the body, in C. Ramazanoglu (ed.) *Up Against Foucault: Explorations of Some Tensions Between Foucault and Feminism*, New York: Routledge, pp. 181–202.

Briggs, A., Claxton, K. and Sculpher, M. (2006) *Decision Modelling for Health Economic Evaluation*, Oxford: Oxford University Press.

Brown, N. and Kraft, A. (2006) Blood ties – banking the stem cell promise, *Technology Analysis and Strategic Management*, 3: 313–27.

Brown, N. and Michael, M. (2003) A sociology of expectations: retrospecting prospects and prospecting retrospects, *Technology Analysis and Strategic Management*, 15(1): 3–18.

Brown, N. and Webster, A. (2004) *New Medical Technologies and Society: Reordering Life*, Cambridge: Polity Press.

Brown, N., Kraft, A. and Martin, P. (2006) Imagining blood – the promissory pasts of Haematopoietic stem cells, *Biosocieties*, 1: 329–48.

Brown, N., Faulkner, A., Kent, J. and Michael, M. (2006) Regulating hybridity: policing pollution in tissue engineering and transpecies transplantation, in A. Webster (ed.) *New Health Technologies: Challenge, Change and Innovation*, Basingstoke: Palgrave.

Buchanan, A. (1995) Privatization and just health care, *Bioethics*, 9: 220–39.

Burke, M. and Fournier, G. (2005) The diffusion of medical innovation: is success in the stars? Southeastern Health Economics Study Group Conference, The Moore School of Business, University of South Carolina, Columbia, South Carolina, 14–15 October.

Burrows, R., Nettleton, S. and Bunton, R. (1995) Sociology and health promotion: health, risk and consumption under late odernism, in R. Bunton, S. Nettleton and R. Burrows (eds) *The Sociology of Health Promotion*, London: Routledge, pp. 1–12.

Burton, J. A. (2001) *Knowledge Capitalism Business, Work, and Learning in the New Economy*, Oxford: Oxford University Press.

Bury, M. (1982) Chronic illness as biographical disruption, *Sociology of Health and Illness*, 4: 167–82.

Bury, M. (1997) *Health and Illness in a Changing Society*, London: Routledge.

Bury, M. (1998) Postmodernity and health, in G. Scambler and Paul Higgs (eds) *Modernity, Medicine and Health*, London: Routledge.

Bury, M. (2000) Health, ageing and the lifecourse, in S.J. Williams, J. Gabe and M. Calnan (eds) *Health, Medicine and Society: Key Theories, Future Agendas*, London: Routledge.

Callon, M., Meadel, C. and Rabeharisoa, V. (2002) The economy of qualities. *Economy and Society*, 31(2): 194–217.

Callon, M. and Rabeharisoa, V. (2003) Research 'in the wild' and the shaping of new social identities, *Technology and Society*, 25: 193–204.

Callon, M. and Rabeharisoa, V. (2004) Articulating bodies: the case of muscular dystrophies, *Body and Society*, 22(10): 183–203.

Calvert, J. (2004) Genomic patenting and the utility requirement, *New Genetics and Society*, 23: 301–12.

Campbell, E.G., Koski, G. and Blumenthal, D. (2001) The triple helix: university, government and industry relationships in the life sciences, *Working Policy Paper of the AEI* – Brookings Joint Center on Regulatory Studies, Washington, DC.

Campbell, E.G., Weissman, J.S., Feibelmann, S., Moy, B. and Blumenthal, D. (2004) Institutional academic industry relationships: results of case studies, *Accountability in Research*, 11: 103–18.

Cant, S. and Sharma, U. (1995) The reluctant profession: homoeopathy and the search for legitimacy, *Work, Employment and Society*, 9: 743–62.

Carers UK (2002) *Without Us . . . ? Calculating the Value of Carers Support*, Carers: UK.

Carpenter, D. (2003) A Polemic for why markets need cops, *Health Affairs*, 22: 253–4.

Carr Saunders, A. and Wilson, P.A. (1933) *The Professions*, Oxford: Clarendon Press.

Carricaburu, D. and Pierret, J. (1995) From illness as biographical disruption to biographical reinforcement: the case of HIV-positive men, *Sociology of Health and Illness*, 17: 65–88.

Casper, M.J. and Berg, M. (1995) Constructivist perspectives on medical work, *Science, Technology, and Human Values*, 20: 395–407.

Castells, M. (1996) *The Rise of the Network Society*, London: Blackwell.

Caufield, C. (1989) *Multiple Exposure: Chronicles of the Radiation Age*, New York: Harper and Row.

CCU (Committee on the Consequences of Uninsurance) (2002) Board on health care services, Institute of Medicine, *Care Without Coverage: Too Little, Too Late*, Washington, DC: National Academy Press.

Chadwick, R. (1999) The Icelandic database – do modern times need modern sagas? *British Medical Journal*, 319: 441–4.

Chakraborty, S. and Harding, A. (2003) Conducting a private health sector assessment, in A. Harding and A.S. Preker (eds) *Private Participation in Health Services*, Washington, DC: World Bank.

Charles-Jones, H., Latimer, J. and May, C. (2003) Transforming general practice: the redistribution of medical work in general practice, *Sociology of Health and Illness*, 25: 71–92.

Charmaz, K. (1983) Loss of self: a fundamental form of suffering in the chronically ill, *Sociology of Health and Illness*, 5: 168–95.

Chatwin, J. and Tovey, P. (2006) Complementary and alternative medicine, in A. Webster (ed.) *New Technologies in Health Care: Challenge, Change and Innovation*, Basingstoke: Palgrave Macmillan.

Chong, S. (2006) Investigations document still more problems for stem cell researchers, *Science*, 311(5762): 754–5.

Clarke, A.E and Leigh Star, S. (2006) The social worlds/arenas/discourse framework as a theory-methods package, in M. Lynch, O. Amsterdamska and Ed Hackett (eds) *The New Handbook of Science and Technology Studies*, Cambridge, MA: MIT Press.

Cohn, S. and Bichard, J. (2005) *Neuroscience Promises: Current and Future Applications of Brain Imaging Technology*, ESRC/MRC IHT Programme, University of York. See www.york.ac.uk/res/iht

Cole, S. and LeJeune, R. (1972) Illness and the legitimation of failure, *American Sociological Review*, 37: 347–56.

Coleman, J.S., Katz, E. and Menzel, H. (1966) *Medical Innovation: A Diffusion Study*, New York: Bobbs-Merrill.

Colgrove, J. (2002) The McKeown thesis: a historical controversy and its enduring influence, *American Journal of Public Health*, 92: 725–9.

Collins, F.S. et al. (2003) Recurrent de novo point mutations in Lamin A cause Hutchinson-Gilford Progeria Syndrome, *Nature*, 422: 293–8, published online, doi:10.1038/.

Collins, H. (1974) The TEA Set: tacit knowledge and scientific networks, *Science Studies*, 4: 165–86.

Collins, H.M. and Evans, R. (2002) The third wave of science studies: studies of expertise and experience, *Social Studies of Science*, 32(2): 235–96.

Conrad, P. (1979) Types of medical social control, *Sociology of Health and Illness*, 1: 1–11.

Conrad, P. and Potter, D. (2004) Human growth hormone and the temptation of biomedical enhancement, *Sociology of Health and Illness*, 26: 184–215.

Corea, G. (1985) *The Mother Machine: Reproductive Technologies from Artificial Insemination to Artificial Wombs*, New York: Harper and Row.

Corrigan, O.P. (2003) Empty ethics: the problem with informed consent, *Sociology of Health and Illness*, 25: 768–92.

Coslett, T., Summerfield, P. and Lury, C. (2000) *Feminism and Autobiography – Texts, Theories, Methods*, London: Routledge.

Cowie, L. (2007) The meaning of medicine, PhD Thesis, Department of Sociology, University of York.

Cullen, J. and Cohn, S. (2006) Making sense of mediated information: empowerment and dependency, in A. Webster (ed.) *New Technologies in Health Care: Challenge, Change and Innovation*, Basingstoke: Palgrave.

Davis, M., Hart, G., Imrie, J., Davidson, O., Williams, I. and Stephenson, J. (2002) 'HIV is HIV to me': meanings of treatments, viral load and re-infection among gay men with HIV, *Health, Risk and Society*, 4: 31–43.

Davis-Floyd, R.E. (1994) The technocratic body: American childbirth as cultural expression, *Social Science and Medicine*, 38: 1125–40.

Dearn, L. (2005) High price of e-health, *The Australian*, 25 January: C01, C04.

Dibben, M.R. and Lean, M.E. (2003) Achieving compliance in chronic illness management: illustrations of trust relationships between physicians and nutrition clinic patients, *Health, Risk and Society*, 5: 241–58.

Dogdson, R., Lee, K. and Drager, N. (2002) *Global Health Governance: A Conceptual Review*, Geneva: WHO.

DoH (2002) *Delivering the NHS Plan: next steps on investment, next steps on reform*, Department of Health, London: Stationery Office.

DoH (2003a) *Delivering 21st century IT support for the NHS: national strategic programme*, Department of Health, London: Stationery Office.

DoH (2003b) *Our inheritance, our future*, Department of Health, London: Stationery Office.

DoH (2004) *Choosing health: making healthy choices easier*, London: Department of Health Publications.

DoH (2005a) *Stem Cell Initiative: report and recommendations*, London: Department of Health Publications, p. 118.

DoH (2005b) *UK Stem Cell Initiative: report and recommendations*, London: Department of Health Publications.

DoH (2005c) *Our health, our care, our say: a new direction for community services*, London: Department of Health Publications.

DoH (2005d) *Self Care – A Real Choice: Self Care Support – A Practical Option*, London: Department of Health Publications.

DoH (2005e) Department of Health, *Commissioning a Patient-Led NHS*, 28 July 2005.

Donaldson, C. and Ruta, D. (2005) Should the NHS follow the American way? *British Medical Journal*, 331: 1328–30.

Ducatel, K. (2000) Ubiquitous computing: the new industrial challenge, in *The IPTS Report*, October, No. 38, Seville: IPTS Publications, pp. 16–21.

Duckett, S. (2001) Does it matter who owns health facilities? *Journal of Health Services Research and Policy*, 6(1): 59–62.

Dunnett, S. (2005) Challenges for translating stem cell research towards the clinic, Paper presented at the Cross Council Stem Cell Workshop, Manchester, 13 December.

Edquist, C. (ed.) (1997) *Systems of Innovation*, London: Pinter.

Ehrenreich, B. and Ehrenreich, J. (1970) *The American Health Empire: Power, Profits, and Politics*, New York: Doubleday.

Ehrenreich, B. and Ehrenreich, J. (1971) *The American Health Empire: Power, Profits, and Politics*, New York: Random House.

Eisenberg, D., Davis, R. and Ettner, S. (1998) Trends in alternative medicine use in the United States, 1990–1997, *Journal of the American Medical Association*, 280: 1569–75.

Elias, N. (1984) *The Civilising Process*, Oxford: Blackwell.

Epstein, S. (ed.) (1996) *Impure Science: AIDS, Activism and the Politics of Knowledge*, Berkeley, CA: University of California Press.

Eriksson, L. and Webster, A. (2007) *Science as Culture* (forthcoming).

ESRC (2005) *Innovative Health Technologies Programme*, www.york.ac.uk/res/iht

Ettorre, E. (2002) *Reproductive Genetics, Gender and the Body*, London: Routledge.

Etzkowitz, H. and Leydesdorff, L. (2001) The dynamics of innovation: from national systems and 'mode 2' to a triple helix of university–industry–government relations, *Research Policy*, 29: 109–23.

European Parliament (2001) Report on the ethical, legal, economic and social implications of human genetics. Temporary Committee on Human Genetics and Other New Technologies in Modern Medicine, Brussels: European Commission.

Fairchild, A. and Oppenheimer, G. (1998) Public health nihilism verses pragmatism: history, politics, and the control of tuberculosis, *American Journal of Public Health*, 88: 1105–17.

Faircloth, C.A., Boylstein, C., Rittman, M., Young, M.E. and Gubrium, J. (2004) Sudden illness and biographical flow in narratives of stroke recovery, *Sociology of Health and Illness*, 26: 242–61.

Farmer, P. (2003) *Pathologies of Power: Health, Human Rights, and the New War on the Poor*, Berkeley, CA: University of California Press.

Faulkner, A. (1997) 'Strange bedfellows' in the laboratory of the NHS? An analysis of the new science of health technology assessment in the United Kingdom, in M. Elston MA (ed.) *The Sociology of Medical Science and Technology*, London: Blackwells.

Faulkner, A., Kent, J., Fitzpatrick, D. and Geesink, I. (2003) Human tissue engineered products – drugs or devices? *British Medical Journal*, 326: 1159–60.

Faulkner, A., Kent, J., Geesink, I. and Fitzpatrick, D. (2006) Purity and the dangers of regenerative medicine: regulatory innovation of human tissue engineered technology, *Social Science and Medicine*, 63: 2277–88.

Ferlie, E., Asbrune, L., Fitzgerald, L. and Pettigrew, A. (1996) *The New Public Management In Action*, Oxford: Oxford University Press.

Fidler, D.P. (2004), *SARS, Governance and the Globalization of Disease*, Basingstoke: Palgrave Macmillan.

Finch, T., May, C., Mort, M. and Mair, F. (2006) Telemedicine, telecare, and the future patient, in A. Webster (ed.) *New Technologies in Health Care: Challenge, Change and Innovation*, Basingstoke: Palgrave Macmillan, pp. 84–96.

Fine, B. (2002) *The World of Consumption: The Cultural and Material Revisited*, London: Routledge.

Fiske, J. (1989) *Understanding Popular Culture*, London: Routledge.

Flowers, P. (2001) Gay men and HIV/AIDS risk management, *Health*, 5: 50–75.

Flowers, P., Knussen, C. and Church, S. (2003) Psychosocial factors associated with HIV testing among Scottish gay men, *Psychology and Health*, 6: 739–53.

Foote-Ardah, C.E. (2003) The meaning of complementary and alternative medicine practices among people with HIV in the United States: strategies for managing everyday life, *Sociology of Health and Illness*, 25(5): 481–500.

Forester, T. (1985) *The Information Technology Revolution*, Cambridge, MA: MIT Press.

Foucault, M. (1975) *The Birth of the Clinic: An Archaeology of Medical Perception*, New York: Vintage Books.

Foucault, M. (1987) *History of Sexuality*, London: Vintage.

Foucault, M. (1988) 'Of Power and Prisons', in M. Morris and P. Patton (eds) *Politics, Philosophy, and Culture: Interviews and Other Writings, 1977–1984*, New York: Routledge, pp. 109–47.

Fox, N.J. (1998) 'Risks', 'hazards' and life choices: reflections on health at work, Sociology, 32: 665–87.

Fox, N., Ward, K.J. and O'Rourke, A.J. (2005) The birth of the e-clinic: continuity or transformation in the UK governance of pharmaceutical consumption? *Social Science and Medicine*, 61: 1474–84.

Fox, N.J., Ward, K.J. and O'Rourke, A.J. (2005a) Pro-anorexia, weight-loss drugs and the internet: an 'anti-recovery' explanatory model of anorexia, *Sociology of Health and Illness*, 27: 944–71.

Fox, S. and Rainie, L. (2002) *Vital Decisions*, Washington, DC: Pew Internet and American Life Project.

Frank, A.W. (1995) *The Wounded Storyteller. Body, Illness, and Ethics*, Chicago, IL: University of Chicago Press.

Frank, A.W. (1996) Reconciliatory alchemy: bodies, narrative and power, *Body and Society*, 2: 53–71.

Freund, P.E.S. (1990) The expressive body: a common ground for the sociology of emotions and health and illness, *Sociology of Health and Illness*, 12(4): 452–77.

Friedson, E. (1970a) *Professional Dominance: The Social Structure of Medical Care*, New York: Atheron Press.

Friedson, E. (1970b) *The Profession of Medicine*, New York: Dodd Mead.

Friedson, E. (2001) *Professionalism, the Third Logic*, Cambridge: Polity Press.

Fuchs, R. and Sox Jr, H.C. (2001) Physicians' views of the relative importance of thirty medical innovations, *Health Affairs*, 20: 30–42.

Fukuyama, F. (1995) *Trust: The Social Virtues and the Creation of Prosperity*, London: The Free Press.

Fuller, S. (1993) *Philosophy of Science and its Discontents* (2nd edition), New York: Guildford Press.

Furedi, F. (2004) *Therapy Culture: Cultivating Vulnerability in an Uncertain Age*, London: Routledge.

Gabbay, J. and Walley, T. (2006) Introducing new health interventions, *British Medical Journal*, 332: 64–5.

Gallagher, C. and Laqueur, T. (1987) *The Making of the Modern Body*, Berkeley, CA: University of California Press.

Galvin, R.D. (2005) Researching the disabled identity, *Sociology of Health and Illness*, 27: 393–413.

Gane, N. (2003) Computerized capitalism: the media theory of Jean-François Lyotard, *Information, Communication and Society*, 6: 430–50.

Garfinkle, H. (1963) A conception of, and experiments with, 'trust' as a condition of stable concerted actions, in O.J. Harvey (ed.) *Motivation and Social Interaction*, New York: The Ronald Press, pp. 187–238.

Germov, J. (2005) Managerialism in the Australian public health sector: towards the hyper-rationalisation of professional bureaucracies, *Sociology of Health and Illness*, 27: 738–58.

Giacomini, M. (2005) *Health Technology As Policy*, IHT/HTAi Conference, Rome, June 20 (see http://www.york.ac.uk/res/iht/events/HTAiRome2005.htm).

Giddens, A. (1990) *The Consequences of Modernity*, Cambridge: Polity Press.

Giddens, A. (1994) Living in a post-traditional society, in U. Beck, A. Giddens, and S. Lash (eds) *Reflexive Modernisation*, Cambridge: Polity Press.

Goffman, E. (1956) *The Presentation of Self in Everyday Life*, New York: Doubleday.

Goffman, E. (1963) *Stigma: Notes on the Management of Spoiled Identity*, New Jersey: Prentice Hall.

Golding, P. (2000) Forthcoming features: information and communications technologies and the sociology of the future, *Sociology*, 34: 165–84.

Goodwin, D., Pope, C., Mort, M. and Smith, A.F. (2005) Access, boundaries and their effects: legitimate participation in anaesthesia, *Sociology of Health and Illness*, 27(6): 855–71.

Gott, M., Seymour, J.E., Clark, D., Ahmedzai, S.H. and Bellamy, G. (2003) Older people's reflections on home as a place of care during dying, Abstracts of the Eighth Congress of the European Association for Palliative Care, The Hague.

Gottweis, H. (2003) Bringing science and medicine back in: olicy studies and the understanding of bio-medical transformations, *Swiss Political Science Review*, 8: 143–9.

Gottweis, H. and Triendl, R. (2006) South Korean policy failure and the Hwang debacle, *Nature Biotechnology*, 24: 141–3.

Graham, F. and Clark, D. (2005) The syringe driver and the subcutaneous route in palliative care: the inventor, the history and the implications, *Journal of Pain and Symptom Management*, 29(1): 32–40.

Graham, H. (ed.) (2000) *Understanding Health Inequalities*, Buckingham: Open University Press.

Graham, H. (2005) Health inequalities: research concepts and policy goals, paper, *What Have We Learned Since the Black Report*, Social Dimensions of Health Institute, University of Dundee, 30 September.

Gray, A. and Harrison, S. (eds) (2004) *Governing Medicine: Theory and Practice*, Berkshire: Open University Press.

Greatbatch, D., Hanlon, G., Goode, J., O'Cathain, A., Strangleman, T. and Luff, D. (2005) Telephone triage, expert systems and clinical expertise, *Sociology of Health and Illness*, 27: 802–30.

Greenhalgh, T., Robert, G., Bate, P., Macfarlane, F. and Kyriakidou, O. (2005) *Diffusion of Innovations in Health Service Organisations*, Oxford: Blackwells.

Grint, K. and Woolgar, S. (1996) *The Machine at Work: Technology, Work and Organization*, Cambridge: Polity Press.

Hacking, I. (1999) *The Social Construction of What?* Cambridge, MA: Harvard University Press.

Haimes, E. (2002) What can sociology contribute to the study of ethics? Theoretical, empirical and substantive contributions, *Bioethics*, 16:89–113.

Hall, D. (2001) *Globalisation, Privatisation and Healthcare*, London: PSIRU, University of Greenwich.

Hanlon, G., Strangleman, T., Goode, J., Luff, D., O'Cathain, A. and Greatbatch, D. (2005) Knowledge, technology and nursing: the case of NHS Direct, *Human Relations*, 58: 147–71.

Hanlon, G., Greatbatch, D., O'Caithain, A., Luff, D. and Strangleman, T. (2004) Risk and the Responsible Health Consumer: The Problematics of Entitlement among Callers to NHS Direct, *Critical Social Policy*, 24(2): 210–32.

Haraway, D. (1997) *Modest Witness @ Second Millenium Female/Man Meets OncoMouse™: Feminism and Technoscience*, New York: Routledge.

Hardey, M. (1999) Doctor in the house: the Internet as a source of lay health knowledge and the challenge to expertise, *Sociology of Health and Illness*, 21: 820–35.

Hardey, M. (2001) 'E-health': the Internet and the transformation of patients into consumers and producers of health knowledge, *Information, Communication and Society*, 4: 388–405.

Harris, B. (2004) Public health, nutrition and the decline of mortality: The McKeown thesis revisited, *Social History of Medicine*, 17: 379–407.

Harrison, S. (1996) The politics of evidence-based Medicine in the United Kingdom, *Policy and Politics*, 26: 15–31.

Harrison, S. and Moran, M. (2000) Resources and rationing: managing supply and demand in health care, in G. Albrecht, R. Fitzpatrick and S. Scrimshaw (eds) *The Handbook of Social Studies in Health and Medicine*, New York: Sage, pp. 493–508.

Hausman, B.L. (1995) *Changing Sex: Transexualism, Technology, and the Idea of Gender*, Durham, NC: Duke University Press.

Healthcare Commission (2005a) Primary care trust: survey of patients 2005, Commission for Healthcare Audit and Inspection, London.

Healthcare Commission (2005b) Healthcare Commission's Report on the review of NHS foundation trusts, www.healthcarecommission.org.uk

Heaton, J. (1999) The gaze and visibility of the carer: a. Foucauldian analysis of the discourse of informal care, *Sociology of Health and Illness*, 21: 759–77.

Heaton, J., Noyes, J., Sloper, P. and Shah, R. (2005) Families' experiences of caring for technology-dependent children: a temporal perspective, *Health and Social Care in the Community*, 13: 441–50.

Henderson, J. (2005) Neo-liberalism, community care and Australian mental health policy, *Health Sociology Review*, 14: 3.

Herzlinger, R.E. (2004) *Consumer-Driven Health Care: Implications for Providers, Payers and Policy Makers*, New York: Jossey Bass.

HGC (2005) *Profiling the Newborn: A Prospective Gene Technology?* London: Human Genetics Commission.

Hill, S. and Turpin, T. (1994) Academic research cultures in collision, *Science as Culture*, 4: 327–62.

Hilless, M. and Healy, J. (2001) *Australia, Health Care Systems in Transition* vol. 3, No. 13, Copenhagen: European Observatory on Health Care Systems.

Hine, C. (1998) Information technology as an instrument of genetics, in P. Glasner and Rothman, H. (eds) *Genetic Imaginations: Ethical, Legal and Social Issues in Human Genome Research*, Aldershot: Ashgate, pp. 41–56.

Hirst, J. and Hewison, J. (2006) Hospital postnatal care: obtaining the views of Pakistani and indigenous white women, *Clinical Effectiveness in Nursing*, 10: 20–30.

Hirst, J., Ahmed, S., Green, J. and Hewison, J. (2004) Social and ethnic differences in attitudes and consent to prenatal testing, *Journal of Psychosomatic Obstetrics and Gynecology*, 25(Suppl. 1): 47–57.

Hopkins, M. (2003) What happens when the emergence of new medical technologies does not depend on industry? *SPRU Working Paper*, University of Sussex.

Horton-Salway, M. (2001) Narrative identities and the management of personal account ability in talk about ME, *Journal of Health Psychology*, 6: 247–259.

House of Commons (2001) *The Royal Liverpool Children's Inquiry*, London: The Stationery Office.

House of Commons (2005) *Changes to Primary Care Trusts*, Second Report of Session 2005–2006, 15 December, London: Stationery Office.

House of Commons (2005) *The Use of New Medical Technologies Within the NHS*, London: Stationery Office.

House of Commons (2005) *The Influence of the Pharmaceutical Industry*, Health Select Committee Inquiry, House of Commons, London: The Stationery Office.

House of Commons (2006) *NHS Charges*, Third Report of Session 2005–2006, 6 July, London: Stationery Office.

House of Lords (2000) *Complementary and lternative Medicine*, House of Lords Select Committee on Science and Technology Sixth Report (session 1999–2000), London: Stationery Office.

Human Genetics Commission (2002) Inside information: balancing interests in the use of personal genetic data, London: HGC.

Human Genetics Commission (2003) *Genes Direct: Ensuring the Effective Oversight of Genetic Tests Supplied Directly to the Public*, London: The Stationery Office.

Illich, I. (1975) *Medical Nemesis: The Expropriation of Health*, London: Marian Boyars.

Iriart, C., Merhy, E.E. and Waitzkin, H. (2001) Managed care in Latin America: the new common sense in health policy reform, *Social Science and Medicine*, 52: 1243–53.

Irwin, A. and Michael, M. (2003) *Science, Social Theory and Public Knowledge*, Maidenhead: Open University Press.

Jaggar, A. and Bordo, S. (eds) (1989) *Gender/Body/Knowledge: Feminist Reconstructions of Being and Knowing*, New Jersey: Rutgers University Press.

Jamous, H. and Pelloille, B. (1970) Changes in the French University Hospital System, in J.A. Jackson (ed.) *Professions and Professionalisation*, Cambridge: Cambridge University Press.

Jasanoff, S. (2005) *Designs on Nature, Science and Democracy in Europe and the United States*, Princeton, NJ: Princeton University Press.

Jasso-Aguilar, R., Waitzkin, H. and Landwehr, A. (2004) Multinational corporations and health care in the United States and Latin America: strategies, actions, and effects, *Journal of Health and Social Behaviour*, 45(Suppl. 1): 136–57.

Kanavos, P. and Reinhardt, U. (2003) Reference pricing for drugs: is it compatible with U.S. health care? *Prescription Drugs*, May/June: 16–34.

Kaput, J. and Rodriguez, R.L. (2004) Nutritional genomics: the next frontier in the postgenomic era, *Physiological Genomics*, 16: 166–77.

Karlsson, M. et al. (2006) Future costs for long-term care: cost projections for long-term care for older people in the United Kingdom, *Health Policy*, 75: 187–213.

Kassirer, J.P. (2005) *On The Take: How Medicine's Complicity With Big Business Can Endanger Your Health*, New York: Oxford University Press.

Kawachi, I., Kennedy, B.P., Lochner, K. and Prothrow-Stith, D. (1997) Social capital, income inequality, and mortality, *American Journal of Public Health*, 87: 1491–8.

Kerr, A. (2005) Understanding genetic disease in socio-historical context: a case study of cystic fibrosis, *Sociology of Health and Illness*, 27: 873–96.

Kleinman, A. (1988) *The Illness Narratives. Suffering, Healing and the Human Condition*, New York: Basic Books.

Kolko, G. (1999) Ravaging the poor: the International Monetary Fund indicted by its own data, *International Journal of Health Services*, 29: 51–7.

Krimsky, S. (2003) *Science in the Private Interest*, New York: Rowman and Littlefield Publishers Inc.

Kuhlmann, E. (2004) Knowledge and power in the era of consumerism – negotiations on professionalism in health care, International Sociological Association Interim Conference RC52, *Knowledge, Work and Organization*, 22–24 September, Versailles, France.

Lehoux, P. and Blume, S. (2000) Technology assessment and the socio-politics of health technologies, *Journal of Health Politics, Policy and Law*, 25: 1083–120.

Landzelius, K. (2006) Patient organisations and new metamorphoses in patienthood, *Social Science and Medicine*, 62: 529–37.

Lash, S. and Featherstone, M. (eds) (2002) *Recognition and Difference: Politics, Identity, Multiculture*, London: Sage.

Last, J.M. (1963) The iceberg, *The Lancet*, 2: 28–31.

Laurie, G. (2002) *Genetic Privacy: A Challenge to Medico-Legal Norms*, Cambridge: Cambridge University Press.

Law, J. (1987) Technology and heterogeneous engineering: the case of Portuguese expansion, in W. Bijker, T. Hughes and T. Pinch (eds) *The Social Construction of Technical Systems: New Directions in the Sociology and History of Technology*, Cambridge, MA: MIT Press, pp. 111–34.

Law, J. and Mol, A-M. (eds) (2002) *Complexities: Social Studies of Knowledge Practices*, Durham, NC: Duke University Press.

Lee, S. and Mysyk, A. (2004) The medicalisation of compulsive buying, *Social Science and Medicine*, 58: 1709–18.

Lehoux, P. and Blume, S. (2000) Technology assessment and the socio-politics of health technologies, *Journal of Health Politics, Policy and Law*, 25: 1083–120.

Lehoux, P. (2006) *The Problem of Health Technology: Policy Implications for Modern Health Care Systems*, London: Routledge.

Levin, B.W. and Browner, C.H. (2005) The social production of health: critical contributions from evolutionary, biological, and cultural anthropology, *Social Science and Medicine*, 61: 745–50.

Lewando Hundt, G., Green, J., Sandall, J., Hirst, J., Ahmed, S. and Hewison, J. (2006) Navigating the troubled waters of prenatal testing decisions, in A. Webster (ed.) *New Technologies in Health Care: Challenge, Change and Innovation*, Basingstoke: Palgrave Macmillan.

Lewis, G. (2004) Tissue collection and the pharmaceutical industry: investigating corporate biobanks, in R. Tutton and O. Corrigan (eds) *Genetic Databases: Socio-ethical Issues in the Collection and Use of DNA*, Basingstoke: Palgrave.

Lewontin, R.C. (1999) People are not commodities, *The New York Times*, January 23: A19.

Leydesdorff, L. and Eztkowitz, H. (1998) The triple helix as a model for innovation studies, *Science and Public Policy*, 25: 195–203.

Lippman, A. (1991) Prenatal genetic testing and screening: constructing needs and reinforcing inequities, *American Journal of Law and Medicine*, 17: 15–40.

Lippman, A. (1992) Led (astray) by genetic maps: the cartography of the human genome and health care, *Social Science Medicine*, 35(12): 1469–76.

Lippman, A. (1999) Embodied knowledge and making sense of prenatal diagnosis. *Journal of Genetic Counseling*, 8: 1059–77.

Lock, M. (2001) The alienation of body tissue and the biopolitics of immortalized cell lines, *Body and Society*, 7: 63–91.

Lock, M. (2002) *Twice Dead: Organ Transplants and the Re-invention of Death*, Berkeley, CA: University of California Press.

Louis, K.S., Anderson, M.S., Jones, L., Blumenthal, D. and Campbell, E.G. (2001) Entrepreneurship, secrecy, and productivity: a comparison of clinical and non-clinical life sciences faculty, *Journal of Technology Transfer*, 26: 233–45.

Lowton, K. and Gabe, J. (2003) Life on a slippery slope: perceptions of health in adults with cystic fibrosis, *Sociology of Health and Illness*, 25: 289–319.

Luhmann, N. (1979) *Trust and Power*, London: Wiley and Sons Ltd.

Lupton, D. (1996) 'Your life in their hands': trust in the medical encounter, in V. James and J. Gabe (eds) *Health and the Sociology of Emotions*, Oxford: Blackwell, pp. 157–72.

Lupton, D. (1997) Consumerism, reflexivity and the medical encounter, *Social Science and Medicine*, 45: 373–81.

Lysaght, M. and Reyes, J. (2001) The growth of tissue engineering, *Tissue Engineering*, 7: 485–93.

MacKenzie, D. (1990), *Inventing Accuracy*, Cambridge, MA: The MIT Press.

Mackintosh, M. and Koivusalo, M. (eds) (2005) *Commercialisation of Health Care: Global and Local Dynamics and Policy Responses*, Basingstoke: Palgrave Macmillan.

Majone, G. (1994) The rise of the regulatory state in Western Europe, *West European Politics*, 17: 77–96.

Mamo, L. and Fishman, J.R. (2001) Potency in All the Right Places: Viagra, *Body and Society*, 7: 13–35.

Martin, P. and Nightingale, P. (2004) The myth of the biotech revolution, *Trends in Biotechnology*, 11: 564–9.

Martin, P., Abraham, J., Davis, C. and Kraft, A. (2006) Understanding the 'productivity crisis' in the pharmaceutical industry: over-regulation or lack of innovation? in A. Webster (ed.) *New Technologies in Health Care: Challenge, Change and Innovation*, Basingstoke: Palgrave.

Martin, P., Crowther, S., Watson, P., Frost, R., Benedictus, J. and Enzing, C. (2000) Gene therapy in Europe: exploitation and commercial development. Final project report, Brighton: SPRU, University of Sussex.

May, C. (2000) *A Global Political Economy of Intellectual Property Rights. The New Enclosures?* London: Routledge.

May, C., Allison, G. and Chapple, A. (2002) Framing the doctor–patient relationship in chronic illness: a comparative study of general practitioners' accounts, *Sociology of Health and Illness*, 26: 135–58.

May, C. and Ellis, N.T. (2001) When protocols fail: technical evaluation, biomedical knowledge, and the social production of 'facts' about a telemedicine clinic, *Social Science and Medicine*, 53: 989–1002.

May, C.R., Harrison, R., MacFarlane, A., Williams, T.L., Mair, F.S. and Wallace, P. (2003) Why do telemedicine systems fail to normalise as stable models of service delivery, *Journal of Telemedicine and Telecare*, 9: 25–6.

May, C.R., Harrison, R., Finch, T., MacFarlane, A., Mair, F.S. and Wallace, P. (2003) Understanding the normalisation of telemedicine services through qualitative evaluation. *Journal of the American Medical Informatics Association*, 10: 596–604.

May, C.R. (2005) Chronic illness and intractability: professional–patient interactions in primary care, *Chronic Illness*, 1: 1–15.

McEwan, I. (2005) *Saturday*, London: Jonathan Cape.

McKeown, T. (1976) *The Role of Medicine: Dream, Mirage, or Nemesis?* London: Nuffield Provincial Hospitals Trust.

McNeil, M., Varcoe, I. and Yearley, S. (eds) (1990) *The New Reproductive Technologies*, Basingstoke: Macmillan.

Merton, R.K. (1979) *The Sociology of Science: An Episodic Memoi*, Carbondale, IL: University of Southern Illinois Press.

Miles, I. (2002) Towards the cybereconomy: making a business out of cyberspace, in J. Armitage and J. Roberts (eds) *Living With Cyberspace: Technology and Society in the 21st Century*, London: The Athlone Press.

Miles, I. (2002) Transformations of information society, in S. Inayatullah (ed.) *Encyclopedia of Life Support Systems*, Oxford: Eolss Publishers.

Miller, D. (ed.) (2001) *Consumption: Critical Concepts*, London: Routledge.

Miller, F.A., Ahern, C., Ogilvie, J., Giacomini, M. and Schwartz, L. (2005) Ruling in and ruling out: implications of molecular genetic diagnoses for disease classification, *Social Science and Medicine*, 61: 2536–45.

Mina, A., Ramlogan, R., Tampubolon, G., McMeekin, A., Venetucci, L. and Metcalfe, J.S. (2004) Problemsequences and innovation systems: emergence, growth and transformation of a medical sector, *Working Paper No 67*, CRIC University of Manchester.

Mizrachi, N. and Shuval, J. (2005) Boundary at work: alternative medicine in biomedical settings, *Sociology of Health and Illness*, 27: 20–43.

Moore, L.J.C. and Adele, E. (2001) The traffic in cyberanatomies: sex/ gender/sexualities in local and global formations, *Body and Society*, 7: 57–96.

Moran, P.J. (1999) *Governing the Health Care State: A Comparative Study of the United Kingdom, the United States, and Germany*, Manchester: Manchester University Press.

Mort, M., May, C.R. and Williams, T. (2003) Remote doctors and absent patients: acting at a distance in telemedicine, *Science, Technology and Human Values*, 28: 274–95.

MRC (2005) *The UK Stem Cell Bank*, London: Medical Research Council.

Mulkay, M. and Ernst, J. (1991) The changing profile of social death, *Archives of European Sociology*, 32: 172–96.

NAO (2005) *Choose and Book*, National Audit Office, London: Sationery Office.

Navarro, V. (1976) *Medicine Under Capitalism*, New York: Prodist.

Nelkin, D. and Andrews, L. (1999) DNA identification and surveillance creep, *Sociology of Health and Illness*, 21: 689–706.

Nettleton, S. (2004) The emergence of e-scaped medicine? *Sociology*, 38: 661–80.

Nettleton, S. and Hanlon, G. (2006) Pathways to the doctor in the information age: the role of ICTS in contemporary lay referral systems, in A. Webster (ed.) *New Technologoies in Health Care: Challenge, Change and Innovation*, Basingstoke: Palgrave.

Nettleton, S.J. and Burrows, R. (2003) E-scaped medicine? information, reflexivity and health, *Critical Social Policy* (Special Issue on Social Policy and ICTs), 23: 165–85.

Nettleton, S.J., O'Malley, L., Watt, I. and Duffey, P. (2004) Enigmatic illness: narratives of patients who live with medically unexplained symptoms, *Social Theory and Health*, 2: 47–66.

Nettleton, S.J., Burrows, R. and O'Malley, L. (2005) The mundane realities of the everyday lay use of the Internet for health and their consequences for media convergence, *Sociology of Health and Illness*, 27: 972–92.

NHS (2005) *Connecting For Health*, London: Department of Health.

NHS (2000) *National Plan* 2000, Cm 4818–I, paras 6.1 and 6.5.

Nuffield (2002) *The Ethics of Patenting DNA*, London: Nuffield Council on Bioethics.

O'Neill, N. (2002) *Autonomy and Trust in Bioethics*, Cambridge: Cambridge University Press.

OECD (1996) Special issue on government technology foresight exercises, *STI Review 17*, Paris: OECD Publications.

OECD (2004) *Health Data 2004* (1st edition), Paris: OECD Publications.

OECD (2005) *Health Data 2005*, Paris: OECD Publications.

Ong, B.N. and Hooper, H. (2006) Comparing clinical and lay accounts of the diagnosis and treatment of back pain, *Sociology of Health and Illness*, 28: 203–22.

Opie, A. (1998) 'Nobody's asked me for my view': users' empowerment by multidisciplinary health teams, *Qualitative Health Research*, 18: 188–206.

Orbach, S. (1993) *Hunger Strike*, London: Penguin.

Oudshoorn, N. (2007) The patient as diagnostic agent, *Sociology of Health and Illness*, 29 (in press).

Packer, K. and Webster, A. (1996) Patenting culture in science, *Science, Technology and Human Values*, 21: 427–53.

Pagliari, C., Sloan, D., Gregor, P., Sullivan, F., Detmer, D., Kahan, J.P. et al. (2005) What is e-health: a scoping exercise to map the field, *Journal of Medical Internet Research*, 7(1): e9 URL: http://www.jmir.org/2005/1/e9/

Pakulski, J. and Waters, M. (1996) *The Death of Class*, London: Sage.

Parr, S., Watson, N. and Woods, B. (2006) Access, agency and normality: the wheelchair and the internet as mediators of disability, in A. Webster (ed.) *New Technologies in Health Care: Challenge, Change and Innovation*, Basingstoke, Palgrave.

Parsons, T. (1951) *The Social System*, New York: Free Press.

Parthasarathy, S. (2005) Architectures of genetic medicine: comparing genetic testing for breast cancer in the United States of America and United Kingdom, *Social Studies of Science*, 35: 5–40.

Patterson, B. (2001) Myth of empowerment in chronic illness, *Journal of Advanced Nursing*, 34: 574–81.

Pavitt, K. (2003) The process of innovation, *SPRU Working Paper No 89*, Brigton, UK: University of Sussex.

Petersen, A. (2001) Biofantasies: genetics and medicine in the print news media, *Social Science and Medicine*, 52: 1255–68.

Pickstone, J.V. (ed.) (1992) *Medical Innovation in Historical Perspective*, London: Macmillan.

Pickstone, J.V. (2000) *Ways of Knowing: A New History of Science, Technology, and Medicine*, Chicago, IL: University of Chicago Press.

Pickstone, J.V. (2005) On knowing, acting, and the location of techno-science, *Perspectives on Science*, 13: 267–78.

Pidgeon, N. and Poortinga, W. (2006) British public attitudes to agricultural biotechnology and the 2003 GM Nation? Public debate: distrust, ambivalence and risk, in P. Glasner and P. Atkinson (eds) *New Genetics, New Social Formations*, London: Routledge.

Pinder, R., Petchey, R., Shaw, S. and Carter, Y. (2005) What's in a care pathway? Towards a cultural cartography of the new NHS, *Sociology of Health and Illness*, 27: 759–79.

Pirmohamed, M. and Lewis, G. (2004) The implications of pharmacogenetics and pharmacogenomics for drug development and health care, in E. Mossialos, M. Mrazek and T. Walley (eds) *Regulating Pharmaceuticals in Europe: Striving For Efficiency, Equity and Quality*, Milton Keynes: Open University Press.

Pliskin, K.L. (1987) *Silent Boundaries*, New Haven, CT: Yale University Press.

Prior, L. (2003) Belief, knowledge and expertise: the emergence of the lay expert in medical sociology, *Sociology of Health and Illness*, 17: 41–57.

Prior, L., Wood, F., Gray, J., Pill, R. and Hughes, D. (2002) Making risk visible: the role of images in the assessment of genetic risk, *Health, Risk and Society*, 4: 242–58.

Quigley, R.B. (2002) Waiting on science: the stake of present and future patients, *American Journal of Bioethics*, 2: 3–11.

Rabeharisoa, V. and Callon, M. (2004) Patients and scientists in French muscular dystrophy research, in S. Jasanoff (ed.) *States of Knowledge*, London: Routledge.

Rangnekar, D. and Duckenfield, M. (2002) Drug development and patient groups and drug development: the emerging influence of patient groups, Report for the Patient Groups and Drug Development Seminar, University College London, 16 September.

Rapp, R. (1999) *Testing Women, Testing the Fetus*, London: Routledge.

Relman, A.S. (1980) The new medical–industrial complex, *New England Journal of Medicine*, 303: 963–70.

Rhodes, L.A., McPhillips-Tangum, C. and Markham, C. (1999) The power of the visible: the meaning of diagnostic tests in chronic back pain, *Social Science and Medicine*, 48: 1189–203.

Rich, E. (2006) Anorexic (Dis)connection, *Sociology of Health and Illness*, 28: 284–305.

Richards, D.A., Godfrey, L., Tawfik, J., Ryan, M., Meakins, J., Dutton, E. et al. (2004). NHS direct versus general practice based triage for same day appointments in primary care: cluster randomised controlled trial, *British Medical Journal*, 329: 774.

Rier, D. (2000) The missing voice of the critically ill: a medical sociologist's first hand account, *Sociology of Health and Illness*, 22: 68–93.

Rip, A. (1995) Introduction of new technology: making use of recent insights from sociology and economy of technology, *Technology Analysis and Strategic Management*, 7: 417–31.

Ritzer, G. (1998) *The McDonaldization Thesis: Exploration and Extensions*, London: Sage.

Roberts, C. and Franklin, S. (2004) Experiencing new forms of genetic choice: findings from an ethnographic study of preimplantation genetic diagnosis, *Human Fertility*, 7(4): 285–93.

Rogers, E.M. (1995) *Diffusion of Innovations*, (4th edition), New York: Free Press.

Rood, E., Bosman, R.J., van der Spoel, J.I., Taylor, P. and Zandstra, D.F. (2005) Use of a computerized guideline for glucose regulation in the intensive care unit improved both guideline adherence and glucose regulation, *Journal of the American Medical Informatics Association*, 12: 172–80.

Rose, N. (1999) *Powers of Freedom; Reframing Political Thought*, Cambridge: Cambridge University Press.

Rose, N. (2001) The politics of life itself theory, *Culture and Society*, 18: 1–30.

Rose, N. (2004) Becoming neurochemical selves, in N. Stehr (ed.) *Between Commerce and Civil Society: Biotechnology*, New Brunswick, NJ: Transaction Publishers, pp. 89–126.

Rose, N. (2006) *The Politics of Life Itself*, Princeton, NJ: Princeton University Press.

Rosengarten, M., Imrie, J., Flowers, P., Davis, M. and Hart, G. (2004) After the euphoria: HIV medical technologies from the perspective of clinicians, *The Sociology of Health and Illness*, 26: 579–96.

Rothstein, H., Huber, M. and Gaskell, G. (2006) A theory of risk colonisation: the spiralling regulatory logics of societal and institutional risk, *Economy and Society*, 15: 91–112.

Rozack, T. (1986) *The Cult of Information*, Berkeley, CA: University of California Press.

Saks, M. (2003) *Orthodox and Alternative Medicine: Politics, Professionalization and Health Care*, London: Sage.

Salter, B. (2002) Medical regulation: new politics and old power, *Politics*, 22: 59–67.

Salter, B. (2004) *The New Politics of Medicine*, Basingstoke: Palgrave Macmillan.

Salter, B. (2006) Cultural politics, human embryonic stem cell science and the European Union's Framework Programme Six, in A. Webster (ed.) *New Technologies in Health Care, Challenge, Change and Innovation*, Basingstoke: Palgrave Macmillan, pp. 211–23.

Sandman, L. (2004) *A Good Death: On the Value of Death and Dying*, Buckingham: Open University Press.

Sandywell, B. (2006) Monsters in cyberspace: cyberphobia and cultural panic in the information age, *Information, Communication and Society*, 9: 39–61.

Schiller, D. (1999) *Digital Capitalism: Networking the Global Market System*, Cambridge, MA: The MIT Press.

Scott, J. (1997) *Corporate Business and Capitalist Classes*, Oxford: Oxford University Press.

Scott, J. (2000) If class is dead, why won't it lie down? in A. Woodward and G. Lengyel (eds) *European Societies: Inclusions and Exclusions*, London: Routledge.

Scott, S. (2006) The medicalisation of shyness: from social misfits to social fitness, *Sociology of Health and Illness*, 28: 133–53.

Scott, S., Prior, L., Wood, F. and Gray, J. (2005) Re-positioning the patient: the implications of being-at-risk, *Social Science and Medicine*, 60: 1869–79.

Seymour, J., Ettorre, E., Heaton, J., Lankshear, G., Mason, D. and Noyes, J. (2006) Time, place and settings: negotiating birth, childhood and death, in A. Webster (ed.) *New Technologies in Health Care: Challenge, Change and Innovation*, Basingstoke: Palgrave Macmillan, pp. 131–45.

Seymour, J.E. (2000) Negotiating natural death in intensive care, *Social Science and Medicine*, 51: 1241–52.

Shakespeare, T. (2005) Disability, genetics and global justice, *Social Policy and Society*, 4: 87–95.

Sharma, U. (1993) *Complementary Medicine Today: Practitioners and Patients*, London: Routledge.

Shilling, C. (2002) Culture, the 'sick role' and the consumption of health, *British Journal of Sociology*, 53: 621–38.

Shilling, C. (2005) *The Body in Culture, Technology and Society*, London: Sage.

Sigurdsson, S. (2001) Yin-Yang genetics, or the HSD deCODE controversy, *New Genetics and Society*, 20: 103–17.

Silverman, D. (1987) *Communication in Medical Practice*, London: Sage.

Simmel, G. (1978) *The Philosophy of Money*, Boston, MA: Routledge.

Slade, M. (2001) Are randomised controlled trials the only gold that glitters? *The British Journal of Psychiatry*, 179: 286–7.

Sointu, E. (2005) The rise of an ideal: tracing changing discourses of well-being, *The Sociological Review*, 53: 255–74.

Stacey, C. (2005) Finding dignity in dirty work: the constraints and rewards of low-wage home care labour, *Sociology of Health and Illness*, 27: 831–54.

Stacey, M. (1988) *The Sociology of Health and Healing*, London: Unwin Hyman.

Stanworth, C. (1998) Telework and the information age, *New Technology, Work and Employment*, 13: 51–62.

Stanworth, M. (ed.) (1987) *Reproductive Technologies: Gender, Motherhood and Medicine*, Cambridge: Polity Press.

Starr, P. (1982) *The Social Transformation of American Medicine: The Rise of a Sovereign Profession and the Making of a Vast Industry*, New York: Basic Books.

Strathern, A. and Stewart, P. (1999) *Curing and Healing*, Durham, NC: Carolina Academic Press.

Strong, P. (1979) *The Ceremonial Order of the Clinic*. London: Routledge.

Suchman, L. (2003) Figuring service in discourses of ICT: the case of software agents, in E. Wynn, M. Whitley, M. Myers, and J. DeGross (eds)

Global and Organizational Discourses about Information Technology, Dordrecht, The Netherlands: Kluwer, pp. 33–43.

Thorogood, N. (1996) What is the sociology of knowledge? The example of health education and promotion, in A. Perry (ed.) *Sociology: Insights in Health Care*, London: Arnold, pp. 235–49.

Timmermans, S. (2005) Death brokering: constructing culturally appropriate deaths, *Sociology of Health and Illness*, 27: 993–1013.

Timmermans, S. and Berg, M. (2003) The practice of medical technology, *Sociology of Health and Illness*, 25: 97–114.

Turner, B. (2003) Social capital, inequality and health: the Durkheimian revival, *Social Theory and Health*, 1(1): 4–20.

Turner, B.S. (1995) *Medical Power and Social Knowledge* (2nd edition), London: Sage.

Urry, J. (2000) *Sociology Beyond Societies*, London: Routledge.

Van Lente, H. and Rip, A. (1998) Expectations in technological developments: an example of prospective structures to be filled in by agency, in C. Disco and B.J.R. van der Meulen (eds) *Getting New Technologies Together*, Berlin, New York: Walter de Gruyter, pp. 195–220.

Virilio, P. (1998) *Polar Inertia*, London: Sage.

Vogel, D. (2004) The new politics of risk regulation in Europe and the United States, in M. Levin and M. Shapiro (eds) *Trans-Atlantic Policy-making in an Age of Austerity*, Washington: Georgetown University Press.

Wailoo, K. (2004) Sovereignty and science: revisiting the role of science in the construction and erosion of medical dominance, *Journal of Health Politics, Policy and Law*, 29(4–5), August–October: 643–66.

Waitzkin, H. and Iriart, C. (2001) How the United States exports managed care to developing countries, *International Journal of Health Services*, 31: 495–505.

Wajcman, J. (1991) *Feminism Confronts Technology*, St Leonards: Allen and Unwin.

Wakefield, S. and Poland, E.B. (2005) Family, friend or foe? Critical reflections on the relevance and role of social capital in health promotion and community development, *Social Science and Medicine*, 60(12): 2819–32.

Waldby, C. (2000) Fragmented bodies, incoherent medicine, *Social Studies of Science* 30(3): 465–74.

Waldby, C. (2002) Stem cells, tissue cultures and the production of biovalue, *Health*, 6: 305–23.

Waldby, C. and Mitchell, R. (2006) *Tissue Economies: Blood, Organs and Cells in Late Capitalism*, Durham, NC: Duke University Press.

Waldholz, M. (2000) AIDS discovery spurs some to challenge: a patent ® that boosted HGS stock, *The Wall Street Journal*, 16 March, p. 8.

Wanless, D. (2002) *Securing our Future Health: Taking a Long-Term View. Final Report*, HM Treasury, April.

Warnock, M. (1984) *Report of the Committee of Inquiry into Human Fertilisation and Embryology*, Cmnd 9314 (The Warnock Inquiry), London: HMSO.

Watson, N. and Woods, B. (2005) The origins and early developments of special/adaptive wheelchair seating, *Social History of Medicine*, 18(3): 459–74.

Watson, N. and Woods, B. (2005) No wheelchairs beyond this point: a historical examination of wheelchair access in the twentieth century in Britain and America, *Social Policy and Society*, 4: 97–105.

Webster, A., Brown, N., Nelis, A., Van der Meulen, B. (2002) *Foresight as a Tool for the Management of Knowledge and Innovation*, Brussels: European Commission.

Webster, A. (1991) *Science, Technology and Society, New Directions*, Basingstoke: Macmillan.

Webster, A. (1994) University corporate ties and the construction of research agendas, *Sociology*, 28: 123–42.

Webster, A. (2002) Innovative health technologies and the social: redefining health, medicine and the body, *Current Sociology*, 50: 443–58.

Webster, A. (2004a) Health technology assessment: a sociological commentary on reflexive innovation, *International Journal of Technology Assessment in Health*, 20: 61–6.

Webster, A. (2004b) Risk, science and policy: researching the social management of uncertainty, *Policy Studies*, 25: 5–15.

Webster, A. (2007) Crossing boundaries: social science in the policy room, *Science, Technology and Human Values*, 32(4) (in press).

Webster, A., Martin, P., Lewis, G. and Smart, A. (2005) Integrating pharmacogenetics into society: in search of a model, *Nature Reviews Genetics*, 5: 663–9.

Webster, A. and Constable, J. (1990) Strategic alliances and hybrid coalitions, *Industry and Higher Education*, 4: 225–30.

Webster, F. (1995) *Theories of the Information Society*, London: Routledge.

Webster, F. (2000) Information, capitalism and uncertainty, *Information, Communication and Society*, 3: 69–90.

Webster, F. (2002) *Theories of the Information Society* (2nd edition), London: Routledge.

Welsh, S. (2004) Moving forward? Complementary and alternative practitioners seeking self-regulation, *Sociology of Health and Illness*, 26: 216–41.

WHO (1946) Preamble to the Constitution of the World Health Organization as adopted by the International Health Conference, New York, 19–22 June, 1946; signed on 22 July 1946 by the representatives of 61 States (Official Records of the World Health Organization, no. 2, p. 100) and entered into force on 7 April 1948.

Wilkinson, R. (2005) *The Impact of Inequality: How to Make Sick Societies Healthier*, New York: The New Press.

Will, C. (2005) Arguing about the evidence: readers, writers and inscription devices in coronary heart disease risk assessment, *Sociology of Health and Illness*, 27: 780–98.

Williams, G. (1984) The genesis of chronic illness: narrative reconstruction, *Sociology of Health and Illness*, 6: 175–20.

Williams, G. (2003) The determinants of health: structure, context and agency, *Sociology of Health and Illness*, 25: 131–54.

Williams, R. and Edge, D. (1996) The social shaping of technology, *Research Policy*, 25: 865–99.

Williams, R., Hartswood, M., Proctor, R. and Rouncefield, M. (2001) Building information systems as universalized locals, *Knowledge Technology and Policy*, 14: 90–108.

Williams, S. (2006) Medical sociology and the biological body: where are we now and where do we go from here? *Health: An Interdisciplinary Journal for the Social Study of Health, Illness and Medicine*, 10(1): 5–30.

Witz, A. (2000) Whose body matters? Feminist sociology and the corporeal turn in sociology and feminism, *Body and Society*, 6(2): 1–24.

Wolder, L.B. and Browner, C.H. (2004) The social production of health: critical contributions from evolutionary, biological, and cultural anthropology, *Social Science and Medicine*, 61: 745–50.

Wolpert, H.A. and Anderson, B.J. (2001) Management of diabetes: are doctors framing the benefits from the wrong perspective? *British Medical Journal*, 323: 994–6.

Wood, B. (2000) *Patient Power?: The Politics of Patients' Associations in Britain and America*, Buckingham: Open University Press.

Woods, B. and Watson, N. (2005) When wheelchair innovation in Britain was under state control, *Technology and Disability*, 17: 237–50.

Woolf, S. and Johnson, R. (2005) The break-even point: when medical advances are less important than improving the fidelity with which they are delivered, *Annals of Family Medicine*, 3: 545–52.

Woolgar, S. (ed.) (2002) *Virtual Society? Technology, Cyberbole, Reality*, Oxford: Oxford University Press.

World Social Forum (2005) Annual Meeting, http://www.ukabc.org/ wsf2005.htm

Wynne, B. (2002) Risk and environment as legitimatory discourses of technology: reflexivity inside out? *Current Sociology*, 50: 459–77.

Ziman, J. (ed.) (2000) *Technological Innovation as an Evolutionary Process*, Cambridge: Cambridge University Press.

Zinn, J.O. (2005) The biographical approach: a better way to understand behaviour in health and illness, *Health, Risk and Society*, 7: 1–9.

Zola, I.K. (1973) Pathways to the doctor, from person to patient, *Social Science Medicine*, 7: 677–89.

Zola, I.K. (1997) Medicine as an institution of social control, in P. Conrad (ed.) *The Sociology of Health and Illness: Critical Perspectives*, New York: Worth Publishers, pp. 404–14.

Author Index

Subject Index